The
100 Best
Small Art Towns
In America

The
100 Best
Small Art Towns
In America

Where to Find Fresh Air,

Creative People,

and Affordable Living

John Villani

John Muir Publications

Santa Fe, New Mexico

First edition. First printing September 1994

Library of Congress Cataloging-in-Publication Data

Villani, John.
    The 100 best small art towns in America: where to find fresh air, creative people, and
    affordable living / John Villani.
      p. cm.
    Includes index.
    ISBN 1-56261-180-1 : $12.95
    1. Artist colonies—United States. 2. Artists—Vocational guidance—United States.
    3. Cities and towns—United States. 4. United States—Description and travel. 5. Quality of
    life—United States. I. Title. II. Title: One hundred best small art towns in America.
    NX503.V55 1994
    700'.25'73—dc20   94-19074
                                                                                     CIP

Production: Kathryn Lloyd-Strongin, Chris Brigman
Editorial: Elizabeth Wolf, Jean Teeters
Cover art: Tony D'Agostino
Back cover design: Linda Braun
Design and typography: Cowgirls Design, Taos, New Mexico
Printer: Malloy Lithographing, Inc.

Distributed to the book trade by
W. W. Norton & Co., Inc.
500 Fifth Avenue
New York, New York 10110

To my parents

Life's greatest rewards are reserved for its most creative individuals.

— Maria Thompson

Contents

Foreword

In 1972, as a result of Pete Johnston's article in a Sunday edition of the *New York Times*, the nation's attention was directed to a new experience opening up to travelers throughout America—the country inn. Since then, hundreds of thousands of travelers have assiduously avoided the impersonal, urban, sterile, cookie-cutter hotel/motel scene and opted for the more relaxed, less complicated, friendly personalization of the bed and breakfast (B&B) or country inn. This has been true for both the vacation and the business traveler, many of whom would not leave home without a copy of *Country Inns and Back Roads* in their bags. With the publication of *The 100 Best Small Art Towns in America,* not only will these travelers' suitcases be a little heavier, but all automobile rental companies should consider placing a copy of this work in their vehicles as "standard equipment."

In his introduction, author John Villani asks just how long it will take local governments to realize the economic potential for rural communities in entering into partnership with the arts. The question is both perceptive and timely. The economic impact of the arts in these communities has been profound, and thoroughly documented of late. Earlier this year, the National Assembly of Local Arts Agencies (NALAA) released the results of its three-year study of 33 communities representing all regions of the country. The goal of this study was to demonstrate the positive economic impact of the arts on communities across the country. The NALAA did just that. It found that:

> The arts have a positive impact not only on a community's quality of life, but also on the entire social and business fabric. Arts districts attract business investment, reverse urban decay, revitalize struggling neighborhoods, and draw tourists. Attendance at arts events generates related commerce for hotels, [B&Bs and country inns,] restaurants, parking garages, galleries, and more. Arts organizations themselves are responsible businesses, employers, and consumers. Despite their place in the local economy, however, the arts are repeatedly overlooked as a legitimate tool for economic and social improvement.

In *The 100 Best Small Art Towns in America,* John Villani vividly documents and supports the NALAA's conclusions. Through hundreds of interviews, he has recorded the changing American landscape, focusing on communities formerly characterized as "rural and underserved" which now, though still rural, have become "well-served" by artists acting in partnership with community leadership. His research is broad-based and inclusive. The visual, literary, folk, and performing art forms have idiosyncratically affected the infrastructure and fabric of each community. Villani covers all of these art forms in an easily accessible and reader-friendly work.

John Villani has not written just another chapter in the proverbial chamber of commerce cultural tourism "puff piece." Instead, he has identified the central core of a national trend and placed it in context for economists, the arts community, leaders of governmental units large and small, and the average citizen who wants to learn about new experiences. His free-flowing, journalistic style is refreshingly minimalist, and we are left wanting more. But it is up to us to go out and get it ourselves—and Villani has motivated us to do so.

The author profiles small art towns nationwide, but particularly highlights the Western region. Collaborative initiatives formed among artists, arts organizations, and rural communities in the West are further documented by the Western States Arts Federation (WESTAF). This regional arts organization has been developing arts/community-based partnerships in 12 western states, from Alaska to New Mexico, for more than 20 years. The annual Cowboy Poetry Gathering in Elko, Nevada, organized by the Western Folklife Center ten years ago and funded by WESTAF, is the quintessential Western arts event: It has transformed a community and provided international exposure to a festival uniquely American, rural, and economically positive.

I was born in New York City and moved to New Orleans at age 12. There I stayed for 44 years. In 1990, I moved to New Mexico, giving up a stressful litigation practice to become involved in professional arts administration. When John asked me if I would write the foreword for this book, I knew I had come full circle. As authors John Naisbitt and Patricia Aburdene note in *Megatrends 2000*, art "is a spiritual quest, but its economic implications are staggering." *The 100 Best Small Art Towns in America* fuses the notions of spirit and economy in a work that will grace bookshelves for years to come. It will also serve the weekend or month-long traveler, business executive, or tourist who wishes to discover the joys of a new American phenomenon: creative arts professionals, working arts facilities, and artistically successful festivals located in communities previously unidentified by the Berkshire Traveler.

So hop into your rental car, open the glove compartment, and hope to find this book awaiting you. Or, just to be on the safe side, buy a copy of your own—one of these 100 best small art towns is probably not far from you. Enjoy the pleasures of the confluence of events described in this work. Thanks, John, for identifying these towns and calling them to our collective attention and enjoyment.

As Thulani Davis stated in her keynote address in April 1994 at Art 21: Art Reaches into the 21st Century, "I believe that at times chaos in society is fueled by the absence of art." I agree! It is thus submitted that the 100 best small art towns in America have taken giant steps towards the reduction or elimination of community chaos.

Donald A. Meyer
Executive Director,
WESTERN STATES ARTS FEDERATION (WESTAF)

Santa Fe, New Mexico
April 1994

Preface

When Dan Anthony approached me a few years ago with the idea of doing a story on Loveland, Colorado's annual art festival, Sculpture in the Park, my first thoughts were about who would publish an article about one small town's art festival. Dan, sculptor Glenna Goodacre's business manager (she's the creator of the Vietnam Women's Memorial), assured me that once I got to Loveland, I'd find not only a great story, but something extraordinary.

He was right. The sight of hundreds of realist sculptors and their bronze creations assembled underneath sprawling tents at the foothills of the Rocky Mountains was the inspirational nudge that led to this book. Once I understood that this small farming community had evolved into the home base for hundreds of professional artists, the extent of the arts' impact as an economic development driver in rural Colorado became obvious.

I live in Santa Fe, New Mexico, a community whose economic foundation rests in large part on the employment and commerce generated by its tourism and fine art sectors. When you live in a place like Santa Fe, Provincetown, Carmel, Cannon Beach, or Scottsdale, it's easy to see that art galleries and the business of selling art is a vital component of the high-end tourism experience. What's not readily apparent, however, is the way small communities 20, 80, and 200 miles away have also had the tides of their economic waters raised by the success of these popular tourist destinations.

That's because once a town is on its way to becoming attractive to visitors, once the positive write-ups begin appearing in travel magazines and Sunday newspapers, the costs of living and doing business in that town start rising sharply. While each popular tourist town experiences its own variation of this syndrome, the results are the same: many of the artists who once lived in these towns have high-tailed it out.

That, in turn, has resulted in towns like Las Vegas (New Mexico), Wellfleet (Massachusetts), Cambria (California), Astoria (Oregon), and Bisbee (Arizona), becoming the beneficiaries of an unanticipated economic spill-over, as artists have moved in, purchased homes, renovated vacant storefronts, opened their own galleries, and in general, plugged into these towns as quintessential 1990s entrepreneurs.

How do these artists, playwrights, musicians, jewelers, and dancers survive? Simple: they don't rely on their new hometowns to supply them with a source of income. Instead, they use their existing contacts (galleries, agents, producers, and collectors) to keep their cash flow healthy. Now, in some instances, these new hometowns have become popular places in their own right: either the town has become famous for its annual arts festival—Loveland, Northport (Alabama), Brattleboro (Vermont)—or a respectable tourism business has developed over the past several years. In those cases, the artists living in these communities—Bay St. Louis (Mississippi), Fredericksburg (Virginia), Livingston (Montana), Deadwood (South Dakota), to name a few—have been able to tap into this income source as well.

Other areas, such as New York Mills (Minnesota), Belfast (Maine), and Floyd (Virginia), are arts communities in the more classic sense—where rural living and friendly neighbors were the attractive drawing cards for artists. Small-scale economic transformations in these towns range from the simple establishment of a few new businesses on Floyd's sleepy Main Street to the more complicated takeover of the former town hall and public school in New York Mills and their subsequent rebirth as arts centers.

From one end of the country to the other, small towns are waking up to the fact that there's been an unexpected influx of artists, and that these newcomers are having a positive economic impact on that community's appearance and vitality. Business leaders and Chamber of Commerce members are quickly realizing that in a community whose likelihood of attracting a new computer chip plant or defense industry contractor is practically nonexistent, there is instead a tremendous potential in the economic impact of the arts. We're not talking simply about art galleries and arts supplies stores, but new restaurants, bed and breakfast inns, community performing and visual arts centers, and downtown buildings being restored into housing and work spaces for professionals in the many creative fields.

Think about the possibilities: Imagine yourself on vacation—even just a three-day weekend getaway. You drive to a town you've always wanted to visit, someplace like Asheville (North Carolina), Port Townsend (Washington), or New Hope (Pennsylvania). After checking into your room at a small hotel or bed and breakfast inn, you ask the desk clerk (or consult a guidebook) to select a restaurant for the evening, and maybe even decide to catch a play or attend a chamber music performance. The next day, you tour the town and surrounding area to "get a feel" for the place. And what is it that you do? You go to art galleries, the town museum, visit a craft store, and look at the cultural/artistic end of what the town has to offer.

My point is this: Weekend trips like the one described above are no longer the exclusive domain of a few select cities. This kind of experience is readily found across small town America in the mid-1990s—in unlikely places that you'd never have considered more than a wide spot in the road a decade ago. A place to grab a slice of pie and a cup of coffee, maybe, but never a place to go for affordable, technically superb art, or outstanding musical performances.

This book is an effort to identify and describe the appeal of some of those places—to define what it is that attracts artists to them, and what life is like there. It's a starting point for the culturally aware tourist who is willing to veer off the beaten track—to venture out toward these small towns in search of unexpectedly wonderful art. Some of these places will be familiar to you and, in some cases, there will be more widely-known art towns I've overlooked. This book pays homage to America's new, emerging arts centers.

There have been many wonderful individuals who have helped make this book possible, including Betsy Ostermiller of Loveland, Colorado, Jackie Chalkley of Washington, D.C.; Danny Medina of Scottsdale, Arizona; Denise Kusel of Santa Fe, New Mexico; Lynn Carter of Birmingham, Alabama; Manya Winsted of Phoenix, Arizona; John Dandurand of Denver, Colorado; Sally Ann Holtz and Nancy Cook of San Antonio, Texas; Suzanne Deats of Taos, New Mexico; Harold and Barbara Garde of Belfast, Maine; the wonderfully patient art gallery owners of Santa Fe, who are still trying to teach me to understand and appreciate art including (but not limited to) Phyllis Kapp, Nedra Matteucci, Edith Lambert, Debbye Omlie, Joe and Judy Wade, and Connie Axton; Santa Fe artists Genevieve Wahl, Roger Williams, Phil Navaasaya, Glenna Goodacre, Louisa McElwain, Jack Parsons, Doug Coffin, Bob "Daddy-O" Wade, and Jolene Eustace; the staff at John Muir Publications; Donald Meyer for his unflagging encouragement; and a special thanks to Candelora Versace for her kindness.

Introduction

In 1971, when I left my Connecticut hometown to attend college in Spokane, Washington, I found there were only two restaurants there that served a respectable pizza . . . amazing! Today, when I return to the Lilac City on my annual pilgrimage to the Pacific Northwest, I discover not only that Spokane's pizza shortcomings have been addressed a hundred times over, but it's even easy to find Thai restaurants, cappuccino cafes, and neighborhood restaurants serving Florentine calzones . . . amazing!

What we're in the process of becoming can best be described as "cosmopolitanized." Think of it . . . the generation now taking control of America's government, business, and social structures is comprised of educated individuals who in many cases have traveled to Europe, taken an art class or two in college, survived at least a few rock concerts, and maybe even have had a subscription to *Gourmet* magazine.

It's always been easy to find certain neighborhoods in larger cities that are imbued with a touch of the exotic. One could, since the days of the Beatles invasion, attend a foreign film in Minneapolis, find Guiness on tap in Raleigh, or nibble on fresh-baked French bread in Albuquerque. What's changed is that these mileposts of sophistication, these balms for soothing over life's more mundane qualities, are being created, produced, and served to the public in smaller communities. Want fresh-baked French bread in Boone, North Carolina? Want micro-brewed stout beer in Taos, New Mexico? Want cutting-edge documentary films in Hot Springs, Arkansas? The answers are yes, yes, and yes, and you can have all this and more in 1990s small town America.

As more city dwellers discover that they have to give up less than they thought they would after moving to the country (i.e., rural America), they're doing just that. And what they're finding once they get there are the artists and entrepreneurial risk-takers who blazed similar trails many years ago.

One of my greatest pleasures in writing this book came in the form of a *New York Times* front page headline published during the same month my manuscript was completed: "New York Exports its Talent As a Migration Tide Turns," it shouted. "Well," I thought, "you're only about five years late picking up on *that* trend." Just ask any of the top-name artists represented in art galleries on Madison Avenue, 57th Street, or lower Broadway . . . they'd be happy to tell you (as some have told me) that in their eyes one of the most startling art world trends over the past half-decade is the rapidly increasing volume of their art work that's being sold by art galleries outside "the city."

Guess who's buying this art work? Surprise! It's those wild and wacky urban refugees—the same individuals who once dressed up in their finest black clothes to rub elbows with fellow sophisticates at gallery receptions in uptown, midtown, and downtown. They're the ones who are so thrilled at finding their favorite artists represented at first-rate contemporary galleries in Peekskill, Sun Valley, Northampton, and Mendocino, that they're now doing their art collecting close to their rural homes.

But what's happening in respect to the fine arts in rural America goes much further than that. Yes, the presence in these areas of the kinds of individuals who are capable of making collecting decisions about art is most definitely an asset: the fact that gallery owners in Joseph (Oregon),

Kalispell (Montana), and Loveland (Colorado), can sell original, locally created bronze sculpture costing thousands of dollars is indicative of an important shift in the way Americans are approaching the entire process of buying fine art.

But who could have predicted that an art gallery in St. Simons Island, Georgia, could survive by selling the paintings of contemporary French artists; that abstract expressionism and/or impressionism would prosper in an art gallery in Blue Hill, Maine; that a conceptual landscape artist would thrive in Lawrence, Kansas; or that contemporary paintings by Michigan artists would do well in a Silver City, New Mexico, art gallery?

The yin to these rural galleries' yang is the presence in rural America of thousands of artists—painters, musicians, craftspeople, writers, actors, and storytellers—who not so very long ago would have been compelled to live cloistered in cities (usually in the run-down neighborhoods) if their goals were to survive exclusively on their creative output. Today, the artists you discover living in the country are in many instances astoundingly sophisticated masters of their chosen art forms. In other words, these are precisely the kinds of creative professionals who could, if they so elected, prosper in the competitive milieu that is the artists' lot in a metropolitan area. But living a productive and artistic life in the mid-1990s, means the artist gets to live wherever he or she damn well pleases. More and more, that means a rural community.

Certainly, there are obstacles that must be overcome if an artist chooses to live and work in a rural setting. For a chosen few, those obstacles are no more difficult than having one's sculpture, paintings, or jewelry crated up every few weeks or so and shipped overnight to an art gallery in a distant metropolitan area. Others can survive by keeping one foot planted in their local art markets (i.e., musicians who earn part of their incomes playing at summer festivals held across the country), while dipping the toes of their other foot into the lucrative waters of an urbanized art marketplace (i.e., accepting contract engagements requiring medium-length journeys on the road). Some survive by pasting together a mosaic of teaching engagements, gallery sales, and appearances at regional arts fairs. Many choose a life where their income is earned almost exclusively from regional arts and craft fairs: these are the artists who live in distant rural areas and spend much of their time as 1990s art gypsies.

Another phenomenon of this decade is the establishment of concentrations of creative professionals around active, working art facilities in small communities. Helena, Montana, has a state-of-the-art ceramics center at its Archie Bray Foundation; Round Top, Texas, has a 1,000-seat concert hall and rehearsal facility at its Festival Hill; Loveland, Colorado, has a pair of state-of-the-art bronze foundries that have lured in working sculptors from across the U.S. and Canada; Penland, North Carolina, has a center for the glass arts that's attracted dozens of internationally respected artists to a remote valley in the Blue Ridge Mountains; and the list goes on.

To dedicate yourself to a career in fine art means, in large part, setting out on a track of continual self-examination . . . of probing the creative recesses of your mind in a quest for that individualistic spark of artistic genius that allows an identity to emerge in the form of a creative product belonging to you alone. That breakthrough could be in the form of a technical advance, such as a way to combine materials in a manner nobody previously had been able to achieve (like a jeweler who develops a new way to cut precious stones, or a weaver who extracts undiscovered dyes from the roots of an exotic plant). Breakthroughs also come in the form of improvements on existing creative forms (like the way Stevie Ray Vaughn bent the blues notes formed on his guitar strings, or the way Ellsworth Kelly uses color fields and form to grab a viewer's emotional strings).

Some artists choose to pursue their creative challenges in isolation, while others are finding an increasing number of rural options for living and working in communities that have relatively large numbers of similar-minded arts professionals located nearby. In other words, many rural artists who find themselves trying to work through a problem in their art (be it something on a technical or a creative level), are finding that advice from other artists whose opinions are respected isn't very far away. The artist facing a problem in these small towns can simply pick up the phone and ask a talented colleague over to their studio for a cup of coffee and a chat about what can be done to get them through their creative difficulty.

Sculptors—artists working in three-dimensional forms using bronze, glass, and ceramics—are ahead of the curve when it comes to tapping into this sort of rural art community resource. One of the more startling trends that's evident in the Rocky Mountain region is the way in which communities such as Loveland (Colorado), Joseph (Oregon), Kalispell (Montana), Springville (Utah), and Ruidoso (New Mexico), have been turned into centers for bronze sculpture. In each of these communities the entrepreneurial venture of establishing a privately funded bronze foundry has led not only to jobs that are necessary for the foundry's operation but to an influx of sculptors who have purchased homes and studio facilities; base-makers who carve and sink steel rods into the wood, marble and granite foundations that most sculpture rests upon; shippers who crate and transport the sculpture to art galleries in distant cities; and art suppliers selling everything from buckets of clay to studio lighting systems.

While Kalispell and Ruidoso are communities that also benefit from a healthy tourism industry, towns like Joseph, Loveland, and Springville are able to see the direct correlation between becoming a magnet community for sculptors and a consequent upward shift in the town's economic fortunes. It's this sort of economic revival in rural communities that has caused state art agency administrators, regional art gallery owners, and local artists to realize a change in the ways artists live, work, and sell their art is sending favorable economic shock waves through communities who not so very long ago were completely removed from the art world.

What remains to be seen is how long it will take local governmental bodies to realize the vast economic potential that is poised to revive some rural communities through a partnership with the arts. In many communities the prevailing businessperson's mentality in regard to profiting from the arts is twisted around absurd, small-minded concepts such as T-shirt and "rubber tomahawk" shops, RV parks, and ice cream stores. Towns where this attitude is allowed to prevail soon become boring eyesores, attractive only to tourists on a tight budget. Other communities have been able to come to terms with planning for broader-scale development based on the arts, and it's these towns that are attracting Thai restaurants, charming bed and breakfast inns, active community centers for visual and performing arts, coffeehouses serving as art galleries, and most importantly, well-heeled tourists with money to spend on art, restaurants, and hotel rooms.

If the readers of this book are encouraged to veer off the well-beaten tourist track . . . to put aside their romanticized notions about art towns that have seen their best days disappear into a hazy shroud of development and commercialization (Provincetown, Woodstock, Santa Fe, Carmel, and Newport are in this category), then as culturally aware tourists, they can venture into the smaller, more rural emerging art centers of America. That's what this book is all about.

John Villani   Santa Fe, New Mexico
                                                                                          April, 1994

The

100 Best
Small Art Towns

In America

Northport, Alabama

Location
From its location on the Black Warrior River, the 16,000 residents of Northport benefit from the services and employment opportunities in the nearby university town of Tuscaloosa.

Climate
Escaping from the harsh, northern winter seems to be the motivation for many of Northport's more recent arrivals. Surrounded by the lush, rolling hills of central Alabama, this community experiences a long growing season characterized by an early spring and a long, glorious autumn. While summer tends to be hot and humid, nearby lakes and the Gulf Coast beaches (a 3-hour drive) provide relief.

Living
Family-size, 3-bedroom homes in tree-shaded neighborhoods sell in the $90,000 range. Neighbors in this heavily democratic area tend to be well-educated; lots of college instructors are raising their families in this community filled with parks and bicycle trails.

As could be expected, college sports are nearly everyone's favorite pastime in this area. Lake Tuscaloosa is a prime spot for anyone wanting a day of water skiing or some quiet time angling for bass, with more dramatic waters available nearby in the Gulf of Mexico. The University of Alabama is the area's largest employer, and folks living here enjoy a relaxed lifestyle invigorated by the presence of 30,000 or so college students for three-quarters of each year. The crime rate is lower here than in other southern cities, and anyone wanting a metropolitan fix is welcome to drive an hour into nearby Birmingham (closest large airport) or three hours to Atlanta.

Out On the Town
With the University of Alabama across the river, Northport has immediate access to Tuscaloosa's varied restaurants, nightclubs, and performing arts offerings. Thai food is dished up at the Siam House, while those who prefer to stay on the Northport side of the river can slide up to the bar at the Globe for a cold brew and an active night scene. Natural food is the draw at Manna Grocery and Restaurant, while Johnny's sets Tuscaloosa's standard for hamburgers and shakes. On campus, the Moody Concert Hall is the region's preferred venue for classical music, while downtown's renovated Bama Theater and Performing Arts Center brings in everything from touring Broadway shows to rock concerts.

Economic Impact of the Arts
Having recently been selected as the site for the first North American Mercedes-Benz production facility, this entire community has been given a tremendous burst of pride and confidence. Gail Skidmore, the local art council's director, says she hopes the downtown business community realizes that Northport's visual arts scene and Tuscaloosa's performing arts scene played an important role in attracting the German industrial giant to the region.

Local Arts Agency

Arts Council of Tuscaloosa, P.O. Box 1117, Tuscaloosa, AL 35403, (205) 758-8083.

From its offices in the renovated, 1937 neo-classical jewel that's the Bama Theater Performing Arts Center, the council oversees both a nonprofit art gallery (Bama Theater Gallery) and a performing arts space that centralizes the region's artistic focus. "We're used for rehearsals and performances around 240 days a year," says Gail Skidmore, whose budget includes funds for performing arts residency programs for touring professionals in theater, dance, and music.

Besides serving the cultural needs of the community, the local arts council serves as a meeting ground where Tuscaloosa's African American community is represented as an important component in the region's demographic mosaic, according to Skidmore. "We've expanded into a broad range of arts and art forms, from African dance troupes to school programs where we bring classrooms into the arts center for presentations during school hours." Local schools also interact with the arts center in coordinating artist-in-residence programs that draw from a base of local, regional, and national art professionals.

Galleries and Arts Festivals

In addition to the exhibition space operated by the arts council in the Bama Theater, there are four commercial art galleries in Tuscaloosa and a few open artist studios in Northport. The annual Kentuck Festival of the Arts, held the second weekend in October at Kentuck Park in Northport, attracts 200-plus exhibitors, including dozens of the South's indigenous group of folk artists who create what's come to be known as "outsider art."

What the Artist Says

Craig Nutt, woodworker, lives and has studio space in an artists' complex at the Kentuck Art Center, which offers low-cost work space to professional artists. He has lived in the area since 1968, and says that Northport has the atmosphere of a true artists' enclave. "You get the feeling of being in a small arts town, except that a larger city is right at your doorstep," says Craig, who nationally markets a line of whimsical furniture and wall hangings he refers to as "my vegetable furniture and flying vegetable art."

"Northport has shown a commitment to me and my career, and when critical times came along, the people here were very supportive and made a big difference. I think the business community goes out of its way to try and understand my profession, and the artists in town know who their fellow artists are. There's a lot of interaction among the arts community. Alabama isn't a wealthy state, so to be a professional artist here means you've got to sell outside the state and know where your markets are. Northport has a friendly, comfortable attitude. If you need a small town to live in, this would be a good choice."

Homer, Alaska

Location
Hugging the sloping hillsides of a sheltered harbor at the tip of Kenai Peninsula, Homer (pop. 4,000) enjoys endless views of soaring mountain ranges lying on the opposite side of Cook Inlet.

Climate
Those who grew up on a diet of TV shows about cops and robbers slugging it out in the Yukon will be surprised to learn that one of Homer's most notable features is its moderate (by Alaska standards) climate. More closely resembling the overcast skies of Puget Sound than the bitterly cold tundra of inland Alaska, the climate here is characterized by a wet winter, spring and fall, bracketing four months of moderate warmth and midnight sun.

Living
With its limited supply of housing, homes in Homer tend to be snapped up as soon as they hit the real estate pages of the newspaper—if not before. An average 3-bedroom place sells in the $100,000 range, but because this is the Great North, structures are well-built and superbly insulated. Summer's glacier-gazing tourist season is a make-it-or-break-it time for artists (and most others) who aren't employed in the region's fishing industry, with dozens of gift shops and art galleries open to take advantage of the seasonal rush. During the rest of the year, the performing arts theater inside Homer's new $40-million high school is the heart and soul of this region's arts scene.

Have you ever watched the TV series *Northern Exposure*? Welcome to Homer: a small town where many quirky, yet wonderful, elements of real life come together and somehow manage to peacefully coexist. From the gruff fishermen (and some fisherwomen) who earn their livings from the town's commercial fleet to the summer businesses that crop up like crocuses in spring and then beat a hasty retreat each autumn, Homer manages to hold these and other individualists together as a community. According to Joy Steward, director of the arts council, arts programs are taken very seriously in local schools, with visiting artist lectures and workshops included as a regular part of student learning experiences. "One of our goals right now is to make a strong effort to reach out to Homer's elderly," she says, "and to keep working around the occasional comment we hear about the arts being an elitist pursuit."

Out On the Town
Homer has its share of rough-and-tumble bars, and the scraggly appearance of some locals belies the witty camaraderie pervasive in these shot-and-a-beer sort of establishments. Artists and others looking for a more sedate scene head to Cafe Cups, a restaurant featuring rotating exhibits of work by local painters. Dancing and general good cheer is part of the reason Alice's Champagne Palace is a popular nightclub, while the Glacier Drive-In has Homer's best burgers and shakes. During the summers, the Pier One Theater stages live dramatic performance, but for those wanting classical music and ethnic food it's a 3-hour drive into Anchorage, the state's largest city.

Economic Impact of the Arts

As an oil-rich state, Alaska is forever riding out the ups and downs endemic to states reliant on the energy industry. On a local level, that means in good years (when the price of oil goes up) the state's tax revenues soar to stratospheric levels and everyone's pet projects get funded. Flip that picture over, however, and you get an image of where public funding for the arts presently rests in the 49th state: down in the dumps. Homer's artists and gallery owners have tried valiantly to tap the more predictable summer cash flow of cruise ship tourists who flock to the Kenai Peninsula from late May through mid-September. In turn, that leads to artists struggling with whether they'll create picturesque kitsch for the majority of tourists or attempt to reach a smaller segment of the potential market with more adventurous art work.

Local Arts Agency

Homer Council on the Arts, P.O. Box 1764, Homer, AK 99603, (907) 235-4288. Publishes the newsletter *Behind the Scenes*.

Now that the community has access to the high school's performing arts center, Homer is able to attract a year-round slate of dance programs, music performance, and theater troupes, says Joy Steward. "We're fortunate to have the local business community perceive Homer's artists and galleries as an important reason for tourists being attracted here in the first place, and they're promoting this town as an arts center," she says. "Occasionally, the Anchorage newspaper will send a reporter down to cover one of our performances or a gallery exhibition. The only nonprofit art gallery in town is at the Pratt Museum, which concentrates on natural history exhibits."

Galleries and Festivals

Homer's main arts events are its month-long Spring Arts Festival, which coordinates the opening of extensive gallery exhibitions with performances by nearly two dozen local dance groups, bands, and other performers. During the height of tourist season, the late July run of Summer Street Fair is a zany event pitching belly dancers, local rock bands, and the like—all of whom are set up at one end of downtown Homer's Heath Street, against the booths of 50 or so local artists and craftspeople who compete for tourists' attention and disposable dollars. After the tourists head south, a few art galleries stay open through the off-season, and local artists use the time to create art work and stay in touch with their gallery contacts outside Alaska.

What the Artist Says

Karla Moss Freeman, painter of abstract expressionist landscapes, moved to Homer 14 years ago. "I augment my income by teaching art at Kenai Peninsula College, but Homer is a small community with a true appreciation for the arts. If I wanted to compete with picture windows (and sell more paintings), I'd probably create what some of us artists refer to 'Alaskana,' which from the painter's point of view is a work of art that includes at least one image of a moose and a distant mountain range. To me, Homer's lifestyle is like a continuing meditation . . . you're surrounded by a pristine, spectacular setting, and it prepares you for what you'll find on the 'outside.' Any artists thinking of moving here need to have their markets developed before they arrive, and they need to plan vacations or trips away from Homer at least twice each year."

Juneau, Alaska

Location

Surrounded by the Tongass National Forest and within hiking distance of the Mendenhall Glacier, the southeast Alaska community of Juneau (pop. 28,000) fronts onto the pristine waterways of the Inland Passage.

Climate

The climate is typical northern maritime, which translates into a whole lot of rain and boiling grey skies, interspersed with teasingly brief runs of clear weather. Like the rest of Alaska, Juneau gets a break from the predominant weather patterns each summer, but this isn't the place to move to if you are concerned about sunlight deprivation syndrome.

Living

Juneau is surprisingly cosmopolitan, in a Pacific Northwest sort of way. It has a history of voting Democratic candidates into office, and its downtown streets are filled with the same sort of espresso shops and bakeries more commonly associated with places like Eugene, Oregon, and Eureka, California. Local performing artists make use of Juneau's high school auditorium (which is state-of-the-art), and the town's Perseverance Theater is managed by a core group of experienced professionals. Loaded with gingerbread-trimmed Victorian homes, a 3-bedroom house in reasonable condition will sell in the $135,000 range.

To say that recreational opportunities in this area are limitless is to understate the matter. Perhaps nowhere else in the nation can an individual enjoy skiing, mountain climbing, bicycling, and deep sea fishing—all in one day (providing the body holds up). For those who live here, weather-proof clothing is a must. But when you get past the mental barrier of enjoying yourself in a bit of rain or mist, life here begins to take on real meaning.

The state government, Juneau's largest employer, seems to have a well-paid position for nearly anyone who wants to have one—when oil revenues are high. The kicker comes during lean years for the energy business, which results in a blizzard of pink slips stuffed into those same government payroll envelopes. Overall, Juneau is safe and still affordable, with a refreshing slant on its own style and a charming local take on architecture.

Out On the Town

Benefiting from an ever-growing summer tourist season (they all get here on cruise ships), Juneau's favorite watering holes range from the Armadillo Cafe (where you'll find margaritas and Tex-Mex border town dishes) to the more typically Alaskan ambience of the Red Dog Saloon. Put on your dancing shoes if you head over to catch live music at the Penthouse, and if it's simpler fare of a burger, fries, and a vanilla shake that make your putter flutter, join the locals at the Douglas Cafe or the Channel Bowl Cafe. If a hankering for tofu and soy milk invades your psyche, the place for a more cosmic fix is Fiddlehead's Bakery.

Economic Impact of the Arts

Sure, the summer season in Juneau is a gold mine of opportunity. But what sets this little haven apart from others of its size is a healthy, year-round arts scene and a surprising level of integrity to the work. At the height of tourist season, nearly two dozen craft and fine art galleries swing their doors open to the public—and most of their owners are locals who keep the doors open (figuratively speaking, of course) throughout the year.

Local Arts Organization

Juneau Arts & Humanities Council, P.O. Box 20562, Juneau, AK 99802, (907) 586-2787.

"We support all aspects of the arts," says Natalee Rothaus, executive director of Juneau's arts council. "Writers are very much a part of this town's creative community, as is the region's wonderful Native American heritage of the Tlingit and Haida people. The Chamber of Commerce makes good use of Juneau's arts community as a way of drawing tourists in to see what we've got here. Our summer Arts in the Parks program is very strong, very well-supported by the people who live here. During the school year, we give out annual scholarships for art students and book performers into Juneau who have the time to do workshops at local schools. If the council was not in Juneau, the people who care about having a cultural life would immediately notice the difference."

Galleries and Arts Festivals

Everything from Native American fine art and crafts to challenging contemporary painting is exhibited in Juneau's commercial art galleries. The Alaska State Museum and its extensive collection of historical materials is here as well, and the town's non-profit exhibition space, Artworks Unlimited, is open year-round. While local residents are comfortable enough with art to occasionally buy work produced by Juneau artists, most serious art money comes into town on the cruise ships of summer. The Alaska Folk Festival in April and the Juneau Jazz & Classical Music Festival each May are the town's largest organized arts events.

What the Artist Says

Juan Muñoz, owner of Rie Muñoz Gallery, is a lifelong resident of the area. "Per square foot, there are lots of artists in Juneau," he says. "There's a strong Native American influence, but looking past that you see a number of strong galleries . . . more than a town this size normally can support, and about 15 of them stay open year-round."

His business sells original paintings by various artists and nationally markets the reproductions of art works created by Juan's mother, painter Rie Muñoz. The gallery is strong in the area of regionalist painters, with an emphasis, says Juan, on expressionistic work. "It's not as cold as you think—but an artist has to be of a strong character in order to make it here. Make sure you're happy staying indoors before moving here, because Juneau has a dark, rainy winter. On the other hand, it's a very neighborly place—we need to have more artists become part of this community."

Bisbee, Arizona

Location

If you're standing in the middle of Bisbee at, say, 11:30 a.m. on a typically sunny Arizona day, you'll still have time enough to make it across the border to Naco, Mexico, by noon. Less than a 2-hour drive from Tucson's airport and services, the old mining town of Bisbee is smack dab in the middle of the land that time forgot.

Climate

Yes, it's time to stock up on moisturizers, sunblocks, and lip balm. But you may not need to buy that extra-powerful air conditioner, as Bisbee sits at an elevation of 5,000 feet in southern Arizona's Sierra Vista Mountains. Here, winter is a temperate dream, with cool nights and days that usually prompt locals to wear a sweater right up through noon. While summer can be considered very warm, there are not as many blisteringly hot days here as there are in lower elevation towns like Tucson and Phoenix. Normally, you can count on a temperature difference of 10 to 20 degrees between Bisbee and the desert lowlands.

Living

A thriving mining town up through the 1960s, Bisbee didn't have much time to fall into disrepair between the time miners moved elsewhere to when artists started migrating into homes built along the town's steep, narrow streets. Downtown Bisbee is filled with a curious mix of shops catering to the area's vigorous tourist trade and stores that offer goods and services for locals. The Central School Project, which is housed in a former downtown schoolhouse, offers artists low-cost studio and exhibition space, as well as sponsoring arts workshops and performance space. Sections of Bisbee retain a slice of their rowdy past, but things are changing—perhaps too rapidly for the artists and counter-culture types who came here 20 years ago.

Those in search of a big city fix drive two hours to Tucson, home of the University of Arizona and hundreds of ethnic restaurants, malls, movie houses, and more. An average 3-bedroom home in Bisbee runs $60,000, but is very hard to find. Patagonia Lake State Park and the mountains around Ft. Huachuca are popular recreation spots, while theater-goers and classical music lovers can catch occasional presentations at B.T.V. Theater and the Bisbee Women's Club.

Out On the Town

There are two parts of this town: Old Bisbee, where most restaurants and all the historic buildings are located, and New Bisbee, a more recently built area encompassing residential neighborhoods and shopping malls. For visitors, unless you've just got to eat at McDonald's, there's little reason to venture outside Old Bisbee, and most everything is within a few minutes' walking distance from the heart of downtown. A few bars and restaurants are strung along Brewery Gulch (with alas, no functioning brewery), but the arts crowd tends to favor places like Gianelli's, a restaurant on Shearer Avenue, featuring rotating art exhibitions, and the Good Stuff Cafe on Naco Road. Club

Kilamanjaro on Subway Street has regular bands and D.J. action. The Brewery is a favorite spot for burgers and fries, while Bisbee Co-op supplies natural take-out foods.

Economic Impact of the Arts

No matter where you look in Bisbee, you'll find art. From funky shops hidden down shaded alleyways to paintings hung on the walls of boutiques to more traditional gallery spaces on Main Street, art and artists have obviously been important components in the revival of Bisbee's economic fortunes. Interestingly, this is also a community attractive to literary types, and several well-known authors maintain part-time residences in the quaint Victorian homes faceted into the town's steep-walled canyon. There are nearly two dozen art galleries in Bisbee, along with two nonprofit exhibition spaces. Growth is one of the town's most pressing issues, as is the question of controlling motorhome traffic on the narrow, crowded streets.

Local Arts Agencies

Central School Project, Drawer H, Bisbee, AZ 85603, (602) 432-7688, and Bisbee Arts Coalition, 118 Arizona Street, Bisbee, AZ 85603, (602) 432-5446.

With two active arts organizations in town, nearly all the needs of Bisbee's creative community are being met, in one manner or another. The Central School Project provides strong support to the town's visual artists, offering not only studio space in a classic, 3-story brick elementary school, but also coordinating artist-in-residence programs with local schools and staging arts workshops in one of its many classrooms. The Bisbee Arts Coalition sponsors open studio tours, public performances of dance, music, and theater, and serves as a coordinating point where both the town's artists and its more traditional business community set the arts and humanities agenda.

Galleries and Art Festivals

On the gallery front, Bisbee's exhibition opportunities have never looked better. Certainly, there's an element of what's derisively referred to as the "rubber tomahawk" kitsch sold by local trinket shops. On the other hand, several legitimate efforts at quality art exhibition space have recently marked a maturation in the town's development as an artists' haven. The battlefront in Bisbee is being waged over a familiar issue: how to maintain some level of quality in the art and objects shown in galleries and boutiques. The town's busiest season runs from January through May, and the Artist Studio Tour in early March is an arts event not to be missed.

What the Artist Says

"It's a town that hooks you," says Bisbee artist Tom Kerrigan. "Here, you can work in a fairly uninterrupted way, and there are lots of interesting people coming through from all over the country. We're 50 miles off the nearest interstate and because of the way Bisbee is laid out, development is restricted. Here, artists have an openness to each other, but you need outside contacts in order to survive as an artist. It's a very different lifestyle, so be sure you can handle that before you get here."

Jerome, Arizona

Location
At the edge of Prescott National Forest, a 2-hour drive north of Phoenix, sits the former mining town of Jerome. Characterized by a mining town's typically narrow streets carved into steep hillsides, most of the housing was built prior to 1960.

Climate
Moderated somewhat by its altitude, Jerome's summer climate is typical desert southwest: hot and dry. But while Phoenix sleeps under 45-degree winter nights, Jerome's 500 residents can just as easily receive a dusting of snow. In other words, the weather patterns can vary widely.

Living
Artists and craftspeople make up the majority of Jerome's residents, with a strong mix of '60s refugees and survivalists thrown into the town's diverse population. Residences in Jerome tend to be in need of repair, while those who bought into Jerome in the early days and completed their remodeling projects tend to hold onto their places indefinitely. Some new construction is taking place, but those building tend to favor fitting in with the local architectural schemes, as opposed to the mindless, nouveau-riche flaunting that takes place in towns like Sedona and Scottsdale. An average 3-bedroom home here runs around $50,000, while some studio spaces can be rented above downtown shops for $300 to $600 a month.

With the wide open spaces of Prescott National Forest nearby, some of Jerome's residents enjoy a certain illegal horticultural activity that every now and again causes the local law enforcement authorities to break out their rakes, hoes, and machetes. A liberal hotbed with minimal services, most people in Jerome do their shopping and schooling in nearby towns such as Cottonwood, Prescott, or Sedona.

"I made a lot of sacrifices to live here," says Judie Piner, the director of Jerome's Arts Registry and owner of a local quilting shop. "Serious artists see this as a peaceful place to live and work, but they absolutely must have ways to sell their work outside of Jerome. People come here looking for inexpensive deals, and as a result a lot of Jerome's artists go home hungry each night."

Out On the Town
Those who want a fancy place for drinks and dinner will want to head down the road to Sedona, which also has some ethnic food choices. After dark, Jerome's favorite tell-all kind of place is the Spirit Room, which does double duty as a dance hall and local hangout for the arts crowd. Regular grub (a.k.a. burgers and sandwiches) is served at the English Kitchen.

Economic Impact of the Arts
Once threatened with drying up and blowing away on a stiff wind, Jerome managed to avoid becoming a ghost town when a group of nearly penniless artists and craftspeople moved in during the late 1960s and bought (for next to nothing) the run-down homes owned by old miners seeking

retirement to the Phoenix suburbs. Today, most of the local landowners and businessmen still wear pierced earrings and ponytails, but they watch their investments and know how to take advantage of an economic opportunity. Here, galleries range from dusty and drafty to polished, renovated, and pristine. All things considered, it's a healthy mix of both sides of life that comes off as unpretentious. Lots of visitors come in for Jerome's slate of irregularly scheduled craft shows. Call the Chamber of Commerce at (602) 634-2900 for specific times and dates.

Local Arts Agency

The Arts Registry, P.O. Box G, Jerome, AZ 86331, (602) 634-9621.

Historically a hideout for those who wanted as little to do with the rest of the world as possible, Jerome has attracted artists who have tended to go off in their own directions to work and meditate, which means that only lately has any attempt been made at organizing the community's de facto arts voice. "We also have infrastructure questions to deal with," says Judie Piner. "Growth is taking place, and sooner or later the artists here will have to organize in order to have a voice in the way the community develops." Sociable artists who want to sell their work directly to tourists have opened shops carrying original arts and crafts, but there's also plenty of solitude for those who want it.

Galleries and Arts Festivals

In the past, some gallery owners have come into Jerome with unreasonable expectations as to what the tourist market will buy, says Piner, which explains the regular comings and goings of the town's galleries. The successful businesses tend to be run by artists who emphasize their own work, yet always keep a lot of low-priced objects on hand that sell to tourists. The year's biggest arts fair takes place over the July 4th weekend. Musicians and instrument makers form a considerable segment of the town's creative community.

What the Artist Says

Margo Mandette, a sculptor and painter who arrived in Jerome from Phoenix nearly 17 years ago, lives in the town's former high school (these days, kids are bussed into Cottonwood to attend school). "I think people come into Jerome looking to buy art work directly from the artists . . . looking to get around the galleries and get a better deal. It would be nice to have some sort of light manufacturing business relocate to Jerome, so that the people who aren't artists can have a place in town to work. I think that years ago, before Jerome started becoming popular, the artists here worked together much more than they do now. We need a nonprofit exhibition space for local artists, and to keep the same things in place that attracted artists to Jerome originally: affordable housing and serenity."

Sedona, Arizona

Location

Nestled alongside the Oak Creek, in a northern Arizona canyon slightly more than a 2-hour drive from Phoenix, the nearly 8,000 residents of Sedona live amongst one of the nation's most spectacular natural wonders: a geologic formation of soaring, red rock that look as if it had been painted into place by the Creator himself.

Climate

The area has hot summers and magnificent winters, with a northern enough location to allow for an occasional dusting of snow during January and early February. With plenty of cottonwood trees lining the Oak Creek's banks, Sedona gets a brief taste of spring and a spectacular autumn.

Living

Bring lots of money, because a 3-bedroom home in this artsy town will set you back somewhere in the neighborhood of $200,000. For that kind of dough, you get anything from a sprawling suburban ranch home to a reasonable facsimile of a Santa Fe adobe. Most artists live in the communities surrounding Sedona and come into town to deliver work to galleries or take part in the town's brisk, well-heeled gallery scene. Sedona just formed its own school district, and a new high school is expected to be on line by 1995.

When Sedona was relatively undiscovered, it was populated by the same artists who showed their works in the local galleries; for the most part, these artists produced western realism or cowboy art—the kind of paintings most valued by the group of regional collectors who visited during the town's busy season. Nowadays, with its popularity recognized by a wider spectrum of art collectors, Sedona's galleries exhibit a much broader range of paintings, sculpture, and fine craft objects created by artists working in all forms of imagery. Sedona is now a sophisticated town; a place where Thai food and Northern Italian restaurants are crowded on weekends with visitors from all over the globe.

Out On the Town

The best place to meet your artist pals for a margarita is Rainbow's End, while Canyon Rose is the ideal two-steppin' rendezvous. Burgers and shakes are great at Shuqrues, and natural food is available at New Frontiers Deli. Sedona Arts Center stages an occasional dramatic production.

Economic Impact of the Arts

The arts presence is substantial and elemental in attracting people into Sedona, although selling real estate seems to be every other newcomer's profession of choice. Probably because it's so close to California, Sedona has been under increasing pressure to find an effective way to deal with the many newcomers and their Range Rovers and cellular phones. The town has an arts museum, but most serious art action takes place in the commercial galleries.

Local Arts Agency

Sedona Art and Culture, P.O. Box 30002, Sedona, AZ 86339, (602) 282-9738.

"We're a resource for the town's arts community and try to act as a catalyst in matching people, resources, and needs," says director Lorna McLeod. "One of our goals is to help our new school district beef up its music and visual arts programs, something we plan on doing by bringing more local writers, actors, artists, and musicians into the Sedona schools. We have inadequate facilities when it comes to staging public events like opera, ballet and theater. That's why the plans for the Sedona Cultural Park (52 acres, 5,000-seat ampitheater, festival grounds, etc.) are important. If we can get the park built, it will go a long way toward pulling together the arts resources of Sedona . . . and those are substantial."

Galleries and Art Festivals

With over 40 art galleries playing an active role in Sedona's cultural life, the marketing opportunities for artists living in this area are magnificent. During the busy October-through-April tourist season, galleries here go through a make-it-or-break-it period. Afterward, the collectors head north to Santa Fe, but while they're here, Sedona does a great job with coordinated opening night receptions and frequent outdoors arts events aimed at maximizing the art community's exposure. The year's biggest arts event is the Sedona Arts Fair, held each October on the grounds of the Sedona School. Even so, exhibitions and other art events held in Sedona are strong enough to attract coverage from newspapers in Phoenix and Las Vegas. Obviously, quality sells.

What the Artist Says

Sculptor Susan Kliewer, whose bronzes of western realist images are primarily sold through her Sedona gallery representative, says she likes living in Sedona because of "the tremendous support the people here have shown me every step of the way." Susan came to Sedona 23 years ago, drawn by its mysterious scenery and the existence of an arts community. "I'd been mostly a Sunday painter, but then I signed up for classes at the arts center and became interested in working in clay. Now, I do monumental-size commissions and help organize our successful Sculpture Walk each January. I'm very interested in meeting people, so most days I just go down to the gallery and sculpt right there in front of them. We tend to get a family crowd during the summer months, but our winters are so strong that it more than makes up for slow sales during the rest of the year. Any artist who wants to move here should be ready to work two (or even three) jobs to pay their bills. Success just doesn't happen overnight."

Tubac, Arizona

Location
Once an outpost of Spanish colonialist government, Tubac's 1,000 year-round residents live in the Santa Cruz Valley between Tucson and the Mexican border, at the edge of the Sonoran desert.

Climate
Here, folks like to boast that theirs is the best winter weather in the nation, and with Tubac's clear skies and 70-degree days from December through February, who can blame them? Did I forget to mention those 115-degree broilers during the summer months? Well, if that's when you'll be visiting, make sure you bring plenty of ice tea.

Living
Until recently, Tubac was the sort of frayed-at-the-edges, dusty old town that only an artist could love. But a few years back, real estate developers started scoping out the surrounding hillsides as ideal sites for what are euphemistically referred to as "country club communities." Since then, most real estate prices have escalated and what was once an influx of artists from places west has turned into an influx of retirees from the Midwest. Homes of average size run upwards of $150,000, and those who want ethnic food or a cultural life need to drive north to Tucson. Of course, just down the road, Nogales, Mexico, has several fine dining establishments, but most of Tubac's country-clubbers tend to shun anything more exotic than Red Lobster.

There's fishing in the lakes around Patagonia and Pena Blanca, and cervezas and steaks smothered in green chile just across the border. Locals grab their food at Mom's Place and drive into Tucson for a dose of nightlife. Tucson is also home to the Arizona Repertory Theater and the Tucson Symphony.

Economic Impact of the Arts
To walk Tubac's streets, you'd think the nation was crying out for howling coyotes. Unfortunately, there are more than two dozen so-so galleries and gift shops lined up along Tubac's main drag, and the town's more long-term residents fondly remember the days when buyers looking for art had something in mind other than paintings of smiling Native American toddlers. Even so, there's an active arts center in Tubac, one whose tireless efforts at visual and performing arts education programs seem to bounce off the sun-hardened skulls of many of its newcomers.

Local Arts Agency
Tubac Center of the Arts, P.O. Box 1911, Tubac, AZ 85646, (602) 398-2371.

Wonderfully equipped and presenting a September-through-May slate of visual and performing arts events and workshops, Tubac has the kind of innovative arts center most small towns would sell their water systems for. "The subscription series we put on during the busy winter months is extremely popular," says Marty Spencer, the center's administrative director. "We don't have any schools in Tubac, but we still put on four-week arts programs for kids and make a strong effort to cooperate with the art departments at the schools in Nogales (Arizona). We've got three gallery spaces for visual exhibitions, some studio spaces, and facilities for adult arts education classes."

Galleries and Art Festivals

The year's busiest season runs through the heart of winter, the same time northerners are shoveling piles of snow from their doorsteps. The first weekend in February marks the opening of Tubac's annual Festival of the Arts, a nine-day affair that attracts hordes of visitors to town. The event also draws caravans of tourist trinket-vendors who end up competing directly with some of downtown Tubac's souvenir shops. Lately, the owners of these "legit" shops have started complaining that the flea market types are stealing their best customers! Yet the festival also has a reputation for drawing in some of the Southwest's most proficient craftspeople. Tubac is just one of those towns you've got to visit to understand.

What the Artist Says

"With NAFTA coming in, this place is bound to expand," says western realist artist and gallery owner Bob Shepherd. "I'm just afraid that Tubac isn't going to figure out a way to plan for its growth. I keep a sign on my door telling people this is a fine art gallery, but the tourists we get in this town still come wandering in here, asking for the gee gaws and T-shirts. It's actually surprising to me when someone eventually comes in and ends up buying one of my originals. The Chamber of Commerce doesn't care to promote Tubac as a place that's attractive to artists, although artists were the first ones in here and were the only reason this little town survived. As for the local businesspeople, I get the feeling they'd just as soon see all the artists hit the road. What Tubac needs is a dozen artists coming in here to run their own galleries. If there was a little more helping each other out . . . some kind of effort made to make this town more attractive to people with money, things would be a lot better for everyone."

Eureka Springs, Arkansas

Location

The northwest corner of Arkansas is a land of tall trees, meandering lakes, steep hillsides, and springtime white water rafting. Eureka Springs (pop. 2,000) is a 3-hour drive from the closest city, Little Rock. The Ozark Mountains shelter a number of funky old towns, and while Eureka Springs retains a strong flavor of rural Arkansas living, it has managed to grow into a surprisingly vibrant regional arts center.

Climate

Locals revel in a seasonal explosion of moderate weather conditions covering every possible variation of winter, spring, summer, and fall. Yes, there's an occasional heavy snowfall, but within a few days things will warm up to the point where the white stuff melts and everyone starts planning for the arrival of the area's characteristic extended, tolerably humid summer.

Living

Among Eureka Springs' residents are hundreds of folks who have lived in metropolitan areas and chucked it all for a chance to get back to a semblance of normal, rural living. Here, they've found it. Slightly hip, slightly decrepit, slightly restored, and completely unpretentious, Eureka Springs has housing prices in the $80,000 range for a 1930s, craftsman-built structure. There isn't an arts center, but local folks are pleased with the way the schools are beginning to integrate arts education into student curriculums. Closest NPR station is in Fayetteville, and Little Rock's newspapers seldom give serious mention to the town's arts community.

Artists move here for the region's scenic beauty, says Douglas Stowe, president of Eureka Springs Guild of Artists and Craftspeople. "There's a genuine warmth and friendliness in Eureka Springs. Here, people are tolerant of the differences that exist between individuals. They're able to look beyond that and focus instead on what we can all do together. We've got a strong voice in the way things happen in Eureka Springs, and are definitely respected for our opinions. It's a sophisticated arts scene that goes far beyond what many people think of as being typical Ozark Mountains craft."

Canoeing, water skiing, and fishing are the town's most popular leisure pursuits, most people vote Democrat, and the closest college is the University of Arkansas in Fayetteville.

Out On the Town

Pick up on the local art buzz at the Center Street Cafe (also a good place for live bands and dancing), or join the more sedate scene at Cafe Armagost, the town's best place for natural food. Meet your pals for a drink at the Oasis, and if you leave Eureka Springs without diving into a basket of brisket or chicken at Bubba's Barbecue, well, you haven't really been paying attention, anyway. Occasional live theater is staged at the Eureka Playhouse. Fortunately, many Ozark communities—former health spas—have lovingly preserved their alternative healing legacies; the Palace Hotel and Bath House in downtown Eureka Springs has come a long way from its more freewheeling days as a cat house and gambling joint.

Economic Impact of the Arts

Local businesspeople realize that a few renovated spas aren't bringing more tourists into this remote corner of the state, which is why the arts are being seen for what they clearly are: a money-making godsend. Each year, the town seems to attract at least one or two new quality art galleries or craft stores, joining a restaurant or two, and seeding the renovation of a few more downtown historic buildings. In other words, the pace of change is humanely slow, yet it is definitely taking place. Thankfully, it's improving the quality of life for the entire community.

Local Art Agency

Eureka Springs Guild of Artists and Craftspeople, P.O. Box 182, Eureka Springs, AR 72632. (No phone.)

The local arts group has been around for a number of years and pursues a broad agenda aimed at the general promotion of the town's art and craft professionals. Lately, that's included a strong effort to expand into the area of arts education programs and artist services, says president Douglas Stowe. "We're one of the few arts groups whose members include both younger artists and retired folks who have turned to the arts later in their lives," he says. "The downtown business community has been very supportive in understanding what the Eureka Springs arts community needs to survive and prosper. We're just now opening a nonprofit downtown studio and exhibition space that's largely been funded by the business community."

Galleries and Arts Festivals

There are nearly two dozen art galleries in this small town, and that's a testimonial to the reliable tourist business the arts and business communities have built through the years. Lots of quality work is exhibited, with a special emphasis on craft and furniture, although more visual art has been popping up in recent years. The Arkansas Craft Gallery is a year-round, nonprofit exhibition space. April through October is the busiest time of year for the arts, and the year's largest arts event is the May Fine Art Festival, with nearly a hundred exhibiting artists and craftspeople.

What the Artist Says

Jim Nelson, who owns two Eureka Springs art galleries and still gets around to occasionally completing a canvas or two, says the best way for an artist to survive here is to open a gallery and sell directly to the well-educated tourists attracted to the region. "Our music scene has really taken off in the past few years. . . . Now, there's jazz, blues, and some country music festivals. We love the way Eureka Springs responds to individual creativity, whether that's channeled into a business venture or into the creation of a work of art. We should concentrate on becoming one of the country's leading centers for crafts and art . . . and promote ourselves into the best possible level of quality. If you're thinking of moving here, try not to become involved in Arkansas politics, and take time to get to know the people who live here."

Hot Springs, Arkansas

Location
An hour's drive southwest of Little Rock's shopping malls and airport, Hot Springs is a community of 36,000 residents living in an area bounded on one side by a national park and on the other by the banks of sprawling Lake Hamilton.

Climate
Hot Springs has mild versions of each season, with a long growing season stretching from early April through the beginning of November. The terrain is heavily wooded and farmlands abound, giving painters magnificent landscape inspiration.

Living
The cost of living is very inexpensive, a result of Hot Springs having been exposed to some over-development in years past, and the declining population base of its manufacturing businesses. Forest products and a shoe manufacturer are still the area's largest employers, and with a thoroughbred race track in town, Hot Springs has one heck of a varied local economy. The average 3-bedroom home sells in the $60,000 range. Schools are just starting to reach beyond simple art and music instruction for students (gallery walks are becoming popular with some classes). The Little Rock media regards this area as being within its backyard, so art reviews and coverage of performing art events is thorough.

Traditionally a playground for Arkansans, Hot Springs has plenty of ticky-tacky parlors selling souvenirs and the like. If you've always wanted to play putt-putt golf and ride in a go-kart on the same day, Hot Springs can satisfy those urges several times over. Okay, so there's lots of schlock—but along with that dose of Americana, you also get the arts community: a fairly tight-knit group of individuals who care deeply about art and culture.

Lake Ouchita, just outside of town, offers great fishing and sailing, golf courses abound, and there's also parimutuel betting at the track. Most locals tend to vote Democrat, while most of the towns retirees (and there are lots of them) are Republicans (which probably explains why they largely stick to their own communities).

Out On the Town
You've got the horse racing crowd in Hot Springs, and until the 1960s, casino gambling was legal and prostitution was tolerated (haven't you heard the tale of the two-faced Baptist?). The Arlington Hotel may have seen better days, but it's still some artists' favorite spot for a double Jack Daniels and live music. The Old Country Store serves natural food, while the Shack, in nearby Jessieville, and Hot Springs' Sawmill Depot vie for the area title of best burgers and shakes. Because it's so close to Little Rock, most locals head to the city to catch a theater performance at the Arkansas Rep and a sizzling plate of Thai cuisine.

Economic Impact of the Arts

Getting stronger each year, the dozen art galleries in Hot Springs have recently attracted nearly a hundred serious artists and have spawned the establishment of two nonprofit exhibition spaces. Things started coming together for the town's artists in the late 1980s, when Italian artist Benini moved his operations here from Miami Beach. Since that time, not only has the service and food improved in Hot Springs' Italian restaurants, but other European artists have arrived, along with an influx of creative types from points elsewhere across the U.S.

Local Arts Agencies

THEARTFOUNDATION, 520 Central Avenue, Hot Springs, AR 71901, (501) 623-9847, and Hot Springs Art Center, Park Avenue, Hot Springs, AR 71913, (501) 624-0489.

The existence of two arts organizations in a town the size of Hot Springs attests to the healthy state of the arts in this revived community. THEARTFOUNDATION emphasizes the work of contemporary artists, and is integrally involved in the planning and promotion of the community's annual documentary film festival. The Hot Springs Art Center is more closely identified with the town's large community of realist painters and craftspeople, staging exhibitions as well as lectures, workshops, and coordinating artist-in-residence programs through local schools.

Galleries and Arts Festivals

"The impact of the arts on downtown Hot Springs has been tremendous," says local artist and THEARTFOUNDATION president Lorraine Benini. "Galleries and artists have bought and renovated many turn-of-the-century buildings that had been condemned. Major investments have been made, and now the Chamber of Commerce takes a great deal of interest in what Hot Springs' artists want." The town's biggest local arts events are the Arkansas Celebration of the Arts, held in downtown Hot Springs during early November, and the staging of the Documentary Film Festival in October, and the Spring Gallery Walk in early June.

What the Artist Says

Gary Simmons, a graphic (pen and ink) artist whose primarily figurative creations are sold through fine art galleries across the country, says that the key to an artist's survival in Hot Springs is the willingness to build a career in diverse territories. "Here, galleries are still trying to find the right mix of artists and art buyers, so Hot Springs is still shuffling things around a bit. For artists who are new to the area, there's that need to do some work that's commercial, some that's meant for fairly common tourist tastes, and some that's really from your own heart. You have to give yourself time to grow into the community before you can concentrate on doing only what you want to do.

"Here, you can sense the growing interest from the business community in seeing the arts as a way to bring a more diverse, higher-quality visitor into town. . . . People are becoming concerned about protecting the integrity of the downtown arts community, and still see what's here as being a fragile thing. Local artists are free with their advice and support toward each other, and are quick to help each other out on any matter."

Cambria, California

Location
Along Big Sur, halfway between San Luis Obispo and Monterey, Cambria sits just a mile or so back from the Pacific Coast cliffsides at the edge of a heavily wooded pine forest. A few hours' drive either north or south will land you in San Francisco or Los Angeles.

Climate
Temperatures moderate between 50 and 70 degrees year-round, with some hotter days not uncommon during summer.

Living
Being close enough to Los Angeles to be considered a destination for daytrippers has been a mixed blessing for tiny Cambria (pop. 5,400). There is a large influx of tourists, and housing prices are in the $200,000 range for an average-size home. The local arts organization coordinates changing exhibitions at the Allied Arts Schoolhouse Gallery and stages a half-dozen or so major arts fairs and events annually. The most popular recreational activity is a toss-up between staring at the ocean waves crashing against the rocky shores of Big Sur, and mountain biking though the splendor of San Simeon State Park.

   There are many retirees in Cambria, and most have a sincere desire to contribute to their new community. Local government takes a great deal of interest in promoting Cambria as an arts town, a campaign financed by the town's lodgers' tax. The big tourist pull in the area is San Simeon (also known as Hearst Castle) just a few miles up the road. Cambria is a community full of opinionated, yet concerned, citizens.

Out On the Town
Folks move here for peace and quiet. Many have done their time in the big city and retreat to Cambria for its serenity and unmatched natural beauty. The natural food restaurant, Robins, makes a passable effort at Thai cuisine, but most locals just bide their time and wait for their next trip to L.A. The Camozzi Saloon is a great place to meet over a cold brew, and if you need a burger worth writing home about, try the one at Main Street Grill. About the only place to go after dark is the Cambria Pines Lodge. Morning coffee at Molly's is a must-do.

Economic Impact of the Arts
Nearly two dozen art galleries and craft stores crowd this town's Main Street, and you don't have to be a rocket scientist to figure out that not all the work shown in a town like Cambria is worth a serious look. Nonetheless, the community is home to a hundred or so artists, many of whom bypass the local galleries in favor of selling their work through galleries in larger cities. Local watercolorists, who paint the sort of landscapes visitors most commonly associate with this section of the coast, seem to do best in Cambria galleries. Studio rentals are practically nonexistent; most artists build studio spaces onto their homes.

Local Arts Agency

Allied Arts Association, P.O. Box 184, Cambria, CA 93428, (805) 927-8859. Publishes the *AAA Newsletter*.

"We're looking to build a facility that will allow us to stage performances," says association president Peter Jesness, "because as things are now, San Luis Obispo gets all the theater and performing arts groups that come through the area. Ours is a broad-based arts orientation: a little work with local schools, a few arts workshops, and work with businesses raising money for what the arts community needs and wants to do."

Galleries and Arts Festivals

If you look hard enough, you can find one or two places in town selling cheap souvenirs, but on the average the work represented in Cambria's nearly two dozen galleries represents a fairly proficient level of realism. The year's biggest arts events are the Petals and Palettes show at the end of April, the 427 contemporary art show in mid-July, and the Pinedorado art show in early September.

What the Artist Says

Ken Butterfield, artist, community activist, and environmentalist, is a sculptor whose "psycho-socio, neo-surrealist commentaries" are sold in galleries outside Cambria. After living in Cambria for 20 years, he's aware of the need for this community's need to limit its ever-expanding population if it is to have a shot at retaining its charm and tourist appeal. "We've tried to promote the work of artists doing non-traditional imagery and the local response has been tremendous. Downtown businesses are aware of the need to maintain a certain quality of life here, not wanting to see our hillsides covered with L.A.-style mansions.

"Cambria is a great place to come and work if you want to get away from any distractions—that is, unless you do what I did and get involved in local politics. Artists who come here have to be at a certain point in their careers, and need to watch out for the tendency this place has to take some sort of edge off your work."

Eureka, California

Location

A Pacific coast community with its roots in the logging and fishing industries, Eureka is a town of 25,000 that boasts California's second-largest per capita concentration of artists. A 5-hour drive south gets you to San Francisco, while a 6-hour drive north lands you in Portland.

Climate

Locals like to refer to their weather patterns as "Northern Mediterranean," but that seems a bit generous for a region where 55-degree days are common in most months and not unheard of in others. Summer can be as nice here as anywhere else north of Santa Barbara, but locals know better than to leave home (yes, even in August) without tossing a sweater and umbrella into the trunk of their car. Not as overcast as the Pacific Northwest, the chances of getting a moderately clear (but cool) day during February are much better here than in Cannon Beach, Oregon.

Living

One of the last affordable communities in the state, Eureka's average 3-bedroom home sells in the $100,000 range, with lots of lower-priced fixer-uppers available for the manually talented. Two colleges (one in nearby Arcata) keep a steady flow of talented performers and academicians touring through town, so there are plenty of opportunities to broaden your cultural and intellectual horizons. Several nonprofit exhibition spaces and a decidedly counter-cultural bent make Eureka a place more than simply friendly to the arts—it celebrates them!

This is, after all, California. On top of that, this area is loaded with college students, and the living is relatively cheap (compared to the rest of the state). Ponytails and pierced ears on men have always been in (and will never go out of) style here. Leave your Ralph Lauren shirts at home, or only wear them when you fly home to visit the parents. For women who buck gender roles, this region is nirvana. The town's best art openings are the ones staged by the nonprofit gallery called Ink People. White water rafting on the Mad River is everyone's favorite spring pastime, followed by hiking amongst the redwoods in Redwood National Park, and fishing along the area's many rivers. Freedom and community involvement are equally valued by local artists, who join forces on projects benefiting the area's arts community.

Out On the Town

From Thai restaurants to superb, locally caught seafood, Eureka has an abundance of great dining choices that are uniformly affordable. Artists like to park themselves at a table and catch up with their pals at Ramone's Bakery, while the two most popular nightspots are Club West and Jambalaya's. Star's Hamburgers has the best you-know-what in town, while natural food is best at Spoons, located in the Arcata Co-op. While horticultural experimentation remains one of the area's favorite leisure activities, there are repertory and other theater troupes performing in several locales, and the colleges host regular performances of classical and symphony music.

Economic Impact of the Arts

With its traditional means of making a living (fishing and logging) on the decline, the arts community has moved into Eureka and Arcata with a vengeance, picking up a surprising amount of slack in the local economy. That's not to say the downtown business community is either very aware or very appreciative of the arts community's contributions, as the local fellas seem to be focused more on bringing in a new manufacturing plant, or somehow doing whatever they can to revive the logging and lumber industries. Only recently has there been any significant business support for turning Eureka's historic downtown into an arts district, so the jury is still out on this one.

Local Arts Agency

Humboldt Arts Council, 422 First St., Eureka, CA 95501, (707) 442-2611.

The council's orientation is geared toward visual artists, which is an acknowledgment of the wonderful access this community has to performing arts events staged through the local colleges and semi-professional theater groups. The downtown arts center is being turned into an artists' studio space, because the council is moving its offices into an unused auditorium (also a better spot to hold its Friday concert series). "We have a touring program that goes into local schools," says council president Cathy Ray Pierson. "We call it the Art Bank and have given it a humanities focus on arts education programs. It also tries to reach local teens outside the setting of their school environment. During the summer we offer classes and stage an authors' festival."

Galleries and Arts Festivals

There are hundreds of professional artists counted in the Eureka and Arcata area, with ten local commercial art galleries and three nonprofit exhibition spaces available to those seeking to sell locally. Some of the finest wood craftspeople in the nation live in this heart of redwood country, close to other sources of hardwoods and softwoods. Many artists sell their work outside the area in metropolitan galleries from New York to Los Angeles, or choose to market directly through the craft and art festival circuit. The biggest local arts festivals are Arcata's Summer Arts, the Mad River Festival, Fourth of July in Eureka, and Dell Arté each summer in Blue Lake.

What the Artist Says

"If you come here you'll experience ocean, mountain, and forest environments . . . all in the same hour," says painter Lisa Marie Waters. "And don't miss the Kinetic Sculpture Race (yep!) each fall—that's a true taste of this area. There aren't a lot of local jobs, so bring your own work, and don't forget your mountain bike."

Mendocino, California

Location
The former fishing village of Mendocino sits snuggled atop the Mendocino Headlands, a Q-shaped cliffside that's perpetually battered by waves crashing in from the Pacific Ocean. With redwood forests completing this magnificent setting, the 1,100 residents of Mendocino are a 3-hour drive north of San Francisco.

Climate
Mild, with lots of foggy days and several howling storms during the winter months, Mendocino can also be warmed by sunny skies and weather that's more like San Diego's than San Francisco's. In other words, no matter what time of year you visit, hope for the best, but prepare for the worst.

Living
Hardly inexpensive, Mendocino's stratospheric real estate values are the unfortunate outcome of what originally started as word-of-mouth advertising about an artists' community stuck in a small town along the Northern California coastline. One whispered success story led to another, and within the past two decades the dream of punching out of city life and starting a gallery/boutique/bed and breakfast inn somewhere in Mendocino has been an integral part of Bay Area wage-slave fantasies. For $400,000 or so hard-earned bucks, Mendocinans buy into a community with a vibrant arts center, a thriving gallery scene with a never-ending flow of moneyed tourists, and schools that have managed to stay insulated from the draconian budget cuts sweeping across this state.

Close enough to San Francisco to allow residents regular visits to its art museums and opera house, locals turn to the natural beauty of Mendocino's environment for weekend fun. This can take the shape of a walk out onto the Headlands, a hike along the banks of one of the many rivers and streams cascading through nearby redwood stands, or a bicycle excursion up the Pacific Coast Highway to a secluded sliver of seashore. Fishing is spectacular, no matter where you choose to drop a line.

Out On the Town
As liberal as it is rugged (in a safe, J. Crew sort of way), Mendocino has the variety of cozy restaurants and busy bars you would expect in a town ultra-friendly to well-heeled visitors. If it's ethnic food you simply must have, then drive up the coast to Ft. Bragg. Drinks and dancing to live music are the attractions at the Caspar Inn, while the Mendocino Cafe serves first-rate natural specialties. Burgers are best at the Bayview Cafe, and if you're in town when a play is being staged at the Mendocino Art Center's theater, try not to miss it.

Economic Impact of the Arts
Simply put, without the arts Mendocino would have been just another coastal town where fishermen had fallen onto hard times. But today, with demand for retail and residential space continu-

ing, the fishermen's second-generation families have been turned into real estate magnates, and there always seems to be another retired stockbroker/doctor/auto parts dealer willing to part with a king's ransom for the privilege of moving into town and establishing a new identity. Mendocino promotes itself as an arts center and realizes that if the creative core is pushed out of this community, "Carmel-ization" (the word locals use whenever they talk about T-shirt and souvenir shops) is a distinct possibility.

Local Arts Agency
Mendocino Arts Center, P.O. Box 765, Mendocino, CA 95460, (707) 937-5724.

"One of our main focal points is education," says art center executive director Steve Wiltse. "We've got seven studios with teaching facilities, a foundry and an etching press, and our emphasis can shift from weaving to pottery to painting to printmaking—we had over a hundred classes and workshops in the past year. Local schools come in here all the time (the center is adjacent to Mendocino's high school). We display student artwork, send artists into the schools for workshops, bring students in here for classes, and any educator in the area is welcome to make use of our facilities. The local media is very supportive of anything that takes place at the center since we're an important part of what continues to make Mendocino work as an arts community. We try to provide the artists with any help they need from facility rentals to support groups."

Galleries and Arts Festivals
Hundreds of locals refer to themselves as artists, yet the number who actually make their living from creating art work is still well over the 100 mark. There are 20 commercial gallery spaces in town, with a mix of work ranging from watercolor seascapes to contemporary craft and abstract oil canvasses. Three nonprofit exhibition spaces (the largest is at the arts center) give newcomers and established professionals a place to show work the galleries can't handle. The year's largest arts festival is the one held each August at the Mendocino Arts Center.

What the Artist Says
Charles Stevenson, a painter who moved to Mendocino in the early 1960s, says that while he laments the passing of Mendocino's days as a ghost town inhabited by pioneering artists, he's also pleased to be living in an area where his fellow artists show support for each other. "It's turned into a place that's great for painters selling laser print reproductions and woodworkers who turn out furniture, but Mendocino's galleries can't handle much original work, and that makes things tough on the artists who live here. Artists feel it's wise to keep your business local and there are a lot of creative minds to bounce your ideas off of." His studio assistant, Matt Leach, says that while Mendocino is a good place for younger artists to get an education and work on their technique, anyone thinking of permanently relocating here had best be ready to dig in, work several jobs, and have a realistic attitude about life in a town reliant on art sales to tourists.

Santa Cruz, California

Location

Just over an hour's drive south of San Francisco, Santa Cruz and its neighboring towns of Aptos and Capitola sit on the northern edge of Monterey Bay. The luckiest of Santa Cruz's 50,000 residents live in homes built into hillsides stretching back from the sandy coastline, and ocean views are common.

Climate

Santa Cruz can be hot and sunny, as well as overcast, misty, and bone-chilling. During the winter months, dreary, Seattle-like stretches of weather are common, but they're always followed by blasts of sunny California glory. Summer is spectacular—the area supports a large colony of itinerant surfers—and ocean breezes usually keep temperatures tolerable. Gardening is year-round.

Living

Home prices are typically high, which reflects Santa Cruz's proximity to the Bay Area: Many commuters head into San Jose and San Francisco for the daily grind. The University of California at Santa Cruz brings 10,000 or so students into town for nine months of the year, so rentals can be tight. On the bright side, this is a decidedly counter-cultural community that's very accepting of artists, musicians, writers, dancers, and their ilk. Studio space is available, sometimes in buildings that once served as seafood processing plants. The local arts groups (and there are many) are active, better-funded than most, and have lots of members.

The Santa Cruz lifestyle is what everyone's picture-postcard image of California is about: lots of laid-back, friendly locals who enjoy life in a place that reflects the values of the southern part of this state more than it does the north. Homes tend to be quaint and slightly funky—nobody minds if you paint your doors blue and your window frames yellow. Favorite local activities include surfing, cruising the beach, rollerblading, and sleeping in a hammock. Schools have been hurt by state budget cuts, and the party is over as far as government-funded projects are concerned, but then, who can get too agitated about politics when there's such a wonderful beach practically at your doorstep?

Out On the Town

People here like to cut loose (way loose). As a matter of fact, they consider it their right to break boundaries, live slightly crazy, and be as eccentric as they want. The Mescal and tequila selections in local liquor stores would put a border town mercado to shame. Thai food and East Indian dishes at India Joze are as good as anywhere else in the state. Nightlife selections are fantastic, with live music aplenty and rockin' bars that serve everyone from the area's substantial gay and lesbian population to the Hell's Angels who roar into town whenever the urge strikes. The Catalyst is a favorite place for meeting friends for drinks, and the Bagelry has great natural food. Want a burger? Then head over to Carpo's in nearby Soquel. The university stages a Shakespearean Festival each year, and the needs of this multicultural community's third world music lovers are more than adequately served at the Kuumbwa Jazz Center.

Economic Impact of the Arts

As a college town, Santa Cruz gets its share of young people who graduate with arts degrees, only to set out on a career path of waiting tables and thinking about applying to law school. Nevertheless, hundreds (not an exaggeration) of serious professionals in the fine craft and fine art fields choose to live in the forested hillsides above Santa Cruz, and their work goes on regardless of what takes place down at the beach. There's a local market for art, with buyers coming in from primarily the Bay Area. Artists and craftspeople have a tradition here of bartering for each other's creations and services.

Local Arts Agency

Cultural Council of Santa Cruz County, 7960 Soquel Dr., #1, Aptos, CA 95003, (408) 688-5399. Publishes the newsletter *Art Works*.

With numerous, specialized arts organizations in the community, the local cultural council serves as an umbrella organization for funding and promoting activities, exhibitions, and presentations the organizations want to sponsor. Santa Cruz has recently opened a new arts museum to replace a building destroyed by the 1989 Loma Prieta earthquake.

Galleries and Arts Festivals

The arts scene in this area spreads out to include several towns that dot this end of Monterey Bay. Santa Cruz itself has eight commercial galleries and two nonprofit exhibition spaces. Around the area you'll find at least another dozen commercial galleries, supplemented by many restaurants and banks exhibiting rotating shows of everything from photography to sculpture. The area's largest arts festival (last year it included more than 300 participating artists) is the annual Open Studios Tour, which takes place over three weekends each October.

What the Artist Says

"The one event that's made the biggest difference here in recent years is the Open Studios Tour," says pastels artist Kitty Wallin. "I moved here because Santa Cruz wasn't dominated by a conformist culture. It's a lovely environment that's conducive to creative thought, and a great place for artists who are looking for a location to inspire their work. Sure, change is always in the offing here—if it's not real estate prices going up again, then it's someone's plans to explore off the coast for oil, or build a new highway. But local people are very good at organizing around issues and have shot down many proposals to change things.

"I've been here 25 years, so my work sells well locally, but I also go with galleries outside the area and sell art supplies as a sideline. People go to restaurants expecting to see good work on the walls, and are likely to buy if they see something that appeals to them. For myself, the environment here is an important part of my work: I'm a realist painter and I refer to my work as contemporary impressionism, so water, plants, and birds are all in my paintings.

"Artists who come here should realize that this is a place that's already dense with talent, but someone who is motivated, who knows how to find opportunity and isn't afraid of working hard to establish themselves, can make a living and tap into the local market. You may have to go on the road to sell at fairs—and there are lots of those events in this part of the state. The normal mindset around here will work both for and against you—there will be lots of opportunities to avoid working hard, but there are also lots of locals who care about quality, and that can keep you honest."

Alamosa, Colorado

Location
Wedged into the San Luis Valley, a productive agricultural region in south-central Colorado, the 9,000 residents of Alamosa live in the shadows of two towering mountain ranges, the Sangre de Cristos, and the San Juans. From here it's a 3-hour drive to Denver and a 2-hour drive south to Santa Fe.

Climate
Here, you'll find hot, dry summers, and winters that can seem as if the Almighty One herself left the freezer door open for a few months. Temperatures in Alamosa often vary 20 degrees from those in Santa Fe, a reflection of the valley's location between two ranges of sheltering mountains. Spring and fall are rather brief affairs characterized by the influx of tens of thousands of migrating cranes, geese, and ducks on their ways to points further north or south, depending on the time of year.

Living
Affordability is cited as the main consideration for artists who have made their move to Alamosa, and it's a good jumping off point for those with commercial representation or other interests in both Denver and Santa Fe. A safe, comfortably small community, Alamosa is home to Colorado's highest concentration of Hispanic voters, a legacy of the upper Rio Grande Valley having been administered hundreds of years ago by Spanish colonialists headquartered in Santa Fe. A 3-bedroom home in Alamosa costs about $60,000.

For the outdoors enthusiast this part of Colorado offers uncrowded, easy access into everything from ski areas to trout streams. Several hot springs in the area have been developed into spas with bath houses and mineral pools, and the Rio Grande River cuts right through the town's largest park. On its outskirts, Alamosa has some of the nation's most noteworthy wildlife migratory grounds, and the area is endowed with an infinite supply of pristine, inexpensive water.

Out On the Town
Fortunately for Alamosa's residents, the campus of Adams State University keeps a fair amount of performing art and visual arts activity flowing through the community. Unfortunately, Alamosa lacks an arts center, so the college's programming is essential to the vitality of this community's cultural life. Taos, a diverse arts community just an hour's drive away, has the range of ethnic and high-end restaurants Alamosa lacks, but the town is just getting its first European-style coffee cantina, a development the local artists are looking forward to. St. Ives is a favorite place to meet friends over drinks and a basket of tortilla chips, while the dinner crowd at True Grit Steakhouse knows a thing or two about where to get Alamosa's best burgers and prime rib. A fairly representative college-age crowd can usually be found on the dance floor at Weekends, providing you go, of course, on Fridays or Saturdays.

Economic Impact of the Arts

This end of Colorado never experienced the lows or highs more common to the economies of larger cities on the state's eastern slope, so things weren't so bad here when the regional economy crashed a few years back. The strength and consistency of the area's agricultural economy has inclined the local business community to regard the arts as an interesting, somewhat curious diversion, not something to be improved upon and used as an economic driver for the town's retail sector.

Local Arts Agency

Associated Artists of the San Luis Valley, 10385 County Road 15, Del Norte, CO 81132, (719) 657-2666.

"We're still trying to define what we want to achieve as a community of artists," says Alamosa art gallery owner and ceramicist Carol Mondragon. "The first high-profile project we took on was a portable mural made in response to a proposed (and defeated) water project, and now we're in the process of organizing a couple of local arts festivals. There's room for improvement in the way the business community views the arts in Alamosa—when we do put on an event, the place is usually packed—so we're still building community support for our projects and goals. We're in a multicultural area, and the town of San Luis (20 miles away) has done a much better job of promoting itself as an arts community. We need to make the Alamosa Chamber of Commerce aware of how much can happen through the arts."

Galleries and Arts Festivals

The three commercial art galleries in Alamosa have their own turfs well-defined. One specializes in Western realism sculpture, originals, and prints; another has a strong interest in art more closely defined with the Southwest; and the third has a wide range of original painting, sculpture, jewelry, and fine craft produced by artists from Alamosa and its environs. The college has an active arts department, but not a dedicated exhibition space. San Luis, a small, primarily Hispanic community 20 miles from Alamosa, has two art galleries, a small museum, and a massive display of public sculpture (the Stations of the Cross) that draws tourists in year-round. Alamosa's largest arts event is the Sunshine Festival, which takes place in Cole Park in early June.

What the Artist Says

Charles Ewing, a wildlife painter who moved here during the late 1970s, says Alamosa presents a great package for young artists. "I'm always surprised when I find how well the artists do here in local galleries. It's not anything like Santa Fe, but this town has come light years from where it was five years ago. Alamosa is the sort of town where you can set up your home and studio at a very reasonable cost, become part of an active, supportive group of artists who enjoy sharing information, and find out what you need to do to become part of the commercial art market. I think we're on the verge of getting a lot of attention—we're seeing people move into parts of the valley who have an art collecting background, and they're very supportive about buying local work."

Creede, Colorado

Location
A former mining town in south-central Colorado, Creede is a community of 600 residents who live in the shadows of the towering San Juan Mountains. The closest airport is in Alamosa, about an hour's drive east.

Climate
Bring your snowmobiling gear and a fishing pole. Creede's brief but glorious summer is one of those crystal-clear, spectacular affairs city folks fantasize about. Things take on an *Ice Station Zebra* flavor from around the Day of the Dead through Passover, with many stores boarding up for the winter. Locals respond by either heading to central Mexico for long stretches of landscape painting, or by learning to enjoy the considerable pleasures of cross-country skiing, and keeping a crackling fire going in their living room stoves.

Living
A few miner holdovers (mostly retirees) remain, but for the most part these older families have left Creede, and it's a buyer's market for real estate. A 3-bedroom, wood-frame home with Victorianesque details sells in the $75,000 range, and Creede has plenty of lower-priced, fixer-uppers for those who don't mind the drudgery of drywalling and laying down floors. Local schools work closely with Creede's well-organized arts community (the Creede Repertory Theater serves as a de facto arts center) to offers student programs in dance, drama, ceramics, music, and painting.

Laid-back but wonderfully optimistic, the artists who have in the past several years made Creede their home simply bubble over with enthusiasm—they know they're onto something good and have the unshakable impression things are going to get better and better. Summers here are a wonderful time to experience the glory of Colorado outdoors, and winter sports aren't just fun, they're important for shaking any feelings of cabin fever.

Out On the Town
A small town, Creede has limited offerings, but the good news is that what's here is done with a sophistication and friendliness that'll warm your heart. A few innkeepers have dining establishments that serve visitors during the warmer, busier months. Old Miner's Inn and the Cafe Ole are artist hangouts (and favorites of just about everyone else in town), while the Mucker's Bucket is Creede's burger-and-shake joint. Like any good mining (or former mining) community, there are a half-dozen or so bars lining Creede's Main Street, with mostly friendly folks inside.

Economic Impact of the Arts
If it weren't for the determination of the artists, actors, and arts administrators who have helped get this town back on its feet, Creede would be in far worse shape than it is today. Certainly, what's done here is on a small scale, but nonetheless, the arts community has had an impressive

and obvious impact on this tiny town. In recent years, what once were vacant and dusty store-fronts in stone-walled mercantile buildings have been spruced up and turned into a variety of galleries and shops. Surprisingly, most of the creative product you find in these stores is quite good, although those who really care about Creede (and aren't just looking to make a few fast bucks off other people's hard work) have got to remain vigilant about the influx of vendors selling T-shirts and coffee mugs.

Local Arts Agencies

Creede Arts Council, P.O. Box 269, Creede, CO 81130, (719) 658-2608, and Creede Repertory Theater, P.O. Box 269, Creede, CO 81130, (719) 658-2541.

The council's current primary goal is to promote quality arts programs in Creede schools, which is a reflection of the state government's priority on where and how it channels art funding resources. Creede takes an active approach to promoting its regular schedule of arts events and festivals, occasions where the community works together to attract the kind of tourists likely to make an art-related purchase.

The Creede Repertory Theater is absolutely unique. Somehow having escaped the past century in reasonable condition, the theater has been renovated top to bottom and now stages a full summer program of plays, performance, and art openings. "The people in Creede realize what a difference having this theater has made in their lives," says local businessman Richard Ormsby. "It's what makes us different from other places, and it brings a wonderful quality of visitor into Creede. Make your reservations early!"

Galleries and Arts Festivals

A half-dozen art galleries stretch along the uphill climb of Creede's short but splendidly scenic Main Street. There's even a transplanted Texan (Jenny Inge) who sells elegant jewelry woven from horsehair and decorated with hand-hammered sterling silver clasps. The town's largest arts festivals are the Memorial Day gourmet fest, Taste of Creede, the Mining Competition held on July 4th weekend, and the annual opening weekend of the Repertory Theater in late June.

What the Artist Says

Painter and arts writer Steve Quiller was one of the first artists who staked his claim on Creede, and his downtown gallery space is one of the town's busiest. "We're remote, yet close enough to Taos and Santa Fe to get some of their spill-over," he says. "Creede has lots of energy among its artists and other creative types, yet this is also a town that's wonderfully peaceful. We want it to grow—to be enriched with the culture and influence of people from different backgrounds. More business owners are staying here year-round, giving this town back its heart. Our tourist season is brief but intense: It gives local artists a chance to sell what they've created and then leaves them alone to work uninterrupted for the winter months."

Loveland, Colorado

Location
A hour's drive north of Denver, the artists' community of Loveland is a town of 34,000 in the rolling foothills outside Rocky Mountain National Park.

Climate
Somewhat short blasts of spring and autumn surround a lengthy (but not unbearable) winter and a surprisingly warm summer. Folks living here count on a half-dozen or so major snowfalls each winter and summer afternoons marked by thunderstorms.

Living
Still affordable, a 3-bedroom home is priced slightly over the $100,000 range, but there's a lot of home in the deal, including views of the front range of the Rocky Mountains. Over the past decade, Loveland has become the nation's most vibrant community of sculptors, with several hundred professional artists living in close proximity to two first-rate bronze foundries. Local schools are just beginning to work with the town's large arts community in an effort to bolster student art curriculums, but state budget cuts have hindered such efforts in the past. While Loveland lacks a community arts center, the town's artists are quite friendly and many maintain open studios welcoming guests.

This is a working arts town, unpretentious and singularly dedicated to the creation of quality art. Sculptors are involved with their work at a physical level unapproached by artists working in other mediums, and their overt friendliness and powerful handshakes are a wonderful tonic to the distracted distancing some artists seem to consider their creative psychological license. It's common for fellow sculptors (male and female) to enjoy leisure pursuits, with skiing, boating, hunting, snowmobiling, and high-country hiking ranking at the top of many activity lists.

Out On the Town
With the college towns of Ft. Collins (a 20-minute drive north) and Boulder (a 30-minute drive southwest) nearby Loveland has access to about as varied an entertainment scene as you could imagine, including Denver's professional sports teams. The best place to meet a local artist for a drink and tortilla chips is the Cactus Grille, which also serves up a great burger. Dinners at the Peaks are always good, but if it's ethnic food that tickles your fancy, the best place to go is Boulder. The nightlife in Ft. Collins is usually worth checking out. Loveland has a community theater group, but again, those nearby college towns generally have better offerings.

Economic Impact of the Arts
From the moment you drive into Loveland, observing the many monumental-size bronze sculptures installed along the main routes leading downtown, there's the unavoidable impression that this is a place that takes its artists and art business connections seriously. With several hundred bronze masters (most of whom work in realist sculptural forms) and a few dozen stone carvers,

painters, and other artists in town, Loveland is a somewhat magical place where the presence of art is everywhere. There are hundreds of employment opportunities associated with the arts community in this town—from shipping specialists to sculpture base-makers to art supply wholesalers. Loveland is a town where the arts means j-o-b-s. Around Loveland—from its gorgeous parks to the civic plaza outside city hall to window displays in small businesses—there are dozens of installations of public art, mostly three-dimensional sculpture.

Local Arts Agency

Loveland High Plains Art Council, P.O. Box 7006, Loveland, CO 80537, (303) 663-2940. Publishes the newsletter *Celebrating Sculpture*.

"We keep a tight focus on sculptural arts," says art council executive director Betsy Ostermiller. "That's part of our mission statement. Other arts organizations in this area have more of a Ft. Collins orientation, but here in Loveland the arts are the town's fourth-largest employer, and sculpture has made most of what's been a substantial economic impact. The image sculpture has created for Loveland is unique—we've focused on the business of creating art and not on the marketing aspects of art. That's revitalized the town and has given us a national reputation."

Galleries and Arts Festivals

If you travel out-of-state for only one arts festival this year, try to make it to Loveland's annual August sculpture bash, Sculpture in the Park. Drawing an international group 150 artist exhibitors to a lakefront park a couple miles from downtown, this three-day festival of three-dimensional art has regularly rung up sales totaling in the $500,000 range, according to art council figures. As a matter of fact, the show has been so astoundingly successful at drawing a moneyed crowd of art collectors into Loveland, that a competing show of regional and out-of-area sculptors has popped up on the grounds of a nearby school. There are a half-dozen art galleries in Loveland, and over the past few years their business has greatly improved due to the rising tide of arts awareness in the region.

What the Artist Says

"The key to surviving here is to use your local successes to build entrée into the profitable markets in Santa Fe, Aspen, and Scottsdale," says sculptor Jane Dedecker. "Because so many gallery owners and collectors have fallen into the pattern of coming into Loveland to meet and work with the sculptors here, we're starting to see an influx of painters and other artists who want to take advantage of that access. They realize the local sales are minimal, but this is a better place to pin your hopes on than a lot of other towns. For sculptors, Loveland is fantastic: Everything is at your fingertips, from supplies to skilled assistants to the advice of sculptors who are way ahead of you in terms of their arts careers. If you're thinking of moving here, understand that there are artists who live here who you already have a lot in common with. There's great living space and studio space—Loveland is an arts town on the upswing."

Steamboat Springs, Colorado

Location

Just on the other side of a 9,400-foot pass cut high in the Colorado mountains, the 7,000 residents of Steamboat Springs live a difficult, 3-hour drive from the outskirts of Denver. It's a lot easier driving into Laramie, Wyoming, for your shopping mall fix.

Climate

Decidedly alpine in terms of terrain, Steamboat Springs enjoys a sparkling, pristine climate where clear views of mountains 50 miles away are a part of daily life. Summer weather is occasionally warm enough to be considered hot, while winter is characterized by frigid nights and surprisingly warm (50 degrees isn't uncommon) January days, unless the town is riding out a four-day blizzard (also not uncommon in January).

Living

Practically crime-free, and about as friendly as a community can be, Steamboat Springs exists in a dramatically picturesque setting that's somewhat pricey because of the town's deserved reputation as a winter sports haven. An average 3-bedroom home runs in the $150,000 range. The Eleanor Bliss Center for the Arts is located in what once was the town's train depot and has 1,800 square feet of visual art exhibition space, along with facilities for performance and visual art workshops. Touring productions are presented at the Steamboat Springs high school auditorium, which seats 550.

This is an outdoors activity mecca, with a population that loves to make full use of nature's nearby wonders. Surrounded by one of the nation's most spectacular stretches of unspoiled, high country environment, folks in Steamboat Springs tend to behave as if they're slightly intoxicated by the overwhelming magnificence of Mother Nature. Hitting the trail whenever a spare minute presents itself is something of a civic duty—no matter if it is a snow-covered downhill ski trail in winter, a riverfront bicycling trail in the middle of summer, or an aspen-shaded hiking trail in the foothills of nearby mountains.

Out On the Town

Like any ski town with non-stop (during winter) jet service to places such as Chicago, Los Angeles, and Houston, Steamboat Springs has lots of fine bars, restaurants, and nightspots where its wealthy visitors can spend their clean, out-of-area tourist dollars. The hot spots to meet over drinks these days are two new brew pubs, both of which have staked their reputations on a fine brand of micro-brewed beer made on premises. Guys and gals like to hook horns in the after-dark confines of the Steamboat Saloon, which features live bands and a party atmosphere. Regular food is the specialty at Burger Express, while anyone with a burning desire for a soy milk shake will need to drive several hours to Boulder for vegetarian satisfaction.

Economic Impact of the Arts

A few years ago, Steamboat Springs was selected for a one-time NEA development grant of several hundred thousand dollars, and the art life in this corner of the Rocky Mountains hasn't been the same since. Public art installations have cropped up around town, summer string music festivals have blossomed into major events, local theater has flourished and become much more sophisticated, and local artists have found employment opportunities teaching workshops, working on commissioned pieces, and the like. The arts council estimates there are over a hundred resident artists of all kinds living in Steamboat Springs, many of whom do quite well selling to the town's vibrant tourist market.

Local Arts Agency

Steamboat Springs Art Council, Eleanor Bliss Center for the Arts at the Depot, P.O. Box 774284, Steamboat Springs, CO 80477, (303) 879-9008. Publishes the *Steamboat Arts Council Newsletter*.

"The support the business community in this town shows for the arts is extraordinary," says art council executive director Nancy Kramer. "There's a national promotion of local art, and here everyone sees art as an important draw to Steamboat's tourist industry. It's been estimated that for every dollar spent on the arts by a tourist in Steamboat, another three dollars are spent elsewhere in the community."

Galleries and Arts Festivals

Steamboat Springs' six commercial art galleries are supplemented by the 1,800 square feet of non-profit exhibition space dedicated to rotating exhibitions at the town's arts center. The most popular creative mediums are photography and watercolor paintings, with a strong presence of bronze sculpture created in nearby Loveland, Colorado. Festivals and hoe-downs are a regular part of Steamboat's slightly loony heritage, with something planned at least every other week throughout the year. The busiest arts festival (the one that gives local artists the best opportunity to sell their work directly to the public during the summer season) is the Art In the Park bash held in West Lincoln Park each July. Over 200 artists and musicians participate in this weekend-long event, which attracts buyers from as far away as Texas and Arizona.

What the Artist Says

Eileen Braziel, painter of mixed-media contemporary landscapes, is part-owner of a local art gallery and sells most of her art work to the wide range of out-of-state visitors who make Steamboat Springs a destination for year-round fun. "The attraction for me is the people who live in Steamboat," she says. "The artists who come here seem to share their wonderful sense of community—they manage to be competitive, yet very considerate of the lives of other artists. The town is growing, and as it expands what's selling best in galleries is art that's reflective of the qualities of this area—no matter if it's traditional realism, contemporary abstraction, or somewhere in between. Development is an important issue here, and if another ski area is built, the town will change drastically. It will distance a lot of people from the feelings they have for this community."

Middletown, Connecticut

Location
Snuggled alongside the hills flanking the Connecticut River Valley, Middletown is strategically located within a half-hour's drive from Hartford's international airport. The town's 40,000 residents are equidistant to Boston and New York, either city being a 3-hour drive away.

Climate
The full breadth of each season comforts Middletown's residents and is commonly cited as a prime reason for moving into this central Connecticut town. A spectacular autumn brings out the best in this place, and every few years a long, glorious spring will give the town a substantial head start on tomato growing season. Summer has its share of hot and humid stretches and winter can turn very unfriendly, but overall, the climate here is livably mild.

Living
Because of its proximity to larger cities like Hartford and New Haven, Middletown's residents pay in the neighborhood of $125,000 for a 3-bedroom home. Connecticut's school system in this corner of the state is much better off than in other communities, with comprehensive arts programs reaching students at all levels with supplemental and curriculum-based offerings. There is no arts center, but the nearby presence of Wesleyan University means Middletown enjoys an invigorating program of performing art, musical, and theater presentations staged on the college grounds.

An interesting mix of country and suburbanite casual, Middletown is one of those towns where the average citizen walking down the street is as likely as not to have an advanced degree from an Ivy League school. Visual arts are strong here, and the college's ceramics program rates as one of the nation's best. Lots of local artists are respected names in metropolitan gallery scenes, but don't show their work locally.

Out On the Town
To this former Connecticut resident, among the region's most precious assets are its fabulous pizza joints (see the movie *Mystic Pizza* for more info). Almost every shopping center and downtown is blessed with a pizza joint the likes of which people living in other parts of the country would trade their city halls for. Middletown has so many of these places that to name one as better than another would require scientific reasoning far beyond the scope of this book, so just go try them yourselves! The town's hottest nightspot is a waterfront place called America's Cup, and artists who have a few moments to spare will usually head over to New York Bagel for comfort food (but Middlesex Rotisserie and Atticus are also popular for more complete dinner offerings). Best burgers in town are served at O'Rourke's, while natural foods are the specialty of the house at It's Only Natural.

Economic Impact of the Arts
In many ways, this is a college town, and even though the school is a private and pricey one, there are a number of graduates of its arts programs who have chosen to stay rooted in Middletown.

Usually, they like having access to markets in New York and Boston, and also want to live in a more affordable, less hectic environment than you would find in towns closer to the suburbs. While not blaringly obvious, the presence of the arts and artists in this area is well-known to locals, yet hasn't led to the kind of arts-based tourism found in other parts of the Northeast.

Local Arts Agency

Commission on Arts and Cultural Activities, P.O. Box 1300, Middletown, CT 06475, (203) 344-3520. Publishes the newsletter *Act 1*.

"We deal with everything," says commission arts coordinator Corinne Gill, "from helping a local clown connect with kids' birthday parties to channeling individual grants to artists. Our mandate is to encourage participation in the arts, and we've thrown ourselves into the challenge: We hook up with local arts groups and help them in any way we can to bring art productions and performances to Middletown. We do concerts, cultural exchanges—whatever you need, we've got a handle on it."

Galleries and Arts Festivals

While there are two commercial art galleries in Middletown and one nonprofit exhibition space (the Buttonwood Tree, open year-round), the arts scene is closely tied into what takes place at Wesleyan University. From student exhibitions in campus galleries to occasional shows of art work created by faculty members, what takes place on campus is what locals pay close attention to. The area's best public arts festivals are Hadassah, which occurs in September along Middletown's Main Street, the Junior Women's Arts and Crafts Festival each May at South Green park, City Fest in June at South Green, and Wesleyan Potters Annual Exhibition in December.

What the Artist Says

Long-term resident, Mary Risley, is a ceramicist and instructor in the pottery program of Wesleyan University's art department. "The idea is for artists to use the town's proximity to New York as a way you can show your work to gallery owners and develop the network of collectors you'll need to keep going while living in Middletown. There are lots of local opportunities to sell work to corporations and to do public art commissions around the Northeast, and those are also important ways for artists to develop an income. Our arts museum is strong and active, and the art department at Wesleyan is very well regarded.

"Succeeding here is a matter of locking yourself in for the long run. You've got to have exceptional skills, because the local art work is very skillfully done, and you've got to be active in the community—that's a great place to lay your groundwork and reach for those contacts that will get you exposure in New York City."

Rehoboth Beach, Delaware

Location
A 3-hour drive from Washington, D.C., Baltimore, or Philadelphia, the oceanfront community of Rehoboth Beach is on the east side of the Chesapeake Peninsula, fronting onto the Atlantic Ocean.

Climate
The 2,500 year-round residents of this town sit through a windy winter characterized by bone-chilling breezes alternating with tolerably milder periods. Summers are distinctly Florida-esque, with 90-degree temperatures supplying the foundation for what's historically been a swinging beach scene, when as many as 40,000 part-time residents crowd into town.

Living
Rehoboth Beach has two distinct personalities, depending on the time of year. Jovial beachcombers set the tone in the summer, while the permanent residents enjoy a more low-key, small-town existence most of the time, taking advantage of an active arts center. Rehoboth Beach boasts several fine art galleries, dozens of great restaurants and bars, and a public school system that's just starting to get in synch with the town's fine art talents to supplement student art education programs.

As long as you don't care about living directly on the beach, an average 3-bedroom home runs in the $100,000 range. With its small retail district, studio rentals in Rehoboth Beach are rare, and, with the exception of a few subsidized studios sponsored by the art league, most artists build the dream studios they've always wanted onto their homes (even if they are within earshot of their kids). Surfing, fishing, and sailing are the main activities locals enjoy, with winters taken up by long beach walks, and stretches of hard work preparing for the upcoming summer tourist season.

Out On the Town
Anyone with the urge for a big city fix can either head up the coast one hour to Dover, the state capital, or drive a couple more hours to a real metropolis. But the locals have things pretty good when the tourists and part-timers have left town, with the Blue Moon, Garden Gourmet, and Nicola Pizza ranking high on the list of the town's favorite hangouts. Nighttime action is great at the Road House and Dugan's, with the Camel's Hump being Rehoboth Beach's favorite natural foods store. The town has several active theater groups staging productions at the Baycenter and Possum Point Playhouse, while Sydney's Side Street is the town's favorite jazz club.

Economic Impact of the Arts
Left to its own devices, Rehoboth Beach would likely be well on the path to becoming a refuge for painters, sculptors, ceramicists, and writers who want to live in a beach community that's close (but not too close) to a large city. But in the past couple of decades, this small town has been overrun by summer crowds exiting the steaming sidewalks of D.C. and Baltimore in search of a place to have fun in the sun. As a result, the arts take a back seat to the tourist business, and much of the local business community takes the artists for granted.

Local Arts Agency

Rehoboth Art League, 12 Dodds Lane, Rehoboth Beach, DE 19971, (302) 227-8408. Publishes the *RAL Newsletter*.

"We've been growing steadily for years," says art league director Charles Palmer, "but recently something has made this place a sensational town for artists selling to the public. After 56 years as an art league, we're seeing people coming in here to buy as they've never done before, and I can't tell you what we're doing now that's so different from what we've done in the past. We've got an exhibition space, studio teaching facilities, and a small performing arts space used for children's arts programs and lectures. Local newspapers are very supportive and there's a classical music station, but we're all just shaking our heads in wonder. Life is filled with pleasant mysteries, and the booming art market in Rehoboth Beach is one of them."

Galleries and Arts Festivals

The biggest arts festival in town is the art league's annual RAL Outdoor Exhibition, held the last two weekends in August on the league's art center grounds, attracting nearly 150 exhibitors. Seven commercial galleries and one nonprofit (the Historic Homestead Mansion Gallery) keep the wall spaces around town filled with art work, while local restaurants and banks are glad to work with artists wanting to show their own works on a rotating exhibition basis.

What the Artist Says

Laura Hickman, painter of mysterious images of vacant architectural spaces, is a lifelong area resident who says she owes much of her success to the contacts and sales she made participating in the art league's public art shows. "Having all these Baltimore, Washington, and Philadelphia tourists in here over the summer gives you a great opportunity to get picked up by galleries. I used to own a retail store and cafe, but once my art career started taking off I sold them and just focused on painting. Businesses here are supportive when it comes to putting art on their walls, but the buyers are the people with summer homes, much more than locals.

"Artists tend to isolate themselves over the winter, and I think that's a reaction to all the socializing you're required to do during the summer months. It's quiet in the off-season. The economy is much better now, especially for locals who stay here year-round, but it can still be very quiet and boring for someone who needs to have lots of action."

Key West, Florida

Location
The 24,000 residents of Key West live in a never-never land that's as much its own end of the world as it is a distant province of Florida. The drive into this somewhat Caribbean, somewhat Cuban, and somewhat mysterious place transports visitors over dozens of bridges spanning a hundred miles of crystal clear waters.

Climate
Cooled by ocean breezes, Key West's climate almost never gets too hot, and chilly days are about as rare as snowmen. The biggest weather problem is the hurricanes that, every few decades, roar in off the Atlantic and flatten a city block or two.

Living
While lots of the fixer-upper homes in Key West have been renovated by members of the town's tirelessly optimistic gay and lesbian population, there are still plenty of opportunities for those with the drive and skills necessary to combat what ocean salts and high humidity levels do to wood frame residences. Average 3-bedroom homes sell in the $150,000 range, with lots of lower cost places available as "handyperson's specials." There is no arts center, but a variance of artistic attitudes give Key West an interesting blend of influences, balancing a hard-edged tourism economy against the wills and wiles of those who come here thinking they've discovered Oz.

Make sure you bring industrial-strength sunblock. Any action worth writing home about involves sand, water, and sun. Nightclubs have a seriously partying edge to them, and much of Key West stays open well into the wee hours of the morning.

Out On the Town
In a town so open to gays and lesbians, being "out" on the town in Key West takes on a whole new meaning. Ethnic restaurants of every possible permutation abound, competing for the tourist dollars that flow into Key West from December through mid-May. On Duvall Street, one bar after another pleads for your attention, but Sloppy Joe's is still a favorite with locals. If you're visiting, be sure to stop in at the Chart Room (underneath the Pier House) on Duvall Street. Breakfasts are an unusual affair in this town, with most locals opting to patronize their neighborhood Cuban grocery for a *cafe con leche*. Nightspots run from tame to scandalous, but a reasonably sane crowd can usually be found at Holiday Isle. Dining spots range from Louie's Backyard (the town's most renowned restaurant) to the Bagatelle and Turtle Kraals, both of which serve fine seafoods. If you leave your prejudices at home, and don't judge bizarre-looking people too harshly, you'll have a great time.

Economic Impact of the Arts
Hemmingway aside, this has always been a working town. Realizing that the local definition of work can take on some unusual meanings, from rolling cigars to smuggling bales of ganja, there's

still a large part of the local economy that's hooked into the commercial fishing industry. In a place that has so many T-shirt shops and hotels, the presence of an artists' community, while encompassing a large number of individuals, tends to get lost in all the hustle and bustle. Nonetheless, there are lots of painters, writers, and musicians here who make a good living from their work and are inspired by the town's loony personality.

Local Arts Agency

Monroe County Fine Arts Council, 95360 Overseas Highway, #5, Key Largo, FL 33037, (305) 852-6116.

"The majority of our focus is on the performing arts," says council executive director Parvan Bakardjiev, "from classical music ensembles to jazz groups, dance, opera, and youth programs. Once we get a traveling group down here, we usually send them into as many local schools as possible, or we stage performances in the hotel ballrooms. We have a few artist-in-residency programs that we've privately raised funds for, but politically, the arts just haven't arrived yet in the Keys. There isn't the level of awareness of the the role arts play in the community that we'd like to see. We're battling a laid-back, almost rural mindset."

Galleries and Arts Festivals

Key West has an active, organized art gallery association that publishes and distributes a walking tour guide for art lovers, and serves as the primary sales outlet for local artists. The town has nearly two dozen art galleries, with many more stretched along the larger islands comprising the Key West archipelligo. With a well-organized approach to festivals and events, there's practically no breathing room between the arts fairs and festivals that follow one after another during the tourist season. Mardi Gras, in mid-February, seems to bring the most art-conscious group of tourists into town.

What the Artist Says

"When you get past the veneer of tourism that covers the Keys, what you end up with are a series of small towns," says painter Sandy Kay. "Here, the average buyer isn't a local person, it's that tourist who wants a memento, or someone who may have just bought a second home and wants something nice—something with local flavor—to put up on their walls. We're fortunate to be getting a more upscale level of gay tourist coming into Key West, because that sort of individual is generally better informed about the arts than you average visitor to Florida, and will seriously consider purchasing something that's original and costs more than a couple of hundred dollars. If you want a more typical kind of life, there are other places in the Keys you can move to. Anywhere you go outside Key West you'll find these Sunday painters doing seascapes, but if there's going to be an organized arts community here, it needs to develop some sort of a focus. Expect to have a hard time making a living here, unless you've got galleries in other places that are willing to sell your work."

Naples, Florida

Location
Standing on one of the crystalized, iridescent beaches along Naples' corner of southwest Florida, you get the feeling that sailing down to the Yucatan wouldn't be too difficult. Right frame of mind, but flawed reasoning. Just stay close to the beach and everything will be alright, dude.

Climate
Folks here like to characterize their weather as less severe than you find in other parts of the state. It's definitely a tropical setting, one with languid summers moderated by ocean breezes, and free from the threat of winter frosts.

Living
Becoming more expensive as the east coast of Florida and places like Tampa and Orlando become more crowded, Naples is a community of 20,000 residents who are joined during the winter months by thousands of transient snowbirds. Real estate isn't cheap, with the average 3-bedroom home selling in the $150,000 range. Affordable studio spaces are readily available, with the average monthly rent being $300. Living close to Everglades National Park means the locals have recreational access to one of the nation's most spectacular stretches of natural beauty. It's suntan city . . . with beachcombing for seashells being one of the favorite local pastimes. Southwest Florida has miles and miles of unspoiled beachfront, but is also within easy access to the Everglades National Park. Naples has traditionally attracted a number of Canadian tourists, but lately has been benefiting from European travelers as well.

Out On the Town
Naples' performing arts offerings improved considerably when the town's Philharmonic Center for the Arts opened a few years back. The facility has gone a long way toward putting Naples on the cultural map. Local artists pull into Harold's now and then for a cold brew, and ethnic food choices are good, with Bangkok being Naple's entree into the national Thai restaurant trend. If you're looking for nightlife, try the Oasis and Witch's Brew.

Economic Impact of the Arts
Reflective of the diverse backgrounds of part-timers and relocated full-timers who have elected to live in this corner of paradise, in recent years Naples has developed a deserved reputation as an artsy alternative to the traditional Florida tourist destination. Monumental-scale sculptural installations are just starting to appear in the area, but the community periodically wrestles with the challenge of combining its diverse arts groups into a singular arts community voice.

Local Arts Agency

United Arts Council of Collier County, 1051 Fifth Avenue South, Naples, FL 33940, (813) 263-3830.

Operating from the town's former train depot, the arts council emphasizes programs and services for visual artists in this part of the state. "We see ourselves as a service-oriented organization," says council executive director Carolyn Jansen, "whose goal is to provide affordable access to facilities needed by Naples' visual and performing artists. Naples has a need for more arts education programs for local school children, but the funds are going to have to come from local sources due to cutbacks in state education funding. The town has over 700 registered nonprofit groups, and many of them are formed by out-of-state people with no regard to what local residents need. There should be an emphasis on keeping the arts affordable for the entire community."

Galleries and Arts Festivals

Naples' artists have 30 commercial arts galleries within city limits, so there are numerous opportunities to gain entree into the town's arts market. Many artists who live in the area don't sell their work locally, choosing instead to use Naples' spectacular environment as a base from which their work is shipped to galleries in major cities. Three nonprofit exhibition spaces are fortunate to be able to draw from this talented segment of the arts community. Things start hopping in Naples around Thanksgiving, and don't let up until April. The biggest arts festival is the annual Naples ArtFest in May, with nearly 200 exhibitors.

What the Artist Says

Jonathan Green, one of the nation's most respected regionalist painters and a ten-year resident of Naples, splits his time between here and a home in South Carolina. "Naples is where I do my work—my studio assistant is top-notch, I'm vice president of the arts council, and I conduct free classes for gifted children. It's a great community, is very supportive of artists. I'm a big believer in participation, although I realize many artists don't feel the same way. There's always the tendency to stay private in a place like Naples and just witness nature. I use my time to plan for shows, to reflect on the things that are influencing my work, and to get out and see what the town's younger artists are doing.

"To anyone who might consider moving here, I'd say you need to be straight about your reasons for moving to Naples. It's quite isolated, and might not be a wonderful place for everyone. Know what you're looking for from life before you get here."

Seaside, Florida

Location
The pure white sand and emerald waters of the Gulf of Mexico make the panhandle region one of the most beautiful and inspirational places in the world, according to Panama City artist Paul Brent.

Climate
While summer is hot and humid, the relief of sea breezes and perfect-temperature waters are just minutes away from any point in Seaside or its neighboring communities of Grayton Beach and Panama City. Here, winter can be downright nippy, but the cool weather lasts for about ten weeks, then it's back to glorious warmth.

Living
Being a planned community, Seaside real estate prices are in the upward-range. Three-bedroom homes will command anywhere from $150,000 and up on the open market, while similar residences in Grayton Beach and Panama City sell in the neighborhood of $100,000 (even less for fixer-uppers).

In the Seaside area, the residents tend to be older and more likely to stay close to home for golfing and beach activities. Panama City's younger population has more entertainment options, especially in the area of live theater, which is staged at the Martin Theater, the Kaleidoscope Theater, Marina Civic Theater, and on the grounds of Gulf Coast Community College. Studio rentals are easy to find in Panama City, with the average monthly cost running $200 for around 900 square feet. For those who may tire of beachfront activities, the area offers sheltered bays ideal for sailing and fishing, with numerous lagoons bordering vast stands of Spanish moss-covered oaks.

Out On the Town
On the Seaside and Grayton Beach end of this area, Shades is the spot where locals head for nighttime fun. The ethnic restaurants, from Thai to French (with a strong emphasis on seafood), are located in Panama City. The best place to meet friends for a drink is Sweet Magnolias in Panama City's historic downtown district, a part of town with enough nightlife options to keep even college spring breakers happy.

Economic Impact of the Arts
Seaside and Grayton Beach tend to be where some artists and most local collectors live, while Panama City is more the kind of laid-back, affordable community that artists and others in the creative fields prefer to call home. While at least a hundred artists create and successfully sell their own work in Panama City, there's a somewhat subdued approach to the way local businesses promote and support the arts.

Local Arts Agency

Bay Arts Alliance, P.O. Box 1153, Panama City, FL 32402, (904) 769-1217, and Seaside Institute, P.O. Box 4730, Seaside, FL 32459, (904) 231-2421.

With a newly renovated structure in downtown Panama City, the Visual Arts Center offers the region's visual artists a first-rate exhibition space, as well as studio classrooms where local artists hold classes for children and adult art students. Nearby is the Martin Theater, once an art deco movie palace, but now restored as the town's performing arts venue.

Seaside Institute has initiated an innovative program bringing an artist-in-residence to its facilities. During a several-month stay, the artist conducts classes for Seaside residents and is given living quarters and a studio to create their own art work. Seaside also has an active arts lecture series.

Galleries and Arts Festivals

The Grayton Beach Arts Festival, held each May, is the largest public arts event in the Seaside area. A half-dozen galleries and craft stores are scattered around Seaside's beautifully designed commercial districts. Panama City has a nonprofit exhibition space at its Visual Arts Center, and while its busiest times of the year are the Christmas and summer seasons, the Spring Festival of the Arts in early May is the community's largest public arts happening.

What the Artist Says

"This is still one of the most surprisingly affordable seacoast towns in the country," says Paul Brent, a watercolorist whose work is included in many museum collections. "Waterfront living can still be found in the Panama City area—it's picturesque, affordable, and offers a wealth of the types of inspirational places that creative people find enjoyable."

Seaside's architectural beauty has been written about in many national publications and continues to attract a surprising number of visitors who come to see what all the excitement is about. Annete Newbill Trujillo's craft gallery carries the work of local artists and photographers, selling primarily to second home buyers who decorate their residence with locally significant art, but tend to buy their more expensive pieces elsewhere. "Seaside has a good potential for developing the kind of community that will support a broad range of visual arts and performing arts productions," she says, "but it's not there yet. People are still at the stage where they want things to match their interior designs and aren't seriously looking at work carried in the local galleries."

St. Augustine, Florida

Location

An Atlantic seacoast community in northeast Florida, St. Augustine's 12,000 residents are an hour's drive from Jacksonville.

Climate

For the weeks between Thanksgiving and Lincoln's Birthday, St. Augustine has a mixed bag of weather that can more closely resemble that of North Carolina than South Florida. But all things being equal, outside of a few chilly, overcast skies, the climate here is typically Florida temperate.

Living

With its large population of retirees and a constant flow of tourists (looking for the fountain of youth?), St. Augustine is a historic, picturesque community that's something of a victim of its own success. While there are locals who have either grown up in the area and continue to live and work here, along with younger newcomers who sought to establish their lives in St. Augustine, the community's visitor promotion campaign has resulted in a major real estate development planned nearby for as many as 50,000 new residents by the end of the decade. Presently, family-size homes are priced in the $70,000 range.

The pace is very casual, with golf, tennis, and fishing rating high on the list of how to pass the time on a three-day weekend. Because of its many parks and historical sites, St. Augustine teens manage to swing many seasonal employment opportunities as docents, groundskeepers, and actors in the area's regularly scheduled re-enactments of historical events.

Out On the Town

With the metropolis of Jacksonville just 45-minutes north, people in St. Augustine seldom feel a lack of entertainment or dining options. The local acting troupe, Lime Light Theater, performs in the downtown Bayfront Theater, while Flagler College has a lively performing arts program, with regular recitals and classical music performances. Restaurant-wise, one of the local favorites is the cuisine known as Minorican food, characterized by its spiciness from the area's native-grown datil pepper. As for artist hangouts, Scarlet O'Hara's is a local favorite for drinks, but for nightlife, most folks head into Jacksonville or Daytona.

Economic Impact of the Arts

St. Augustine, like Key West, is one of those wonderfully ethnic-appearing spots on the map that have historically drawn a great deal of artist interest. And like its sister city to the south, the town has changed mightily over the past few decades. Still beautiful and inspiring, St. Augustine has remained more affordable and is an easier, less hectic place to live. Unfortunately, many local business types see the arts as a somewhat frivolous waste of time, despite the fact that a local reputation as an arts community is what draws most visitors here in the first place.

Local Arts Agency

Ancient City Arts Alliance, P.O. Box 2176, St. Augustine, FL 32085, (904) 829-2964.

"St. Augustine is loaded with historical significance (Spaniards settled here in the late 1500s), so there's a great deal of interest in re-enactments of famous battles, treaty signings . . . things like that," says arts alliance president Charlene Peterson-Parish. "We were formed as an advocacy agency, but we're trying to become an educational group so we can help to bring more quality to the area's arts community. The arts groups still need a better organizational structure to insure that the arts don't get overlooked when it comes time for the government to make broad decisions on spending and development."

Galleries and Arts Festivals

Being north of the year-round tourist traffic pulled toward Disney World in Orlando, St. Augustine is able to skim off a steady stream of summer visitors who stop in for a day or two of seeing the area's historical sights. Add to that the regular busy season that begins at Christmas and continues through April, and you come up with a lot of opportunities for galleries to sell art to visitors. Twenty or so galleries do business in St. Augustine, with a nonprofit exhibition space serving the needs of the town's younger or part-time artists. Busiest local arts events are the Arts and Crafts Festivals held over Palm Sunday weekend and in early December.

What the Artist Says

"Most local artists aren't concerned about selling to tourists," says furniture craftsman Bill Long, "because the serious artists in St. Augustine can't stand to paint the repetitive street and beach scenes tourists come here to buy. It's a quaint, uncrowded spot on the map—a place where you can head out sailing after doing a full day's work. I do eight retail craft shows each year and like dealing with the public at the shows, but when I return to St. Augustine, it's to work and enjoy life."

Enzo Torcoletti, a 23-year resident of St. Augustine, is a sculptor working primarily in carved stone. "It's like a little European town: a bit manicured, but a very quiet, attractive community for artists who are serious about their work. The kind of tourist who has the desire to buy original art is the same type of person who may spend two or three nights at a bed and breakfast inn. St. Augustine is friendly and safe, but realize there aren't many opportunities to sell your own work."

Vero Beach, Florida

Location
At the halfway point along Florida's eastern seaboard lies the bustling community of Vero Beach, an art-friendly community of 18,000 residents with a balanced population of families, retirees, and wintering snowbirds.

Climate
If you took a year's worth of temperature variations and averaged out the highs and lows, Vero's weather would clock in at a perfect 72.4 degrees. Every few years, a northern front will barrel into the area, wreaking havoc on the citrus crop, or a stretch of summer will turn particularly hot and humid. But in this part of the country weather patterns change quickly, so patience is rewarded.

Living
The local arts center is one of the most active small-town arts facilities in the nation, with large areas dedicated to working artists, art exhibitions, student instruction, and the performing arts. Outside of resort communities populated by the winter home set, real estate remains affordable, with a 3-bedroom home selling in the $100,000 range. Local schools have a progressive, pro-active approach to blending arts education into student curriculums.

Vero Beach residents consider themselves fortunate to be living in an area that's both beautiful and free from the serious crime and drug problems plaguing many parts of the Sunshine State. They refer to their area as the "Treasure Coast," alluding to the substantial number of local tales of pirates and buried treasure, but just as easily applying to the region's long stretches of unspoiled beachfront. Long-range prospects for a continued high quality of life in this community look favorable.

Out On the Town
Because there are a few planned, high-income communities on the town's outskirts, and being the off-season home of the L.A. Dodgers, Vero has a much more sophisticated restaurant scene than most communities of comparable size. There's also an active community theater organization, and regularly scheduled musical performances at several venues within the town's borders. Two restaurants, Waldo's and Bobbie's, are the community's favorite places to meet friends over drinks or lunch, while Eddie's is the best leg-shakin' place to hit after dark. For more diverse ethnic foods (other than Vero's many Italian and Chinese restaurants) head north for a 45-minute drive to Melbourne.

Economic Impact of the Arts
Not so much an arts marketplace as a community with a high level of arts awareness, the presence of the arts in Vero Beach is an integral, rather than parallel, aspect of what has come to be expected from the region. The community has a disproportionately large number of individuals who refer to themselves as artists, but even if you weed out all the Sunday painters and home crafts folks, there's still a strong group of art pros who choose to live and work in Vero, marketing outside the immediate area.

Local Arts Agency

Center for the Arts, 3001 Riverside Park Drive, Vero Beach, FL 32963, (407) 231-0707.

"We're operating a full-scale operation on 8 acres right now, and are in the middle of a $6-million campaign to increase our size," says center education curator Sherry Spires. "What started off primarily as a visual arts center has expanded into many other aspects of the performing arts and humanities—activities that are held year-round to address the needs of the town's permanent residents, but which also increase in number to accommodate the area's part-time people.

"One of our most important focal points is education. We have school administrators on our board, bring classes into the center for exhibitions and performances, send presentations out to the area schools, and fund youth scholarships for students who are gifted in the arts. We also have arts programs aimed at this area's large population of migrant workers. We've found that in Vero Beach the local residents are committed to having strong arts programs to benefit their kids."

Galleries and Arts Festivals

If you take into account the town's good, bad, and ugly commercial galleries, the numbers reach somewhere above 20 art outlets. At least a few of those are galleries carrying worthwhile work by regional artists, with buyers tending to be the surprisingly few second-home owners whose taste goes beyond trite, simplistic realism. The busiest time of the year is from New Years Day through April, which is about how long Tommy Lasorda's boys of summer are in town. Vero's largest public festival of the arts is Under The Oaks, held each March.

What the Artist Says

Haydn Llewellyn Davies, a Canadian sculptor who, for the past two decades has spent many of his winters holed up in the warmth of a Vero suburb, keeps his local profile at a minimum while he creates sculpture for his gallery representatives in Toronto and New York. "Here, I can work outside all winter long and not have to breath in the gasses and fumes that are created when you work with metals," he says. "I've done an artist-in-residency program at the arts center, but my main interests lie in large-scale commissions from my Toronto gallery and creating more personal-size works for my New York gallery. I've found that there are many artists living here who feel the way I do—that you can work just as well in a warm climate as you can in the snowy north.

"There are lots of interesting elements starting to come together here, which is creating cultural opportunities that Vero Beach hasn't had in the past. There are some very knowledgeable individuals moving in who have a great deal of interest in the arts, and that's going to give many local artists better opportunities to sell their work."

Brunswick, Georgia

Location

Surrounded by the extraordinary scenic beauty of St. Simons Sound, the 17,000 residents of Brunswick live in a sheltered Atlantic seaboard setting, protected from hurricanes by a string of barrier islands, including St. Simons and Jekyll Islands. Brunswick is located along Georgia's southeast coast, an hour's drive north of Jacksonville, Florida.

Climate

A perfect balance of cool winters, followed by predictably long springs leading into moderate, humid summers have historically attracted as many mid-year visitors into the area as it does winter snowbirds.

Living

This region is called the Golden Isles, an area encompassing not just the population center of Brunswick, but the outlying resort communities and barrier island nature preserves and parks as well. Three-bedroom homes in Brunswick run in the $100,000 range, while a similar place in St. Simons is slightly more expensive. A strong arts center in Brunswick plays an important role in addressing the arts needs in the region, with many commercial galleries selling works by local, Southeastern, and international artists.

The Golden Isles region has an interesting mix of income levels, minority groups, somewhat sleepy city areas, along with several of the country's most attractive state parks, national seashores, and historic monuments. Those who come here for a fresh start couldn't do much better, as this area is growing in a manageable way, yet somehow retaining the most significant aspects of what has made it desirable. Golf, that quintessential pastime of the leisure class, is high on the list of some locals, while those who shy away from the canned camaraderie found on the links tend to stick to water sports, with sailing the St. Simons Sound a favorite.

Out On the Town

Like any commercially vibrant community along the coast, there are several dozen restaurants, bars, and nightclubs keeping locals and visitors entertained year-round. The local nightlife centers around hotel clubs, which tend to be down along the waterfront, presenting the typical live music scene found in other parts of the country. In Brunswick, Poor Stephen's is a popular place to meet for drinks and dinner, and the Cloister rates as a local nightlife favorite.

Economic Impact of the Arts

Brunswick tends to be popular among the area's artists as an affordable, less hectic place to live, where art work, not necessarily geared to tourist eyes, can find exhibition space in one of the town's several nonprofit galleries. The performing arts are stronger in Brunswick than in other parts of the Golden Isles. Several clusters of art galleries dot the developed stretches of St. Simons, with most galleries selling locally created images taken directly from the landscape. A worthy exception to this rule is the Left Bank Gallery, run by a local couple with deep roots in the community. Their specialty is the work of contemporary artists from France, several artists from elsewhere in Europe, and Mildred Nix Huie, an active, 88-year-old impressionist painter.

Local Arts Agency

Golden Isles Arts and Humanities Association, The Ritz Theater, 1530 Newcastle St., Brunswick, GA 31520, (912) 262-6934. Publishes the newsletter *The Spotlight*.

From its offices in the renovated Ritz Theater, association executive director Helen Alexander oversees "an active organization that stages everything from comic opera to five touring theater companies each year, dance, piano recitals, and much more. We also work with the organizations in the area, providing training programs so that their own group can be more successful when working with their arts constituencies." The association actively enlists school classes in attending events staged at the Ritz Theater, and sends performers to schools around the region. St. Simons' theater troupe is the Island Players, active through the busiest months of the year.

Galleries and Arts Festivals

The area's dozen or so art galleries are supplemented by a number of nonprofit exhibition spaces, spread along the Golden Isles region. The year's largest local arts event is the Golden Isles Arts Festival, which takes place during the second weekend in October.

What the Artist Says

Margaret Bastin, an impressionist-style painter of local landscape and wildlife scenes, has found the creative life in St. Simons Island to be one presenting great opportunities for everything from affordable studio space to selling originals through galleries to second-home buyers. "I enjoy the town's sense of being a fixed, stable community. I think local art sells well because people have made a commitment to living here. The galleries are generally quite good. I'm a naturalist painter, so the environment of this area is an important influence in my work.

"Artists seem to have a willingness to share critiques and gossip about the galleries, and to provide each other with information on shows. There are always exhibition possibilities in a place like the Golden Isles, but if you're a contemporary artists you may have trouble finding a place to show your work locally. This is a traditionalist stronghold, so if you work along those lines what you do will be readily accepted."

Sautee Valley, Georgia

Location
Tucked into the northeast corner of Georgia, the small community of Sautee defines itself in terms of its surrounding area (pop. 13,000). A 2-hour drive out of Atlanta, the Sautee Valley spreads into Chattahoochee National Forest and is characterized by numerous lakes, rivers, and springs.

Climate
Spring arrives a bit later to this part of the Southeast than to other, more low-lying areas. The terrain is distinctively part of the Appalachian Mountain region, complete with regionalized weather patterns. Winter snows are common, but once summer sets in, the warm, humid weather stays around well into November. The area has lovely transition seasons.

Living
Very countrified, this is a place where family roots extend back through the centuries, and land holdings pass from one generation to another. Houses are somewhat hard to find, and many newcomers prefer building places of their own. If you can spot a 3-bedroom home on the market, it will probably be priced in the $75,000 range. The area has a regional arts center that works with school districts to both bring art to students, as well as getting students in to the center.

Surrounded by mountainous, wooded terrain, there are a number of great hiking, fishing, and bicycle touring opportunities in the area. Here, life is practically crime-free, yet locals take their time when it comes to extending themselves to new arrivals. Once accepted into the community, artists find themselves living in a place that "looks out for its neighbors."

Out On the Town
As rural a community as you can imagine, the folks here realize that a night of entertainment and dining out includes a 90-minute drive to Athens, home of the University of Georgia, or a trip all the way to Atlanta to make a weekend out of it. There is a limited selection of restaurants in nearby Clarkesville.

Economic Impact of the Arts
Traditional folk crafts have always been strong in this part of the state, but in recent years, a number of more contemporary artists who sell their work independently of the local art fairs have quietly started moving into the area. There are several galleries scattered around the region, selling mostly traditional craft, that have lately started to incorporate some of this more contemporary, locally-made work into their inventories

Local Arts Agency

Sautee-Nacoochee Arts and Community Center, P.O. Box 66, Sautee, GA 30571, (706) 878-3300.

"We've emphasized the performing arts . . . theater, dance, and music," says art center executive director Jimmy Johnston. "In our rotating art gallery exhibits we work with museums around the state, and every year we have an auction set up for the purpose of raising funds to support visual art programs with Valley artists." The art center is housed in a 4,000-square-foot former schoolhouse, and its presence has motivated several of the region's art-related businesses to expand their operations. Visitors are drawn to the region for stays at rural bed and breakfast inns, which includes excursions along the country roads leading to art galleries, craft stores, and open artist studios. The arts center sponsors reduced-rate performances for students whenever a performing arts event is programmed, and works to match artists-in-residency participants with regional schools.

Galleries and Arts Festivals

Galleries do exist here, but you may have to hunt them down. Expect to see lots of traditional folk crafts, furniture, and hand-sewn quilts. The year's biggest arts festival is the Echota Performing Arts Festival held each July. Most tourists visit in spring, and especially autumn, when mountain foliage colors are the brightest, but summer weekends can also find local inns filled with guests.

What the Artist Says

John Byron, a glass craftsman who moved into the Sautee Valley nearly 20 years ago, says he left St. Augustine, Florida, for the north Georgia mountains, to enjoy the secluded nature of the place, with its affordable land, and to live in a place "where you can pretty much do whatever you want and nobody will bother you." He's not reliant on the local market to sell his hand-blown vases and vessel forms, choosing instead to spend several months each year on the road, selling directly to buyers at craft and art fairs stretching from south Florida to northern Michigan.

"For me, one of the nice things was that the Sautee Valley is close to the University of Georgia, a place where I have friends," says Byron. "You can look around here now and see that things in the Valley are changing. It's becoming a more popular tourist area—we've got lots of campgrounds and RV parks. People living here have family connections to practically all the other people living in the area. It takes a long time to make friends, but you can't take that personally. . . . It's just different from other places, not less friendly. We've got clean air and the country's best spring water, and this is a wonderful place to raise kids. But artists who move here need to have their markets developed before they arrive—there aren't any jobs, and not much to do but work and raise your family."

Driggs, Idaho

Location

Driggs sits along the west slope of the Grand Tetons. Folks living here wake up each day to in-your-face views of 13,000-foot mountains. Driggs is turning out to be eastern Idaho's success story. Simply spectacular!

Climate

The area is mountainous, with all the implications as to a cold, snowy winter and misty, cool shoulder seasons. Summer, for those who haven't had the chance to experience life at 9,000-feet, can be glorious and almost hot one day, followed by a light snowfall the next. "We count on at least a little dusting once or twice during July and August," say locals.

Living

The cost of living is affordable in this very rural, scenic town within an hour's drive of the tourist mecca of Jackson, Wyoming. While real estate prices are steadily increasing (due to spill-over from the other side of Teton Pass), a 3-bedroom residence on a few acres runs less than $100,000. Driggs is a safe, crime-free place, but it's also remote, lacks services, and is just starting to wake up to the need for improved schools, roads, etc.

Isolated to the point of being lonely, Driggs is the kind of town where those who don't participate in year-round outdoors activities risk a serious case of cabin fever. The growing season is very short, so gardeners must have greenhouses to give summer vegetables a head start. This is also a hunter's paradise, and many local artists find the fall deer season to be a handy way of supplementing the family food budget through the winter. There's a downhill ski area close by, the cross-country skiing and snowmobiling are always great, and summer brings local streams alive with brown and rainbow trout.

Out On the Town

In this corner of Idaho, each small town has one or two places to eat, and that's it. Anyone who has a few extra bucks burning a hole in their pocket can finds lots of variety in Jackson. There's a natural foods store, Table Mt. Foods, in Driggs, as well as Mike's Eats, the local burger and fries mecca. Morning coffee at Teton Bakery is a good way to catch up on chit-chat with friends, and if you're out lookin' for love after sundown, pull your rig into the parking lot at the Knotty Pine in the nearby town of Victor.

Galleries and Arts Festivals

Artists living in Driggs are usually tied into the nearby gallery scene in Jackson, but also try to find gallery outlets in regional art centers such as Bozeman, Montana, and Sun Valley, Idaho. There's been talk about the area's artists organizing a summer arts and crafts festival, but for now the laid-back attitude of Driggs seems to be blanketing many artists in a haze of procrastination. Hey, folks . . . wake up! The galleries in Jackson don't have to take a 50-percent cut on your art work!

Local Arts Council

Teton Valley Community Arts Association, Rt. 1, Box 3370, Driggs, ID 83422, no phone. Publishes the *TVCAA Newsletter*.

"We're still a young and growing community," says Deirdre Cassidy, the association's president, "and while we want to promote the arts and increase people's art awareness here in the valley, it's all just starting. Most of the local artists once lived over the pass in Jackson, and moved to Driggs when Jackson became too crowded, too expensive, or they got too good an offer on their home.

"Right now, we're concentrating on putting together a spring film festival, which we'd like to coordinate with a children's art show. Later on, we need to work out a way to give artists an opportunity to have an arts and craft festival here in the valley. Local schools don't have art instruction, so we're looking at coordinating an artist-in-residency program and at getting performing artists into local schools. Local businesses still see the artists here as newcomers, so we're working to build that bridge."

The association publicizes its events through paid advertisements in the local newspaper and free announcements on the public radio station in neighboring Rexburg.

Galleries and Arts Festivals

There are no galleries or exhibition spaces yet, and the association's first events are scheduled to take place in 1994.

What the Artist Says

"Even the Jackson market isn't enough to keep an artist going—if you're going to survive as an artist in this area, you've got to figure out how to sell directly to the public," says Driggs glass artist Ralph Mossman. Working in hot glass, he's made his professional reputation creating vases, perfume bottles, and Christmas ornaments for galleries around the Rocky Mountain region. But during the off-season, he's usually found on the road, selling his hand-crafted glass beads to craft shows and collectors as far away as Santa Fe, New Mexico, and Portland, Oregon.

"One of the nicest things about Driggs," says Mossman, "is that as an artist you can do whatever it is you want to do here, and there's plenty of space to do it in—it's a beautiful, peaceful place. The one drawback is that we really don't have a local market for our artwork, but like everything else in this part of the country, that will probably change. Unless you stay focused on your work you can feel empty and depressed in a place like Driggs. I'm hopeful that now that we have an active arts council there will be more interaction among the valley's artists."

Sandpoint, Idaho

Location

The Idaho Panhandle region is an area of mountains, lakes, cascading rivers, and soaring trees. The 6,200 residents of Sandpoint live next to Lake Pend Oreille, a nearly 20-mile-long body of water that is the region's year-round recreational focus. Sandpoint is slightly more than an hour's drive northeast of Spokane, Washington.

Climate

Sandpoint has a long, snowy winter with typically Northwestern transition seasons (lots of rain and overcast skies). Summer is glorious and crystal clear, with the average day's temperature hanging somewhere in the 80s.

Living

If you've ever fantasized about building your own log home somewhere in the woods, Sandpoint will seem like paradise. Commercial log home manufacturers abound, land is still very affordable, and your neighbors adhere to the local tradition of respecting people's privacy. Home prices are rising steadily, but a 3-bedroom spread on a bit of land can still be found in the $90,000 range, provided you don't insist on lakefront property.

As open a countryside as you can find in this corner of the Northwest, the Panhandle has everything from a first-rate ski area to fabulous fishing streams, lakes for sailing and sunbathing, and scenery that overwhelms with its beauty. The point of living in this area is not simply to enjoy the outdoors, but to absorb it, and for an artist that means taking the natural assets important to your eyes, using them to inspire and direct your work, then finding the right market to allow collectors a chance to see what you've created.

Out On the Town

During the summers, when northern Idaho is swamped with out-of-state visitors, things in Sandpoint and the nearby resort community of Coeur d'Alene couldn't be better: restaurants, golf courses, pony rides, water skiing—you can have your pick. Winters tend to see locals take long vacations, with many shops either closing down entirely or reducing hours to part-time status. In any case, as quiet as locals want their home base to be during the off-season, anyone who needs an ethnic food fix or some shopping mall action simply makes the drive to Spokane. In Sandpoint, locals stop in at restaurants like the Garden, Ivano's, and Bradley's to meet and greet pals, but Gregory's remains a favorite with the beer-and-chips crowd. Nighttime action can be rustled up at the Kamloops Bar & Grill, the best burger in the area is the char-grilled version up at Serv-a-Burger, and Trudy's Health Food Store is the local headquarters for the non-meat crowd.

Economic Impact of the Arts

A number of this area's visual arts professionals prefer to stay at home, working in their studios and sending their creations to galleries outside the region. There are also a sizable number of

Hollywood types, including actors, screenwriters, producers, and technical directors, who maintain summer homes in the region, slipping into Sandpoint unnoticed for recuperative stays in its unspoiled environment. In recent years, there's been an awakening to the powerful economic impact the arts can exert on a local economy, as a very popular summer music festival and several new art galleries have given an identifiable shape to the creative community that's quietly lived here for years.

Local Arts Agency

Pend Oreille Arts Council, P.O. Box 1694, Sandpoint, ID 83864, (208) 263-6139.

"We're not in an arts center, but we do have an exhibition space available to us in a local bank and a refurbished old theater," says Ginny Robideaux, the council's executive director. "So you could say we try to do it all—keep visual exhibitions rotating in and out of the gallery space, produce anywhere from eight to ten performing arts events each year at the Panida Theater, and work with schools on anything from art teacher volunteers to bringing through performing arts workshops when the opportunity presents itself. We're seen as an important asset by the business community—the area's promotional campaigns cite Sandpoint's arts community as one of the reasons people consider visiting or moving here. Our summer festival fills all the hotels and restaurants."

Galleries and Arts Festivals

Popping up like a spring crocus, the art gallery scene in Sandpoint has been a source of pride to this community. Eight commercial galleries compete for attention, with one nonprofit exhibition space being run by the local art council. Some of the area's more prominent artists who don't show their work locally will schedule annual open studio visits for the entire community. The biggest arts draw is the annual Festival at Sandpoint, a three-week celebration each August, featuring musical styles from classical to Cajun. Arts-wise, collectors won't want to miss the Sandpoint Arts & Crafts Fair, which pulls a hundred exhibitors into town for a two-day run in mid-August.

What the Artist Says

"When I first moved here, the area had a reputation as a center for wildlife artists," says Sandpoint painter and ten-year resident Bob Lindemann. "But in the time since, what's really impressed me is the number of first-rate craft artists, nationally known painters, and sculptors who have come here for the area's beauty and isolation. Some artists are making a good living selling regionally inspired work to the art-conscious newcomers. Realistic work and fine craft sells well here. We've got a number of contemporary artists, but they're not focused on the local arts scene. Their work is shipped out to galleries on the coast. Artists who may want to move here need to realize the seasonal nature of the area. Unless you have galleries established before you get here, you may find it difficult to make a living from art—you've got to have a good understanding about marketing."

Nashville, Indiana

Location

In the rolling hillsides of south-central Indiana, an hour's drive outside Indianapolis and 20 miles east of the university town of Bloomington, Nashville's 700 residents live on the edge of Brown County State Park, within a few minutes of Monroe Reservoir, a 20-mile-long lake.

Climate

Blizzards and near-zero temperatures are common winter occurrences, usually followed by a long, gradually warming spring, and a hot, humid summer. Nashville's surrounding region bursts with color during the traditionally long, Indian summer-like autumn.

Living

Many local residents are employed by the University of Indiana, so housing prices tend to be slightly higher than in other, similar sized Indiana towns. A 3-bedroom home sells in the neighborhood of $75,000, but there are a lot of opportunities to buy nearby fixer-uppers for considerably less.

For the Midwest artist, Nashville is a small town offering not just the presence of a strong community of artists and craftspeople, but also reasonable access to major population centers in several states. This is the Indiana Hill Country, a place where trees spread a shady canopy across gentle hillsides, and camping in one of the many nearby state parks is a favorite pursuit. The artist's colony that once called Nashville home is long gone, having been replaced by a more commercially oriented group of trained painters and traditional craftspeople, while increasing tourism is causing wear and tear on the nerves of many locals. There's an art museum in town, named after art colony founding member T. C. Steele, and if you search hard enough, Nashville's galleries have some strong, regionalist work worth collecting.

Out On the Town

With so many restaurants, nightclubs, and performing arts options right down the road, Nashville residents never want for something to do (unless, of course, they're stranded by a foot or two of new snow). The University's departments sponsor everything from European concert pianists to touring Broadway plays. The nearby town of Columbus has a vibrant community performing arts center, whose 37,000 square feet also house a regional branch of the Indiana Museum of Art. In Nashville itself, a favorite spot to meet and greet friends is Hob Nob Corners, while a coffeehouse, the Daily Grind, has become another place where artists relax.

Economic Impact of the Arts

Nashville is still trying to decide whether it's going to build an identity as a budget tourist town or as a place where fine art is taken seriously. In recent years, the tourist-trade crowd has set up shop along Main Street, threatening to drive out the several galleries that have been gamely making a go of things over the past couple of decades. It's another one of those situations where artists moved in long ago, turning a forgotten town into a place where word-of-mouth eventually led to the development of a fairly healthy trade in original art work and traditional, locally-made crafts. Once the local wheeler-dealer types caught wind of it, they moved in with plans for fast food dives, and started slapping together shops to sell imported junk to the unwary. The battle has been joined and Nashville's future hangs in the balance.

Local Arts Agency

Brown County Art Guild, P.O. Box 840, Nashville, IN 47448, (812) 988-7303.

This small town has a surprising number of artists, some of whom try to make it locally, and others who are more closely associated with galleries in Indianapolis and other regional centers. There are also a number of folks living here who are associated with Indiana University's fine arts department. The guild's primary focus is organizing the rotating shows that fill its nonprofit exhibition space.

Galleries and Arts Festivals

The six commercial galleries in Nashville are patronized by art lovers from across Indiana, some of whom are interested in buying original art. On the outskirts of town is the Little Nashville Opry, a performance facility owned by bluegrass picker Bill Monroe. However, those who are attracted to Nashville for a country and bluegrass music experience aren't necessarily focused on art. The year's largest arts and traditional crafts events are the Redbud Festival each spring, and the Winter Art Fair in later November.

What the Artist Says

Amanda Kirby, a watercolorist and oils painter who has lived in the area since the 1950s, says what Nashville once had going for it was a reputation for quality. "What made Nashville popular with tourists was the non-commercial attitude of the town—we had wonderful antique stores, and a good reputation as an arts colony, with collectors coming in from all over the country. Now, the art you see around Nashville is repetitive and uninteresting. In many stores you find cheap, tourist-oriented material. There needs to be a return to the critical foundations of what made this place work in the first place.

"The town's reputation is still viable, but an appeal has to be made to buyers with more discriminating eyes. I'd like to see more non-objective work in the galleries—art that's created by Indiana's very best painters.

"Businesses are supportive. You see local artists' work displayed in banks and restaurants. The artists who do well here are careful about paying attention to their careers outside the area, showing their work in juried exhibitions around the country—and that's precisely the kind of artist who should be encouraged to move here. The art openings are big social events that many artists turn out for, and we're fortunate to have a wonderful bookstore."

Lawrence, Kansas

Location
Eastern Kansas, a region of sprawling farms carved from lands that once were the prairies of the Great Plains, is a countryside of low, rolling hills punctuated by lakes and rivers. The university town of Lawrence and its 65,000 residents are an hour's drive west of Kansas City.

Climate
Folks here refer to their corner of the nation as having four distinct seasons, which is a nice way of saying winter seems to overstay its welcome and summer skedaddles before everyone gets their fill.

Living
College towns are fortunate to have built-in populations of young, aware students who continually bring new ideas into the community. In Lawrence, they can do so in a town that's historically been more liberal and accepting of change than other Midwestern cities. The cost of living is moderate, with 3-bedroom homes selling in the $110,000 range. It's a safe, low-crime area with a broad range of performance and entertainment opportunities presented through the University of Kansas, the town's largest employer.

You're out on the Great Plains, so forget about mountain climbing and enjoy some of the country's best biking terrain . . . anywhere! Plenty of nearby lakes give residents several choices for sailing, water skiing, or just dropping a line into the water. Quiet during the summer, Lawrence bursts to life each September, when the students return and football season begins. College sports, especially Kansas University basketball, are the town's number one topic of conversation.

Out On the Town
Living here is like being in a suburb of Kansas City, but with so much going on in Lawrence, most local residents prefer staying close to home to enjoy the action in Lawrence's many bars, restaurants, and theaters. The best new hangout (for everyone who is anyone) in town is the Free State Brewery and Pub, a micro-brewery with great salads, chicken wings, and burgers, but Lawrence's most acclaimed burger and shakes are dished up at Johnny's Tavern. Rock'n'roll clubs are jammed with college students, so locals who want a dance floor not dominated by generation X'ers head to Cadillac Ranch, a country and western dance hall. Natural foods are best at the Full Moon, but Lawrence has many dining spots that cater to the vegetarian crowd.

Economic Impact of the Arts
In Lawrence, everyone takes a back seat to what's going on at the ivory towers on the University campus. The big bonus for local artists is that the school's arts department is filled with friendly, talented people with lots of energy and ideas. These same teachers and administrators are integral to the health of the Lawrence arts community, and work hard at making sure the benefits of art are permitted to spread around the region. This is a community where artists find inexpensive living

and studio facilities, along with a well-informed, concerned local population. The arts center is extremely active, local government has a percentage-for-the-arts program, the university art department opens its arms to the community, and schools are very pro-active in incorporating arts programming into their curriculum.

Local Arts Agency

Lawrence Arts Center, 200 West 9th, Lawrence, KS 66049, (913) 843-ARTS. Publishes the newsletter *The Arts in Action*.

"What's really helped us to break through the barriers of getting our kids involved in the arts, is that we're located in what used to be the town's library building," says Ann Evans, executive director of the arts center. "A lot of what we do involves education and performance programs centered around kids, but we're also very committed to classroom programs in visual and per-forming arts for adults. Each of our schools has an art and music teacher, and we do artist-in-resi-dency programs, dance performances, and visual art exhibitions. Lawrence's newcomers point to the town's cultural events as one of the reasons they were attracted to the area. Business and civic leaders sit on our boards, and they always help us with financial and moral support."

Galleries and Arts Festivals

Even though Lawrence has more than a dozen galleries selling art and fine craft, it seems as if locals can't get enough visual stimulation in their lives. nonprofit exhibitions take place at the Lawrence Arts Center and several other sites, the Spencer Museum of Art on the Kansas University campus has an extremely ambitious exhibition schedule, and the Haskell Indian College has one of the nation's finest programs training contemporary Native American artists in all fields. The Lawrence Indian Art Show, held each fall, attracts over 200 exhibitors, and there are many arts and crafts festivals held in town parks throughout the spring and summer.

What the Artist Says

Stan Herd, a ten-year resident of Lawrence and environmental artist, whose gigantic images are cut into crop fields, has been featured in ads for Absolut vodka. "Artists move here from unlikely places, and it always astounds me when I run into someone who has just relocated from San Francisco or New York, but that just goes to prove the point that in order to do well in the art world you don't need to be part of a major city's social scene," he says.

"The borders of Lawrence are changing, and there's talk of putting in a freeway bypass, but artists really enjoy life here. The local market for art isn't reliable, but it's the unique nature of the town—this hotbed of liberalism in a conservative part of the country—that makes Lawrence an interesting place to live.

"The town is starting to perceive itself as an arts community: a place where the art conscience goes beyond the obvious, past just having nice work in the restaurants or installed in public places. I could tell things were changing in Lawrence when I started seeing local politicians at the art openings. We're coming into view as something that's important about this town, and that's nice."

Berea, Kentucky

Location
Less than an hour's drive south of Lexington, the 10,000 residents of Berea live in a part of Kentucky characterized by hilly terrain, spring-fed streams, and farmlands.

Climate
Every few years, this part of Kentucky gets hit with a serious snowstorm or two. Spring usually arrives in mid-March, leading into summer with a profusion of redbud and dogwood blooms, while summer itself tends to kick into a hot and humid stage by mid-May. Autumn is the wet season, but even so, the colorful canopy of trees in central Kentucky draws a steady stream of visitors into Berea.

Living
A refreshingly inexpensive, safe, and friendly place to live, 3-bedroom homes in Berea cost $60,000, with older fixer-uppers running even less. Close enough to major population areas to allow day trips into Cincinnati and Louisville, and Berea's proximity to Lexington makes it practically a suburb to the country's thoroughbred capitol. This is country living at its best: low unemployment, a strong local tradition of high quality crafts, and the influx of many artists and craftspeople who care about each other and their work. Hiking and fishing are favorite leisure pursuits, with live theater and musical performance taking place on the campus of Berea College.

Out On the Town
Bet you'd never have guessed that Berea has its own Thai restaurant, but lo and behold, the Wen Pen not only survives, it prospers! Lots of college kids call Berea home, so expect a disproportionate number of pizza parlors, with the most popular being Papaleno's. Local residents who catch the dancing bug, head over to the Acton Folk Art Center, where the atmosphere is somewhat like you would expect from an Appalachian dance hall (Lexington, home of the University of Kentucky, has the usual selection of generic college pubs). Forget about natural food while you're in Berea, but if the urge for a burger strikes, it's time to slide into a booth at the Dinner Bell. As with most colleges, the campus offers a strong, year-round program of theater and live music performances.

Economic Impact of the Arts
Substantial and fundamental to the continuing health of Berea's economy, the direct relationship between the health of this town's arts and crafts community and the way everyone's financial affairs are impacted is well known to local residents. Many of Berea's jobs are, at one point or another, tied into the town's arts economy.

Local Arts Council

Berea Arts Council/Berea Craftspersons Association, P.O. Box 556, Berea, KY 40403, (606) 986-2540.

"The town has a very strong performing arts tradition—there's good community theater, a strong drama department at the college, and an arts council that's done wonders for bringing performances of classical musicians and dancers into Berea," says Gary Barker, marketing manager for the Berea College Student Crafts Program. "It's a very friendly community toward the arts, all around—the banks make most of the loans artists use to open up galleries, art and craft work is exhibited in local restaurants, and there are artists on the city council. Berea is getting ready to build a new, 4,000-seat performing arts and convention center, and the schools have formed a very strong partnership with the arts community. Arts education is fully incorporated into most student curriculums."

Galleries and Arts Festivals

Okay, so you've got this smallish town with one college and a flood of professional artists selling in one of Berea's 25 galleries and craft stores. What's going on, you ask? Just the best word-of-mouth about an arts community this side of New Hope, Pennsylvania, that's all. Gallery owners, and that goes for painting and fine craft as well as traditional craft and weaving, have been keeping Berea as one of their very closest secrets for years. Its craft and art galleries are along the lines of those walk-in, sit-and-watch, ask-all-the-questions-you-want types of places that aren't simply inspirational, they're also cleverly disguised selling outlets where the artist or craftsperson gets a chance to turn on the charm and close the sales.

It doesn't hurt that Berea College also has a working crafts industry (one whose hand-sewn brooms with hickory handles are known to fine craft galleries across the country) which makes dozens of items that are marketed as a way for students and the school itself to pull in needed income.

Berea is an absolute arts haven, in the purest sense of the word. The year's largest art and craft festivals are the two annual affairs staged by the Kentucky Guild of Craftsmen and Artists (May and October), and the Berea Craft Festival, a July event produced by locals.

What the Artist Says

The functional ceramics created by Jeff and Sarah Culbreth are sold at shops across the country, through a mail order catalog, and from their home-based studio on the edge of Berea. "Our visitors are highly aware that they come here for a quality, hand-crafted object—nobody wants a T-shirt, they want something to collect," says Sarah. "There are a wide range of places they can visit, and the artists go out of their way to be patient, friendly, and informative. There may be some emphasis put on teaching adult visitors how to make craft items of their own, but any program of that kind will have to come through the college. Here, artists are busy, independent, and dedicated to achieving quality in their work. Berea is getting better all the time, and you'll be welcomed if you want to come on down."

Hammond, Louisiana

Location
An hour's drive north of New Orleans, the 18,000 residents of Hammond live in what was once the Mississippi River flood plain—the flat pine forests and farmlands common to parts of the South.

Climate
What passes for winter in this part of the world is a season amounting to three months of moderate temperatures punctuated by some icy rain. Otherwise, Hammond's climate is humid and hot.

Living
Because it's within easy driving distance of New Orleans, Hammond's real estate prices tend to be a bit higher than those found elsewhere in rural Louisiana. Still, a new 3-bedroom home will run in the $85,000 range. Lots of fixer-uppers are available.

Louisiana is a state where enjoying the great outdoors is so much a part of its culture that license plates carry the motto "Sportsmen's Paradise." Fishing and hunting along the many waterways and bayous found in the region is by far a favorite activity. Those who wish to take in a day at the beach can take a short drive over to the Mississippi coast, and nearby New Orleans is, after all, the nation's best party town. Hammond has an historic downtown, and it's safe at night.

Out On the Town
While most local residents look to New Orleans for their fun, Hammond, and the neighboring community of Ponchatoula, are home to the region's Acadian (Cajun) culture, which translates into lots of community dance halls, wonderful cooking, and a zest for life unparalleled in the country. Hammond's most popular dinner spot and watering hole is Brady's Oyster Bar, but if you don't drive out to one or more of the many small town dance halls surrounding Hammond, you'll miss the point of coming here in the first place.

Economic Impact of the Arts
Hammond is the home of Southwestern Louisiana University, the area's largest employer and most prominent cultural institution. Residents can count on regular presentations by performing arts groups in the fields of theater (Hammond is loaded with stage professionals), classical music, and dance. Nearby Baton Rouge (a half-hour drive) has an opera and symphony.

Local Arts Agency
Hammond Cultural Foundation, P.O. Box 2974, Hammond, LA 70404, (504) 542-7113.

"Because the college does such a superb job of bringing performing groups to town, we've focused on children's programs," says Kay Wainwright, cultural foundation director. "We've been able to bring other groups into our facility, mostly arts groups from around the region, and let them use this place as a venue for the kinds of programming they specialize in. There's also a strong base of artists to draw from in this part of the state, and one of our most important tasks is to give them an opportunity to be part of visual arts exhibitions at the foundation's gallery. Our outreach programs bring the arts into the schools around the region."

Galleries and Arts Festivals

There are four commercial art galleries in Hammond, supplemented by the Hammond Cultural Foundation's own nonprofit exhibition space, and the nonprofit Mail Car Art Gallery in nearby Ponchatoula. The local college has student art exhibition space, and also stages the region's most popular arts festival, the Southwestern Louisiana University's Celebration of the Arts and Humanities, held in October. In recent years Hammond has developed a moderately strong tourist economy, drawing in day-trippers from this corner of the country.

What the Artist Says

Painter and writer Gloria Ross moved here two decades ago after spending most of her life in New Orleans. "Hammond reminds me of what New Orleans was like in the 1960s. The potential to turn the assets of this town into a real attraction are here, and there's a great deal of local support for all the arts. There are a few local people who collect, and the university art shows are good sales opportunities for some teachers. I'm still represented by galleries in New Orleans and Mississippi, and most of the area's professional artists have to look elsewhere for the majority of their sales.

"Louisiana's swampiness is perfectly beautiful, and I spend a lot of time painting the spooky black waters in bayous. It's a flat landscape, but there's a lot there to inspire your work. As far as I'm concerned, this area could use a lot more artists painting swamp scenes and less artists painting magnolias.

"Hammond is a nice place to live, a real community. If local people became more interested in collecting, I think more artists would be interested in relocating here. There's some wonderful work being done with children's art programs—once those kids grow up, we'll have the art collectors most places can only dream of."

Belfast, Maine

Location
On the Penobscot River, Belfast is a community in transition, switching from an industrial base to an economy more dependent on the arts. Its 6,000 residents live within a half-hour drive of Bangor, the regional population center.

Climate
Typical Maine: nine months of weather ranging from crisp, autumn breezes to winter freezes that would make Sgt. Preston feel right at home. Summer is brief, but glorious, which is why local residents are so militaristic about enjoying themselves in June, July, and August.

Living
Because this is a town with a working-class background, Belfast is loaded with not just affordable housing (a 3-bedroom place runs $60,000, with fixer-uppers going for much less), but lots of housing and, more importantly for artists, an abundant supply of cheap, well-equipped studio space. Similar in many ways to the economic transformation underway in Astoria, Oregon, Belfast's traditional industries of fish and poultry processing are in transition, consolidating operations elsewhere, and thereby displacing many of the families who have lived here for years.

Underneath the surface of Belfast locals lurks a thinly disguised resentment toward the out-of-state artists, musicians, and craftspeople (a surprising number of whom have moved into the area on a full-time basis) who have come into town with income sources not tied to the fluctuations of the local economy. However, as more people in the creative fields move in to replace those seeking employment in other parts of the state, Belfast has the potential to turn into one of the Northeast's premier art towns—the infrastructure for supporting thousands of artists is in place, and the doors are swinging wide open.

Winter activities focus on more traditional rural pursuits such as hunting, curling, cross-country skiing, and ice fishing, while the action in summer involves heading to the shore and enjoying whatever it is that comes naturally to skimpily-clad people laying about in the sun.

Out On the Town
As more creative types move here on a full-time basis, Belfast's restaurant and entertainment scene is rapidly shaping into something like that of a small college town . . . without the students. Most artists hang their hats (Okay, berets), at least for a couple of hours each week, at Darby's Restaurant. If they're out for a night of leg shakin', there's always the music and boot-scootin' at the Blue Goose in nearby Northport. A night out on the town in Belfast usually requires at least one margarita at Dos Amigos, rumored to have the best enchiladas north of La Grange, Texas. Oh, and vegetarians have heart! (of celery, that is, and much more at the Belfast Coop and Cafe). Local theater is nothing to be ashamed of, with the Belfast Maskers putting on a year-round slate of somewhat bizarrely staged productions, and classical music performance is wonderful in nearby Camden.

Economic Impact of the Arts

While the art community may keep a reasonably low profile, Belfast is one of those towns that people up and down the East Coast are starting to quietly talk about, which probably has a lot to do with the fact that since lots of local homes are selling in the $50,000 range, even someone with an average income can afford to buy in, sublet, and build for the future. As time goes by, we'll no doubt start seeing more artists moving to town, and as they come to know and appreciate their creative neighbors who have lived here for years, they'll start moving in permanently.

Local Arts Agency

Belfast Arts Council, 58 Union Street, Belfast, ME 04915, (207) 338-5814.

"One of the things that's really made a difference here was giving the Belfast Maskers their own building down at the waterfront—they're popular with just about everybody in town," says Belfast gallery owner Rosemary Frick. "For the past few years the galleries have coordinated their opening nights, and that has encouraged people to come into Belfast in groups, see the new work that's in the galleries, go out to dinner at one of the restaurants, and maybe take in a show at the theater. It's done a lot to spread arts money to more businesses, and it's made people aware of the possibilities."

Galleries and Arts Festivals

"Belfast is very fortunate to have galleries showing strong work," says Rosemary Frick, "which makes artists who are dedicated to quality sit up and take notice—they want to be represented in good galleries, and that brings in an educated, monied sort of tourist." Belfast has three serious art galleries, and more are expected. The town's nonprofit exhibition space is ArtFellows, located in a converted industrial building on the Belfast waterfront. The area's most popular arts event is the Maine Arts Festival held each August at Thomas Point Beach in nearby Brunswick.

What the Artist Says

Harold Garde, painter of contemporary images, has lived in Belfast nine years. "What's nice about the galleries in Belfast is that they give the artists a fair chance to show their work. There's some coming and going, but overall it gives us an incentive to work. I sell well here in Maine, but need to keep a presence in galleries in Santa Fe, New York, and Florida in order to survive. Local artists have renovated a lot of buildings that were in very bad condition, and I think that's given us some respect from the community. In the warmer months, Belfast is a wonderful place to live, and we're seeing an influx of professionals who are supportive of fine arts and music. If you're 'from away,' you'll have an opportunity to meet artists in a community that's interested in your work, and will be quick to include you in their social circles."

Blue Hill, Maine

Location

From its east-facing waterfront, the community of Blue Hill fronts onto the Blue Hill Bay, the body of water separating this town of 2,000 from Acadia National Park on Mt. Desert Island. Blue Hill is situated along the northern end of Maine's coast, about a 3-hour drive from Portland.

Climate

Yes, the summers along Maine's coast are legendary for their beauty, attracting many thousands of visitors escaping the heat and humidity of Boston, New York, and places south. Autumn's arrival is always early, leading into a brief, but spectacular, season that's followed by an unrelentingly difficult winter that refuses to give up the ghost until well into April.

Living

The influx of New Yorkers and Bostonian urban refugees has pushed prices upward for just about everything in the area—to the point where it's now difficult to find anything resembling a 3-bedroom home for less than $150,000.

From Memorial Day through late August, Blue Hill jumps with action, and afterward, it enters a nine-month hibernation until the tourists and part-timers return. Lots of businesses are shuttered during winter, which is seen as a time for Maine natives to go about the business of running Maine—until the tourists are back and it's time to earn enough money to get through the coming slim months of winter.

Playing this form of musical chairs is a local art form. If you're a summer person from "outside," you get to enjoy anything and everything in the area just about all the time, while if you live here year-round, you quickly come to terms with the inconvenience and isolation of the off-season. During the nine months of winter and near-winter weather, local residents favor dressing in flannel shirts and lined blue jeans. About the only activity you can pursue in clothes like that are chopping wood and hunting, two things, it turns out, that locals enjoy pursuing. Cross-country skiing and snowmobiling are also popular, while the action shifts to sailing and hiking during the summer.

Out On the Town

Down at Blue Hill's town hall, there's a fairly regular schedule of the folk dance form known as contra dancing. And if you want to bump into an artist or two during a moment of relaxation, try dropping in at Pie In the Sky Pizza, which does double duty as the community's vegetarian restaurant. Burger and shake cravings send locals over to the Fish Net, but if your palate yearns for anything more ethnic in flavor, a 20-minute drive to the nearby town of Ellsworth is your prescription for gustatory satisfaction. Ellsworth also happens to be the home of this area's most active theater group. Blue Hill, a place of refuge for many a musician, stages regular recitals and chamber music performances as part of its own concert series, which runs through the winter months. Across the brief span of summer there are many seasonal places that disperse the dining action, from lobster shanties to blueberry pie stands. So if you're here during the best time of the year, make sure you drive the two-lane roads, looking for something promising.

Economic Impact of the Arts

While the presence of arts in Blue Hill is one of the primary reasons the region has successfully drawn a well-heeled, art-wise tourist trade, what takes place during summer cannot be sustained throughout the year's bleaker months. So, for three months there's a substantial economic impact felt from the arts in Blue Hill, followed by many months when the arts are a mere blip on the screen.

"The arts bring a good, decent individual into Blue Hill," says local gallery owner and artist Judith Leighton, "and I think the people who come into town and spend money on the arts don't want to see much about it change. So far, the arts have brought business to nearly everyone in Blue Hill, yet we've managed to avoid becoming another Maine tourist town, and the people who live here year-round seem to be pleased with that."

Local Arts Agency

Union of Maine Visual Artists, P.O. Box 215, Bowdoinham, ME 04008, (207) 737-4749. Publishes the *U.M.V.A. Newsletter.*

In this rural area there isn't a local arts center. The UMVA, which runs its own nonprofit gallery and acts as a clearinghouse for information on workshops, public art projects, and sources of grant money, is located in a separate part of the state from Blue Hill. Nearby Ellsworth has interesting theater and cinema, and Blue Hill's public library has recently been renovated to include exhibition space for nonprofit art shows.

Galleries and Arts Festivals

While there are four art galleries and one nonprofit exhibition space in Blue Hill, many of the surrounding communities have their own galleries selling fine art and the very strong fine crafts made by the area's traditional and contemporary craftspeople. During the busy summer season, fairs and festivals take place all over this part of the state, with the Fourth of July being an especially promising weekend for gallery exhibitions and local art fairs.

What the Artist Says

Robert Shetterly, a painter and printmaker who has made his home in the Blue Hill area for 23 years, has a high opinion of the art created by Blue Hill's permanent and part-time artists. "We're culturally sophisticated, with loads of galleries and a diverse group of creative people. The artists are supportive, enlightened, and avoid being petty. It's unlikely an artist could survive here just on the local market, but this is also a good place for artists who want to meet vacationing gallery owners from all over the East Coast."

Nantucket, Massachusetts

Location
Nantucket's 6,350 residents live on Nantucket Island, an island paradise accessible only by a 3-hour ferry ride from the southern shore of Cape Cod (or by private plane). This is a place where everything runs on "island time," which is another way of saying that life here is the epitome of laid-back.

Climate
Because it's so far from the mainland, Nantucket's weather is often vastly different from what's being experienced an hour away. Here, ocean currents pushing northward from Bermuda bring warmer waters and unpredictable weather patterns: It's not uncommon for Nantucket to have sunny skies while Cape Cod gets a cool rain. Spring tends to cling on into mid-June, which is also when the local thermometer usually starts hanging in the 70-degree range. Through the summer, nights remain cooler than on the mainland, but autumn weather on Nantucket is a creature of its own, with higher temperatures from September through Christmas, and a generally milder winter than those found in the rest of New England.

Living
Studio spaces are available as summer rentals, but for your $350 or so you get around 500 square feet unsuitable for anything but working and storing materials. (By the way, it's important to bring plenty of supplies to the island.) Most artists try to find a summer rental apartment or house (average cost: $900 per month) that has an extra room suitable for conversion into a studio space. Homes on the island are expensive, which is partly a reflection of the town's cachet, and partly a response to the higher building costs on an island 50 miles offshore. An average 3-bedroom home runs in the $250,000 range. Many of the island's creative professionals are painters, but there is also a very strong music community, which includes several of the nation's most respected maritime music masters.

Rules of Nantucket art life: Hunker down during the winter, create a lot of art work, and maybe do a show or two someplace where it's warm. Work like hell during the summer, hit all the big parties, develop new collectors, and sock away as many greenbacks as you possibly can. If you need a break, go crash on the beach or rent a sailboat.

Out On the Town
Try having morning pastries and a cup of joe at Espresso Cafe, a Main Street institution with outdoor seating and local art work on its walls. In the evenings, there are frequent poetry readings at the X Gallery. The best burger and fries are served at the Atlantic Cafe, which also has a few Mexican dishes on the menu. Chin's is owned by a gentleman from Thailand, and its menu combines both Thai and Chinese specialties. Nighttime fun for the reggae crowd is at Le Box, while a less diverse group gathers at the Muse for dancing and brews. Want to spend a few bucks on great food? Then your best bet is the Second Story, chef David Toole's outpost of first-rate regionalist dining.

Economic Impact of the Arts

"There's a funny relationship here between some of the powers-that-be and the arts community, " says local artist Graham White. "Even though our local planning and economic development commission has targeted the arts as an area where there's a potential for a broader employment of local residents, the prevailing attitude is that the arts and artists are some sort of alien influence. But thankfully, that's beginning to change. What's helped is a lot of local people doing craftwork as a secondary source of income, which has convinced some that the arts are a plus for the town's economy."

Local Arts Agency

Nantucket Cultural Council, Nantucket Town & County Building, Nantucket, MA 02554, (508) 228-7272.

"The council can grant funds to all aspects of the community's cultural needs," says Graham White, who is also chairman of the council. "We don't have an arts center, but there are lots of organizations that have their own memberships and areas of expertise. There are also two theater groups in town that we support and a chamber music center." With over a hundred artists in the community, these groups (such as the recently formed Nantucket Arts Alliance) are more directly involved with artists' careers and concerns and are expected to play a crucial role in fostering the development of Nantucket's creative community. During the busy summer season, the town comes alive with street performers and summer stock theater.

Galleries and Arts Festivals

While most of the Nantucket galleries operate seasonally, during the height of summer there are as many as two dozen galleries selling locally created paintings, contemporary and traditional crafts, and jewelry. Because tourists tend to take their art seriously, the quality of work found in Nantucket galleries tends to be quite impressive. The year's most popular arts festival is Arts Alive!, a week-long bash of visual and performing arts held during early October. There are smaller arts events and gallery exhibition openings held throughout the summer for visitors from as far away as Chicago, Florida, and Texas.

What the Artist Says

"People buying second homes tend to want to fill those places with locally created art and furniture from Nantucket craftsmen," says painter, writer, and poet George Murphy. "Local businesses collect art, people want murals in their homes, and there's a good deal of local art exhibited in Nantucket banks and businesses. Much of the art dollar spent here goes toward traditional work, and that's the type of work you see in the galleries.

"Artists who come here have to make some adjustments in their lifestyles, and most make sacrifices in their careers, but this tends to attract a person whose main priority isn't financial success. Maybe they're more concerned about a safe place to raise a family, or just want to be isolated. What we could really use in Nantucket is a progressive, contemporary gallery, and an artists' cafe—a place for poetry readings and experimental art work. Maybe we should just tow the island into Manhattan Harbor!

"Artists get together to form co-op galleries or do other things aimed at exhibiting their work, and art openings are the main way artists get together. If you come here, don't have any Disney-esque notions about living on an island. It's expensive and off-season work is hard to find."

Northampton, Massachusetts

Location
Nestled along the banks of the Connecticut River in west-central Massachusetts, this town of 32,000 was once known for its manufacturing and textile industries, but in recent years, Northampton has experienced an arts explosion that's turned it into much more than your run-of-mill college town.

Climate
Hundreds of miles inland from the coast, you can count on winter in this part of the state being much more severe, while Mother Nature makes up for this slight with a spectacular, lengthy autumn. Summer is moderately warm and humid, with a short spring wedged between winter's chill and the start of softball season.

Living
Less expensive than areas closer to Boston, the average 3-bedroom home in Northampton sells in the $140,000 range. Studio space is readily available in the town's business district, with an average space costing $500 per month. The community has many local groups representing almost every facet of the art world's spectrum, and several nearby colleges that are extremely active in presenting performing arts events.

Oriented toward activities such as bicycling and hiking in nearby state forests, the opportunities for outdoor fun in this part of the state are enhanced by the presence of many summer festivals, including the summer residency of the Boston Symphony in nearby Tanglewood. Winters are seen as times to ski in Vermont resort areas, or just to stay in the studio and work.

Out On the Town
Choices abound in any college town, but with a dozen institutions in the immediate area of Northampton, the list of dining and entertainment options from one weekend to the next seems too good to be true. The nightclub scene is very strong, with big-name concerts rounding out a strong local music community and many venues for all ranges of musical talent. Try Pearl Street Nightclub for its touring bands and large dance floor, but if the entertainment there isn't to your liking, stroll over to the Iron Horse. There are dozens of stores, cafes, and restaurants dedicated to natural foods, but Northampton's most popular vegetarian restaurant is Paul and Elizabeth's. The burgers are best at Packard's.

Economic Impact of the Arts
The arts economy is substantial, and as more artists and collectors start realizing the quality and consistency of what's being created in the area, the arts scene's growth potential is limitless. "Businessmen in the area understand that one of the reasons Northampton's economy is doing better than other towns in the region is because of the arts," says local arts council member Bob

Cilman. "When you take a look at the local newspaper and see that there are tons of things taking place here all the time, you realize that unless there was a lot of support coming from all sectors of the community, that level of activity couldn't be sustained."

Local Arts Agency

Northampton Arts Council, City Hall, Northampton, MA 01060, (413) 586-6950.

The town's arts council is oriented toward making certain there's a strong mix of cultural programming in Northampton. Funds are allocated from state and regional sources, while the council also stages events aimed at channeling its own raised funds into community arts programs. Craft is a pursuit taken very seriously by local artists, and it's rated by the council as the town's most popular creative pursuit, followed by painting and dance. There's a local artist-in-residency program coordinated through the town's public schools, but with state cuts in funding having been so severe in recent years, the program hasn't been funded to the satisfaction of local arts educators.

Galleries and Arts Festivals

Galleries tend to come and go, but the numbers stay fairly constant, with eight seemingly able to stay active as centers of the town's commercial arts scene. A nonprofit exhibition space is run by the local arts center. While there are art and craft festivals taking place throughout the warmer months, Northampton's arts council considers the town's premier arts event to be First Night, held during the frozen winter months.

What the Artist Says

Landscape painter Scott Prior says the area's attraction for artists "is the degree of comfort you feel here. It's that rural sense you get from the landscape and the urban conscience brought into town by the students at the colleges. I can walk from my house, which has a large garden and wildlife, and in a few minutes nearly be in the middle of town.

"Northampton used to be depressed and blighted, but now it's been fixed up with the help of many local artists and craftsmen, and I'd have to say it's lost part of its charm. Hopefully, the town's savvy city government will realize the need to preserve what we've got, and won't go out and push for more development. Our crafts community has the biggest commercial presence in town and is cited as one of the groups that brings a bundle of arts dollars into Northampton."

Silas Kopf, a furniture craftsman whose specialty in marquetry has led to his work being carried in several metropolitan area galleries, says that working conditions for artists are great. "I've got a studio in an old, converted factory building, and all around me are studios filled with artists and craftspeople. Northampton understands that the cottage industries started by artists and furniture makers are important to the health of the local economy. Here, people enjoy the best of both worlds—it's a safe and small place filled with wonderful music, theater, and film, yet there's the progressive mindset, an openness to concepts coming in from other places and other cultures. I think that most of the local artists would, like myself, be thrilled to see more creative professionals move into town—it could only enhance our diversity."

Wellfleet, Massachusetts

Location
Near the tip of the Cape Cod peninsula, Wellfleet has traditionally been an artists' haven, and artists having always shared space with the town's business community and fishermen. Wellfleet's summer population approaches 28,000, while year-round residents clock in somewhere around the 2,200 mark.

Climate
Legendary as one of the nation's original summer resort areas, Cape Cod's climate is warm, breezy, and pristine from mid-May through September. While the unspoiled nature of the region stays the same from one month to another, winters tend to be very cold, which is due as much to the constant wind as to the Cape's northern latitude. Spring and autumn, months when the weather starts moderating into the 60s and 70s, tend to be favorite times for local residents since visitor traffic is only slightly busy during weekends.

Living
Real estate prices have been on an upward climb since the days of Kennedymania, and if you want to buy into a town like Wellfleet, be prepared to spend in the $165,000 range for a 3-bedroom home (it's even more expensive in nearby Provincetown). What you get here are great local schools, spectacular scenery, and a local population that's cultured, well-traveled, and likes to buy art.

Very oriented toward activities on the beaches, marshes, and sand dunes Cape Cod is famous for, watersports such as sailing, jet skiing, and ocean fishing are favorite ways locals spend a three-day weekend. Wellfleet is also famous for its succulent oysters, so if you enjoy a good slurp every now and again, this place will seem like paradise. Anyone wanting a city fix is obliged to make the drive to Boston, which is roughly two hours away. During the summer, nobody who lives here full-time wants to leave, as if putting in time over a cold stretch of winter obligates full-timers to soak up every last ounce of summer's glory.

Out On the Town
Provincetown, just up the road, is one of the country's oldest art centers, where everything from African music to Thai food is part of the local cultural mosaic. Unfortunately, as rents have continued their steep escalation there's been an outflow of galleries and artists and an inflow of T-shirt shops, pizza parlors, and souvenir stores, a syndrome also seen in Key West. Thankfully, Wellfleet hasn't yet been invaded by the green slacks and topsiders of real estate speculators and developers, which explains why it's becoming the Cape's center for high-quality commercial galleries.

Favorite local hangouts are the Tavern at Duck Creek (also doing double duty as a right spot with live music) and Aesop's Tables. The best hamburger is the one served at P.J.'s, and vegetarian specialites dominate the menu at Flying Fish. As for local theater, residents have come to expect the controversial and unexpected from the performers at Wellfleet Harbor Actor's Theater.

Economic Impact of the Arts

Long overshadowed by its more crowded, pretentious, and hectic neighbor to the north, Wellfleet was content to shape its identity as a working town unbeholden to the fickle nature of the tourist economy. Now that several of the art galleries that once did business in Provincetown have relocated to Wellfleet, the local community is responding with anything these new businesses need.

Local Art Agency

Wellfleet Art Gallery Association, P.O. Box 916, Wellfleet, MA 02667, (508) 349-2530.

"Up until about 20 years ago, art hadn't really caught on in Wellfleet," says Larry Biron, association president. "But that's changed, and now it's an area that's conducive to what artists are looking for in a place to live and work. The art gallery scene is still developing, but the reputation of Wellfleet is considered to be quite good. As the arts continue to become more important, the town is becoming increasingly involved in promoting what's here. Restaurants and businesses have rotating shows of local art work, which has helped the artists to take more of an interest in becoming involved in the community."

Galleries and Arts Festivals

For a fairly small town, Wellfleet has a tremendously disproportionate number of fine art galleries, which is a reflection on this community's strength as a center for art collectors seeking out serious art not pandering to the sensibilities of casual tourists. Twenty-two galleries now call Wellfleet home, and while Provincetown has more galleries and even a couple of nonprofit art exhibition spaces, the general perception is that it is the collectors themselves who most prefer Wellfleet's more casual, unaffected approach to the business of selling art work. Each July, the Wet Art Contest held at the Cape Cod Art Museum draws large crowds of the art-conscious, while summer weekends searching for finds at the arts and crafts fairs in Wellfleet (held at the town's drive-in theater) are a Cape Cod tradition.

What the Artist Says

Judith Shahn, a figurative painter (whose family members include father Ben Shahn, a seminal figure in New England art history), says that part of the region's attraction for artists is its location. "We're close enough to New York that artists who live there can come up to the Cape for a few weeks, bring work back down to their galleries, then return for another stretch of summer painting.

"One of the most pressing local issues is the building of homes that are too large for the landscape, too ostentatious for anyone with good sense or good taste. One of the nicest things about Wellfleet is that it was always the kind of town where an artist could find a place in the sun, and I hope nothing we see happening here will change that.

"Local barter is alive and well: Artists can get anything from electrical work to cabinetry done by exchanging their paintings with the craftspeople. People come into Wellfleet in a spending mood, and as a result many artists do very well selling locally."

Midland, Michigan

Location

Near the center of Michigan, about a 3-hour drive from Detroit, the 38,000 residents of Midland live in a town that's home to two large corporations, each with an arts consciousness aimed at improving the cultural and artistic lives of its residents.

Climate

If it's winter, get out your snowmobiling boots. If it's summer, dust off the fishing pole. Midland is just a short drive from the shores of Saginaw Bay, which makes sailing and water skiing one of the town's most important recreational outlets. Weather is cold to the point of abominable during much the winter, with a long, mild summer perfect for growing its famous cherries.

Living

With the Dow Corporation its largest employer, Midland has a housing stock ideally suited for the company's large, white-collar work force. Still, an average 3-bedroom home lists in the $75,000 range. Schools are way above the norm in terms of cultural programs and art facilities. Downtown Midland has lots of studio space renting out in the $300 per month range.

The outdoors life in this part of the country involves enjoying wide open spaces where the population is dotted onto small towns. Sanford Lake, a few minutes drive north, is a favorite spot for fishing and canoeing. Lake Huron, which during the summer months takes on the qualities of a warm, freshwater ocean, offers a few beaches and busy recreation areas, including the popular one at Bay City State Park. Winter ice fishing is also a favorite with the area's dedicated anglers.

Out On the Town

With lots of live theater, and an arts center that's very active in bringing touring musicians, dancers, and other performers to town, Midland always seems to have a big-name event currently performing or on the coming week's calendar. Don't bother looking for much ethnic diversity among Midland restaurants, since this is still the kind of town where vegetarian food is hard to find. Those out for a night on the town head over to the Holiday Inn for live music, otherwise the best advice is to plan a trip into Lansing. The most popular lunch spot is Frick's, a restaurant famous for its hamburgers, as is the Boulevard Lounge.

Economic Impact of the Arts

In this town, the arts are seen as an important aspect of the community life, not so much for their ability to communicate an artist's inner vision, but because they present an opening in the cultural scene of an isolated, conservative part of the upper Midwest. In other words, the main interest here is in being entertained and occupied by artistic pursuits, rather than in oohing and aahing over the vision of an important figure in the visual arts field. That's not to say painters, sculptors, and craftspeople are ignored in Midland, a town in which they receive much local support. It is just that performing arts are in the driver's seat, and for an understandable reason.

Local Arts Agency

Midland Art Council, 1801 W. St. Andrews, Midland, MI 48640, (517) 631-3250.

"We've got all the performing and visual art spaces the community needs," says Maria Ciski, executive director of the art council. "We work from a building that's part gallery, part studio school, and part performing arts center. Every year we have shows of art by public school students. The kids get great art instruction in the schools and we bring them in here for more specialized things like printmaking, theater, and music. Midland has wonderful opportunities for kids. We're given support by the town's two major corporations. It's a well-off community and the arts have a big impact."

Galleries and Arts Festivals

While there's only one commercial gallery in town, the four nonprofit exhibition spaces in Midland give everyone from Sunday painters to serious contemporary artists an opportunity to show their art work. The year's most popular arts festivals are those held during the summer months, including the Midland Art Council Summer Art Fair, held in early June, drawing nearly 250 exhibiting artists.

What the Artist Says

Arnold Kolb, an artist who is retired from his science responsibilities at Dow, says the attraction of Midland is in its sense of community. "We've enjoyed an extensive level of involvement by local artists in all forms of the arts. Midland's professional approach to the arts is remarkable, and the way the city responds to all artist needs is exemplary. Here, you've got a comfortable, safe environment with parks, lakes, and colleges close by."

Leslie Parsons, a ceramicist and local businesswoman, says that one way in which the local arts scene could improve is in sales. "The executives still have that idea about going to New York or Chicago to find really great art. There's even a higher regard for what's shown in Ann Arbor than there is locally. We need to break through that outdated concept of prestige associated with out-of-area work, which is why Midland isn't a great place to come if you're a young artist still establishing your career.

"Many artists work for Dow, and some have made astounding breakthroughs in their art work based on the research they've done for the company. Our artist groups tend to be informal and very supportive of each other. Our arts center has great programs in education and the performing arts, much better than you'd find in similar size communities. Michigan's most successful artists use their base here to build gallery contacts elsewhere, or to reach the region's summer art shows— you've got to be inventive to survive."

South Haven, Michigan

Location

Protected by miles of long, narrow sand dunes, the lakefront communities of western Michigan have one thing in common: great views across open water. South Haven, a town of 13,000 in the state's southwest corner, is an hour's drive from Kalamazoo and nearly two hours from Grand Rapids.

Climate

If you've never spent a summer on the Great Lakes, your life is not yet complete. One of the best climates to be found anywhere is in this part of the country during the period between Memorial Day and the start of the major league baseball playoffs. A long, subtle spring helps snap local residents back to life after surviving the bitter cold of winter, and those localized weather patterns referred to as "lakefront effect snows."

Living

Housing is still affordable, which is surprising in light of South Haven's three-hour proximity to Chicago. Weekenders have been coming into this area since the turn of the century, and many of the craftsmen's style, 3-bedroom retreats they had built as part-time homes remain, selling in the neighborhood of $80,000. Art instruction still takes the back seat in the curriculums in local schools, as some South Haven old-timers prefer to wistfully glance backwards at the town's lost or declining manufacturing past, refusing to face the future with innovative approaches aimed at improving job prospects in the depressed local economy.

Outdoorsy and friendly, South Haven residents revel in their lakefront setting. This area is ideally suited for bicycling through its low, rolling hills, and the local fishing is great. The per capita boat ownership figures in South Haven are among the highest in the nation, so if you arrive in summer, be sure to bring the water skis.

Out On the Town

To many visitors, South Haven is the southern end of an artsy resort area that's anchored at its northern end by the quaint village of Saugatuck, a magnet for art galleries and gift shops. With its working class past, South Haven tends to be the grittier of the two, and the town where most artists have found living to be more affordable. As summer populations swell with part-time residents, a number of summer stock theaters open up for business, but if it's November and you want a stage fix, driving into Kalamazoo is the ticket. Clementine's, a downtown South Haven eatery located in a restored historic building, is the local favorite for drinks and burgers, while anyone seeking vegetarian (or more ethnic) food will drive to nearby Holland, or eat at the China Palace for Cantonese.

Economic Impact of the Arts

In years past, South Haven was home to a summer colony of artists who primarily came in from the Chicago area. Over time, there was a desire to find a place better suited to the resort-style living preferred by city folks who came this way for summer. That somewhere, which had to be other than South Haven's manufacturing-oriented environs, turned out to be Saugatuck. What's sprung up in South Haven are T-shirts shops, a couple of low-key galleries, and lots of artists looking for a place to call home, while Saugatuck has developed into the gallery marketplace South Haven's artists needed, and the summer fun spot for the upscale second-home crowd.

Local Arts Agency

South Haven Allied Arts Association, P.O. Box 505, South Haven, MI 49090. (No phone.) Publishes the *AA Newsletter*.

Serving a community of 50 local artists, the association operates from offices in the South Haven Center for the Arts, which is also where the town's nonprofit art exhibition space is located. In Saugatuck, the heart of the arts community is the Oxbow School, a facility operated seasonally as the summer programs center for the Art Institute of Chicago. "The center's focus is broad-based, bringing in shows by artists with national reputations," says South Haven artist Kathy Catania. "Lately, that's expanded into more of an educational emphasis, bringing school kids in for classes and performances, and also using the arts center (located in the town's former library building) as a place to hold adult classes in the evenings."

Galleries and Arts Festivals

Even though the presence of South Haven's artists has drawn the well-heeled, art-conscious tourist to town, local businesses don't seem to actively participate in attracting more of these visitors, since South Haven's downtown storefronts are filled with souvenir shops. Hopefully, someone in local government will get a handle on the situation before South Haven blows the one good chance it has for attracting tourists with money to spend on art. A good focus for increased community support is the town's most popular arts event, the South Haven Summer Arts Fair, which takes place in early July.

What the Artist Says

Edward Dickerson, a painter, sculptor, printmaker, and inventor, says that artists in this area have to be energetic in order to survive. "There really isn't much of a local market in South Haven, and the business community's support for the arts in this town is so minimal it makes you wonder what they must be thinking. Even in Saugatuck the art in galleries is very uneven. Art collectors have to go into the towns and actually find the good artists, because the galleries just don't seem to care about quality. Here, if you're trying to make it as an artist, you've got to be an heroic type of individual—you've got to make it by working hard, selling outside the area, and working like crazy during the winter."

Grand Marais, Minnesota

Location
If this town were any further north, the road signs would have to be printed in both English and French. Grand Marais is a Lake Superior community of 1,300 that faces south, looking at the rest of the U.S. from its perch at the far northern tip of Minnesota.

Climate
Three guesses . . . and the first two don't count. Okay, so it's the kind of town where temperatures near zero are considered tolerable. Summer arrives in early June, bringing a 100-day splurge of clear, pollution-free days with average temperatures in the high 70s, but regularly climbing into the low 90s. In winter, the action shifts onto the frozen surface of Lake Superior. Can you say "mukluk"?

Living
Because it attracts a strong tourist business during the year's warmer months, housing in Grand Marais ranges from the expected, $70,000 for a 3-bedroom home in town to a newer place with lakefront views for $150,000. Schools have active arts education programs, and use the town's community of professional artists as a teaching resource. There's also an arts magnet school being developed through the Grand Marais high school, a program expected to attract talented arts students from across the state. Minnesota is a state that takes its art community quite seriously, and in recent years government has allocated increasing funds for arts program development from one end of the state to another.

"Grand Marais is set on Lake Superior, adjacent to the Boundary Waters Canoe Area Wilderness in the real north woods. The adage is that there are more artists here per capita than anywhere else in the country," says Jay Andersen, local artist and director of the Grand Marais Art Colony. Winter activities in this region include the sport of ice boating, a seemingly insane pursuit that hurls wind-powered sleds across frozen lake waters at speeds approaching 80 m.p.h.

Out On the Town
Like most small communities considered to be regional centers, Grand Marais has done a good job of developing its own performing arts programs. Taking advantage of the recent arrival of a number of professional musicians in the area, the North Shore Music Association presents a year-round slate of classical music performances, recitals, and jazz groups at various locations. During summer months, the Grand Marais Playhouse swings in to its repertory mode. Grand Marais has a fine Chinese restaurant, One World Cafe, a vegetarian cafe that's open in summers, and the local burger and shake palace, Blue Water Cafe. Local residents who want a drink after the lights go out, head down to Sven & Ole's, or make tracks for the Birch Terrace Lounge.

Economic Impact of the Arts

Artists, musicians, and writers seeking a remote place to dream, create, and plan for the future have given Grand Marais a long-standing reputation as an arts haven, largely based on the existence of the Grand Marais Art Colony. Established decades ago by artists from Chicago, Minneapolis, and other Midwest cities, the colony remains a living testament to the town's outstanding artistic legacy. "Local government funds art activities across the community," says Jay Andersen. "We've historically brought in a strong tourist business and Grand Marais realizes the impact we have on the economy. The people who come here for the art colony are the same ones who eat dinner at the restaurants and buy fishing gear at the sporting goods store."

Local Arts Agency

Grand Marais Art Colony, P.O. Box 626, Grand Marais, MN 55604, (218) 387-2737.

"We're oriented toward the visual and performing arts, and if things fall into place, Grand Marais will in the near future, have its own performing arts center," says Jay Andersen. "We have no trouble asking the legislature to fund far-reaching arts projects. They understand what the arts can do for a community. One of Grand Marais most active arts organizations is its musical association, and if the performing arts center is built, I can see the town turning into a national center for music."

Galleries and Arts Festivals

Grand Marais has five commercial art galleries and expects more. Showing mostly the work of local artists and craftspeople, the quality of work exhibited here is commensurate with what you would expect from a community with a long-standing tradition as an arts colony. The year's most popular arts bash is the Grand Marais Arts Festival, attracting nearly 100 exhibitors, held the weekend following the Fourth of July.

What the Artist Says

Betsy Bowen, a printmaker and children's book illustrator, creates images of the regional landscape and social scenes. "Living this close to Lake Superior is fascinating, and it's a constant challenge to try to capture the changing nature of the lake," she says. "Artists are able to sell their work in local galleries, and it's the work that's identifiable with the area that seems to do best with the tourist crowd. Others, who may work in a more contemporary type of painting, find markets elsewhere. The visitors who come here arrive from Canada and Minnesota, especially Minneapolis. Grand Marais is slowly growing, its housing market is strong, and in the past two years several galleries have decided to open up. Local artists are a mixed group—there are several critique groups that meet—and overall the feeling is easy, supportive, and casual . . . there's lots of camaraderie."

New York Mills, Minnesota

Location

The 1,000 or so residents of this revived community in west-central Minnesota live an hour's drive east of Fargo, North Dakota, and a 3-hour drive from Minneapolis.

Climate

It's usually a bit nippy during the winter months, with three-day blizzards and howling winds that can peel the roofs off of barns. In summer, the mosquitos arrive in organized formations, launching coordinated attacks on the exposed skin of local Scandinavian descendants. Spring can be a long, subtle climb toward the year's warmer months, punctuated by spikes of heat intended to tease locals into a false sense of security, only to be followed by yet another spell of snow and ice. Autumn, which arrives like clockwork on September 1st, and lasts all of five weeks, is the ricing and duck hunting season. (Yes, that's "ricing"—harvesting wild rice.)

Living

As affordable an arts community as you can imagine, the average cost of a well-insulated, 3-bedroom home in New York Mills is in the $30,000 range. For this amount (about the cost of a Honda Accord), newcomers buy into a town with a strong, caring, and spanking new school system; a place that's so safe locals can't readily remember the last time there was a crime other than teenage pranks; an outdoors environment that's brutally cold in winter, but is considered moderate by those who live here; and an arts scene that's bursting out sideways at the seams.

"We're a picturesque community on the boundary between the Great Plains and the Great North Woods," says John P. Davis, director of the regional cultural center. "We have lakes, family farms, and everything that's peaceful and inspirational about country living. What's here is small town hospitality, a sense of community, a progressive approach to life, and a liberal local forum for ideas. Plus, inexpensive housing and affordable farmland."

Out On the Town

Fargo, a short drive away, is home to two colleges and a number of ethnic restaurants—it's also where New York Mills residents get their shopping mall fix. But being a town that knows how to use the arts in the context of improving community life, there's both live theater and music performance at the New York Mills Regional Cultural Center. The artists in town prefer meeting friends down at Muggs Pub for pool, or getting together at the bowling alley for some more active fun. Weekend nights are the time to hit the Blue Horizon Ballroom for some leg shakin', and if it's time for a burger and fries fix, the favorite spot for locals is Eagles Cafe.

Economic Impact of the Arts

Things never were all that bad around New York Mills, with a boat manufacturing plant employing 300, and many family farms still running very strong . . . it's just that the town realized they needed to do more in the way of economic development. The New York Mills Cultural Center opened in 1992, and since then the community has formed itself into a place that's not simply supportive of the arts, but one that's downright excited about them. Once the arts center was launched, a bed and breakfast inn opened for business, the local cafe expanded, a few new businesses moved in, and New York Mills was able to pitch the existence of its arts center as an inducement to lure two new cottage industries into town.

Local Arts Agency
New York Mills Regional Cultural Center, 24 N. Main Avenue, New York Mills, MN 56567.

"We're housed in an historic, 1885 brick building," says director John P. Davis, "with gallery space and performance space downstairs. Our emphasis runs from jazz to film to literature, visual arts, poetry, and anything that can take the arts into people's everyday lives. Our summer festivals give local nonprofits an opportunity to raise funds for their own programs, and the town has been quick to see the potential in promoting New York Mills as an arts center. We sponsor an artist-in-residency program, and we've made inroads into the area's agricultural community, doing whatever it takes to get people to step inside this building. As the arts have started to strengthen the local economic climate, artists are being given more of a voice in the community."

Galleries and Arts Festivals
There are two stores selling local art work, a genre that includes woodworking, jewelry, painting, sculpture, and traditional crafts. This year's most anticipated arts event is the Continental Divide Music and Film Festival, a community-wide event that features as many as a hundred artists and craftspeople selling their creations at Smith Park, concert performances by several musical groups from Minneapolis, Chicago, and elsewhere, and a film festival showing the work of a half-dozen Midwest film makers. The festival takes place during the third weekend in August.

What the Artist Says
Cindy Linda, a silversmith and jeweler who owns a shop in town and also travels to a dozen craft fairs each year, says New York Mills is changing. "We're attracting attention from Minneapolis artists and gallery types, and I think the vision of building a regional arts center is making people curious about what's going to happen next. Now, the artists are on the bandwagon and we feel as if we're exploring new arts in the context of a rural community. Who knows, one day we may get into science and technology. One of the best things people get together on is the town's annual Philosophy Competition. I know that sounds strange, but we had hundreds of people attend the competition matches leading up into the finals last year. Heck, we had 120 competitors come in from seven different states for a philosophy contest—don't try to tell me there's nothing unusual about that. This town is going places!"

Bay St. Louis, Mississippi

Location
If it were any closer to New Orleans, Bay St. Louis would be a suburban community. As it is, this town of 7,000 splits its identity between the conservative mindset of its own state and the uninhibited funkiness of the metropolis resting a short distance to the west.

Climate
Fortunately, the residents of this town have the clear, blue waters of the Gulf of Mexico right at their doorstep. Summers are, for the uninitiated, long and arduous. Winters are very mild, with an occasional cold snap that lasts only a day or two. There is lots of rain, year-round, and it's almost always humid.

Living
Artists take advantage of the unused commercial space in the business district, renting out second-story studio spaces for $200 or so per month. The average 3-bedroom residence sells in the $80,000 range, which is a bit high for the area, reflecting the town's proximity to New Orleans.

"Dockside gambling has come into town, and we don't know if this is going to help or hurt us," says local artist Jan Hutchison. "Especially when you consider the town's small dinner theater. Our population is accommodating of the artists, using the arts as a way to promote tourism in the area. Art has influenced a lot of things here, but in a subtle way that indirectly benefits all businesses. There are art shows in the public park, and big Christmas shows of local art work. There's not much of a local market, but most artists sell outside the area, anyway. The arts have suffered a great deal in the local public schools—there's good instruction, but it's been cut way back."

Out On the Town
There's a little of everything in town, with Ruth's Bakery serving as one of the community's favorite places for breakfast and lunch. Those wanting a bit more scenery and a great burger, walk over to the Dock of the Bay. Vegetarian is always the catch of the day at Mississippi Natural, while after dark the town's favorite music and dancing place is the Good Life, providing that you're able to resist the pull of the nearby city.

Economic Impact of the Arts
The arts community is significant, and becoming more influential each year. A number of artists, musicians, and writers have moved into the area for a number of reasons: to escape the higher tax rates found in New Orleans; the area has always been tolerant of individuals whose personal or political preferences veer away from the mainstream; the area is developing a reputation as a viable art market; and the New Orleans crime and drug problem has created an atmosphere of fear amongst that city's creative types. They're moving to a safer place that's still within an easy drive of the city's arts scene.

Local Arts Agency

Second Saturday, P.O. Box 183, Bay St. Louis, MS 39520.

"We're just getting our start," says local artist Tony Eccles, a member of the town's fledgling arts organization. "We would like to have all the galleries coordinate their opening exhibitions, which is a better way to draw in the art buyers from New Orleans. Hopefully, by summer (historically the town's most popular time for visitors) we'll have seven openings taking place on the second Saturday evening of the month. And if it really comes together, we'll have musicians at the galleries, restaurants staying open later than usual, and the artists hanging out at the galleries to get people interested in their work."

Galleries and Arts Festivals

The seven art galleries in Bay St. Louis sell work that ranges from the affordable (appealing to the town's visitors) to contemporary and skilled landscapes (priced for those who understand the value of a professional artist's time and creative vision). Serenity Gallery owner Jerry Dixon says the community has a great respect for people in creative fields and that there is a place being made for the arts in Bay St. Louis. The busiest time of the year for visitors is during the weeks from early November to Christmas, and during the three months of mid-summer, a time when urbanites looking to escape New Orleans' heat flock into town and patronize art businesses. The most popular arts event is A Place of Art, held in the old town section of Bay St. Louis during the second weekend in September.

What the Artist Says

Tony Eccles, a sculptor and painter who moved to Bay St. Louis several years back, says that the local arts scene is still developing. "From here, what's happening in Ocean Springs looks very sophisticated and accomplished. We're still in our warm and friendly state, and haven't gotten to the point where there's an excitement for the arts. Since I've moved here, I've seen an influx of coffee houses and art galleries, and the artists are trying to get together their version of an arts crawl, but they don't want to become precious or pretentious.

"I tell artists to just go ahead and move here—the schools aren't great, and you need to get in and out of New Orleans for a lot of things, but it's affordable and safe. There's some walk-in trade during the summer, but the artists living here sell their work all over the country."

Folk artist Alice Moseley, a painter whose prints of the Bay St. Louis railroad depot are sold at galleries throughout the region, manages a business that ships reproductions of nearly three dozen of her paintings to collectors and galleries nationwide. "I've noticed the revival of this area's folk art forms since I moved here five years ago," she says. "This is an appealing, quaint town, but there are 18 casinos planned for the area—that's going to ruin this place. Artists who come here to make their careers need to do the flea markets, art fairs, and tourist galleries . . . whatever it takes to survive and get the financial freedom to do your own kind of work."

Ocean Springs, Mississippi

Location
A Gulf Coast community of 15,000, Ocean Springs is a friendly town filled with parks and historic homes. Across the Mississippi Sound from Biloxi, Ocean Springs is an hour's drive west of Mobile, Alabama.

Climate
Not far enough south to be considered tropical, yet protected from winter weather patterns by the Gulf's warm waters, Ocean Springs has a lengthy, humid summer with average temperatures in the low 80s, followed by a mellow winter with brisk, windy days and an occasional stretch of frost.

Living
Many residents of Ocean Springs are in some manner connected to the military-related industries in nearby Gulfport. The town has an interesting population mix, with a strong community of writers and painters. The average 3-bedroom home sells in the neighborhood of $72,000. Activities in Ocean Springs are oriented toward the community's spectacular seacoast. Gulf Islands National Seashore protects properties both on the mainland outside Ocean Springs and on the barrier islands that lie a few miles away from the town's waterfront. Anyone wanting their fix of metropolitan action drives a couple hours to New Orleans, but if they just want some isolation and natural beauty, chances are they'll paddle a canoe along some local bayous, or sail out to one of the barrier islands.

Out On the Town
While the diversity of Biloxi and Gulfport (a simple drive across the Bay Bridge) provide Ocean Springs with access to everything from a community college to ethnic restaurants and a shopping mall, and the local dining scene makes it well worth staying close to home. One of the town's favorite lunch spots is the Tato Nut Shop, where the patron's Southern accents are as entertaining as the food itself, and Henrietta's is a local favorite for meeting friends over drinks. While Ocean Springs is due to get its first Thai restaurant later this year, the area's barbecue is always worth trying, no matter which of the Southern states you're visiting. Since the recent arrival of riverboat gambling, Ocean Springs has joined the ranks of Gulf Coast towns whose waterfronts now have full-fledged casino action. Certainly, this has given everyone in town a place to enjoy things like night club entertainers and fancy restaurants, but it's also made them wary of what sort of people will be attracted in for the action.

Economic Impact of the Arts
Ocean Springs decided several years back that its image as an arts community could be predicated on the legacy of local artist Walter Anderson. The late artist's home has been turned into a

museum, which is also the community's most popular draw for the culturally inclined. The local theater troupe calls itself the Walter Anderson Players, and the community's cultural life benefits from classical music programs staged at the Ocean Springs Community Center, the stage shared by most local performing arts programs. Ocean Springs has been successful at building the image of being a wholesome, relaxed town that's receptive to those making their living in the creative fields.

Local Arts Agency

Ocean Springs Art Association, P.O. Box 136, Ocean Springs, MS 39564, (601) 392-8630.

"We're still a volunteer arts group," says Margaret Miller, the association's vice president, "and we don't have the kind of funds it takes to produce performing arts programs—we have to rely on what the state arts board sends our way. Our big push is on arts and education, which involves working with the area's four school districts in administering a corporate grant to fund a pilot art instruction program."

Galleries and Arts Festivals

The town is somewhat top-heavy with gift shops and tourist-oriented art galleries, but the bottom line is that Ocean Springs' painters and craftspeople have more than a dozen places to exhibit and sell their work, including a very contemporary gallery showing work from New Orleans and other Southern art centers. The local museum operates a gallery that exhibits both touring exhibitions and shows geared to the work of the area's art talents. The year's largest arts wingding is the Peter Anderson Arts and Crafts Festival, which takes place during the last week in November, bringing in more than 125 exhibiting artists.

What the Artist Says

Trailer McQuilkin, a sculptor who moved to Ocean Springs from New Orleans, says it's the area's environment that attracts artists. "Ocean Springs is still affordable. The artists living here tend to be the type of individuals who can become inspired by the environment, finding a way to incorporate it into their art work.

"We would like to see more galleries come into town—places showing the work of strong regional artists would help to change this town for the better. I co-own a gallery in the middle of downtown, and when it got started people realized there was a change coming to the area. Now, we've got a couple of great cafes, a jewelry store selling original, one-of-a-kind work, and some more galleries. We've gotten the attention of the town's business community, which approves of what we've done.

"Artists who sell in the local galleries do best with work that's priced in the $500 to $2,000 range . . . anything higher than that and they'll prefer to head into New Orleans. Most of us seek out commissioned work, and a lot do the craft fairs. The arts community has a tradition of putting together nonprofit shows that are aimed at raising the town's awareness of its artists, to create the word-of-mouth we needed to make up for the money we lacked to do out-of-town advertising, and now, that work is starting to pay off!

"It's a great place to live, the people are fun, and there's something going on all the time. Try to plan your visit between November and April, to get the best weather."

Branson, Missouri

Location
Southwest Missouri is a land of high, rolling Ozark Mountain hills bisected by meandering lakes. Amongst this natural beauty is the fast-growing community of Branson (pop. 3,700), once known as a regional arts and craft center, but more recently gaining fame as the western outpost of the Nashville music industry.

Climate
Every seasonal change is felt in this part of the country, which gets full blasts of summer, spring, fall, and winter (winters tend to be moderate, but occasional storms roll in off the Great Plains, grinding the place to a halt).

Living
There's a little bit of everything in Branson, from the miles of lush lakefront lining the banks of Table Rock Lake (picnics and swimming at Table Rock State Park are a favorite local pastime) to the steep slopes of the Ozark Mountains stretching south to Arkansas. Residential housing prices have been rising: A 3-bedroom place currently sells in the neighborhood of $80,000, but anyone wanting a place on the lake should be prepared to spend twice as much.

With good weather working in Branson's favor, this region has an outdoors activity season that covers nearly nine months. Golf ranks as a primary local interest, with water skiing and sailing coming in a close second and third during the year's five warmest months. Music's role in Branson as both entertainment and an industry shouldn't be underestimated—the town has 35 performance venues, and regards its performers with the admiration accorded to sports heroes in large cities.

Out On the Town
Did you say entertainment? Branson is an American anomaly, a place where entertainers like Wayne Newton and Dolly Parton have staked their claims, building performing arts palaces that bring local residents a year-round schedule of slick stage shows aimed at keeping the turistas satisfied. Today, Branson gets tourist dollars flowing in from not only across the country, but also from Canada and Europe (hey, after all, this is Wayne Newton we're talkin' about), so restaurants abound. If you live here, chances are your favorite hangout is Rocky's Italian Restaurant, which not only serves a mean dish of rigatoni, but also has one of Branson's most relaxed, unrehearsed bar scenes. On the other hand, if boot-scootin' is your pleasure, there are no less than a dozen semi-authentic, live music, country and western bars. McGuffin's Diner is the best burger-and-shake place, but if your tastes veer toward vegetarian fare, hop on the highway to nearby (1 hour) Springfield, Missouri.

Economic Impact of the Arts

If life in Branson had gone along without the country music boys deciding this was going to become Nashville West, the town would probably be described today as sort of a Eureka Springs North. Of course, with the tourist masses having hit town, lots of artists and craftspeople have figured out a way or two to skim a few bucks off the top (important skill in the country music business). If you've got to be overshadowed, this is the best way to meet that particular fate . . . at least there's room for everyone at the table.

Local Arts Agency

Branson Arts Council, P.O. Box 1309, Branson, MO 65615, (417) 337-7203.

"We play a coordinating role for the arts in Branson," says council executive director Susan Marcussen. "Everything from honoring the people who are the town's largest arts patrons to coordinating art-in-the-park festivals and taking out ads in regional papers for our events. Performing arts are interesting here: We bring in at least one national act a year, but our local talent is so good (many musicians are accomplished pros with years of Los Angeles and Nashville experience) that we don't need to look outside of Branson for performers to work with our regional programs. We're strongly linked to the local school system—the city is the main funding source for art education programs, and we've got programs for kids in theater, music, and dance."

Galleries and Arts Festivals

Crafts are still the strongest regional visual arts form, with pottery especially popular. Branson has one sophisticated art gallery, and a bundle of shops selling everything from local fine craft to pink howling coyotes made in Guatemala. Here, the key to surviving as an artist is to participate in the many local craft fairs held not only in Branson, but at just about every small town in the area. The year's busiest season lasts from March to December, drawing somewhere in the area of 5 million tourists. Reaching them directly (not having to pay a gallery commission) is the difference between surviving full-time on your art, or having to take a job punching tickets part-time to supplement your art habit.

What the Artist Says

Sculptor Tim Cherry, an artist whose bronze realist forms are sold in galleries in Santa Fe, Scottsdale, and Jackson (Wyoming), says that while there isn't much of an organized local arts scene for an artist of his stature to plug into, the town's recent surge of residential and commercial construction activity has provided him with a range of opportunities for both commissioned projects and sales of his fine art pieces. "We're still in the convincing stage here in Branson—trying to convince local people that art is something they want to spend real money on. Here, I'm away from the influence of an art center and can develop my work free from distractions. The local attitude toward fine art is changing, and the opportunity to do well is on the horizon. We really need galleries committed to selling quality art work. Our music scene gives us a unique situation: The late night jam sessions at Rocky's are outstanding, filled with musicians and performers kicking things out after a hard night of work."

Bozeman, Montana

Location

Bozeman is located in south-central Montana, on one of the main routes into Yellowstone National Park, and is home to 23,000 full-time residents and thousands of students at Montana State University.

Climate

People residing here have a sense of civic pride about living in the southern part of the state, going so far as to refer to this area as the "banana belt." This may seem a bit silly to most of the country, but really hits home with the envious, frozen souls in Great Falls, Butte, Missoula, and Helena.

Living

Once the national press caught on to how good life was in Bozeman, the rush was on . . . and it hasn't stopped since. Real estate prices have risen sharply, and what was once an affordable, 3-bedroom home in one of the community's better neighborhoods now fetches anywhere from $125,000 on up—and you've got to be ready to battle for the right to be first in line. Because it's a college town, Bozeman's school system is much better than average, but its arts program is just starting to play catch-up with mainstream areas in science and technology.

   With its easy access into the wilderness areas of Yellowstone National Park and Gallatin National Forest, residents of Bozeman have no trouble heading into nature's realm for a day or two of camping, fly fishing, hunting, or cross-country skiing. Sure, the town is concerned about growth, but that's a problem the entire Rocky Mountain region is having to come to terms with. The best thing new arrivals can do is to find a way to blend in with their new neighbors. Remember, if you want to be accepted by the community, Montana is not the place to flaunt wealth.

Out On the Town

Montana State University sports are a big draw for local residents, with the men's basketball and intercollegiate rodeo programs being extremely popular ways to pass the long, dark winters. Bozeman has expanded its restaurant diversity in recent years (courtesy of newcomers), and there's now a Thai dining spot (New Asia Kitchen), slugging it out with the somewhat expensive (say locals) new places featuring everything from Northern Italian osso bucco to Tex-Mex enchiladas. Your basic local Bohemian type artist likes spending time at the Leaf and Bean, and the best burger is served at Fuddrucker's. Several vegetarian spots are located close to the campus, and for night life, Bozemanites head down to Willy's Saloon.

Economic Impact of the Arts

Overshadowed by Bozeman's college culture and the real estate boom still sweeping through its neighborhoods, the arts scene has a presence here, although it's a rather quiet one. Growing rapidly to accommodate both its influx of tourists and newcomer residents, Bozeman has so far emphasized quantity over quality in terms of what's shown in its newer, arts-and craft-oriented retail stores. There are, however, three bonafide galleries in town that emphasize the original work of the state's many fine artists.

Local Arts Agency

Montana Arts Foundation, P.O. Box 1872, Bozeman, MT 59771, (406) 585-9551.

"Don't even consider moving here unless you like low wages, isolation, and lousy weather," says John Barsness, the foundation's executive director. "Really, people seem to move to Bozeman without having the slightest idea what life is like here and find it's not what they assumed it was. We're the statewide management organization for a number of Montana nonprofit organizations and our programs range from exchanges coordinated with the Russian Academy of Arts to promoting the development of a Native American museum adjacent to Custer's Battlefield. Our downtown business community has yet to understand how art can improve the economy, and there's not much done to promote art as something that would attract bigger-spending tourists."

Galleries and Arts Festivals

Downtown Bozeman has a number of gift shops and even a smattering of tourist oriented stores, but only three downtown gallery spaces take the original art of local artists seriously. The college's arts department is an outpost of contemporary and experimental creative thought, and the exhibitions held on campus at Haynes Gallery tend to reflect those values. There are nonprofit galleries at the Beall Park Art Center and at the Emerson Cultural Center. The biggest arts bash of the year is the annual Sweet Pea Festival, held at Lindly Park in downtown Bozeman during the first weekend in August.

What the Artist Says

Susan Blackwood, a wildlife and landscape artist who sells her originals and reproductions in several galleries around the country, moved here for the environmental beauty. "I was in Colorado before this, so I know how I handle eight months of winter . . . I love it! My favorite pastimes are cross-country skiing and skating. Here, you've got beauty, isolation, and wonderful people. I'm not dependent on the local market, but I realize there aren't many sales opportunities here. We do have a number of great, hot-selling artists, but they're making their livings elsewhere. People move here looking for something, and they end up being disappointed—it's a conservative, low-paying town, and if that sounds like something you can't handle, think twice before coming. Bring your job with you and be sure you can handle the cold."

Helena, Montana

Location

Helena, the state capitol of Montana, is a community of 25,000 residents living in an area bounded by mountains, wilderness regions, and the Missouri River.

Climate

Subject to extremes in temperature change, from sudden breaks of 70-degree warmth in March to an occasional August dusting of snow, Helena's weather is characteristically cold and windy during its long winter, followed by dry, almost desert-like heat during the summer months.

Living

As the region's center for state and federal government, Helena has enjoyed the sort of stability offered by an economy whose employment sector encompasses a large civil service component. Here, artists have one of the nation's most affordable housing markets at their disposal, with plenty of downtown studio spaces renting for under $200, and prime retail space for artist-owned galleries readily available in the downtown business core. The local school system is very strong, and in one of Helena's many safe, serene neighborhoods a 3-bedroom residence can be bought for less than $70,000.

Local residents feel as if Helena is a place that's been fortunate to escape the influx of out-of-staters (especially Californians) who have flocked into Big Sky Country over the past few years, and in a way, they're right. When people get a sense of how difficult Montana winters can be at this corner of the state, they usually turn southward in search of a place less prone to such long and severe stretches of sub-freezing temperatures. Helena residents may have to travel a ways to find a challenging ski area, but the nearby streams and lakes hold as many great fishing opportunities as anywhere else in the state.

Out On the Town

With lobbyists and legislators making this their base of operations, Helena has a number of the wood-paneled, downtown dining establishments that seem most conducive to whispered discussions about the best way to divide up people's hard-earned tax dollars. Don't bother looking for ethnic food choices more exotic than Cantonese restaurants and pizza joints. One of the favorite places for artists to swill a couple of brews and shoot a rack or two of eight-ball is the Corner Bar. If it's time for some nighttime action—the sort of leg shakin' cowboys and cowgirls do before heading out to the rodeo corrals—then be sure to stop in at the Silver Spur. A good place for a burger and chocolate shake is the Windbag, while the Real Food Store is Helena's best place for vegetarian goodies.

Economic Impact of the Arts

The arts in Helena are dominated by the community's teaching and nonprofit institutions. The Archie Bray Foundation, a school focused on ceramic arts, plays a central role in the life of the town's arts community. Helena is also the location of the Holter Museum of Art, Montana's state museum and showcase for contemporary art as well as traditional art forms and artifacts. A performing arts center and a larger auditorium, the Helena Civic Center, make the community's arts scene one of the most active in any Rocky Mountain city.

Local Arts Agency

Archie Bray Foundation for the Ceramic Arts, 2915 Country Club Avenue, Helena, MT 59601, (406) 443-3502. Publishes the *Archie Bray Foundation Newsletter*.

Located on a 27-acre manufacturing facility that once served as a brickyard, the foundation occupies a half-dozen (brick, of course) structures. Its mission is to serve as a center for the development of artists working in the ceramic field, a mandate covering both functional and sculptural ceramics. It has even set out to build a museum dedicated to the history of ceramics in North America. "Helena's outlook on the arts is progressive," says foundation director Josh DeWeese. "The downtown business association is active in promoting the arts, you see art works being installed in downtown retail windows, and art walks take place throughout the year. Schools request workshops for different grade levels and there's art instruction in all the schools."

Galleries and Arts Festivals

The six commercial art galleries active in Helena exhibit the usual range of art work, from first-rate western to suspect southwestern, along with that of regional painters and the fine ceramicists trained at the Archie Bray Foundation, which maintains a nonprofit gallery on its campus grounds for exhibiting work by its current students and out-of-area artists. Touring art shows are offered as part of the regular program at the Holter Museum of Art. Helena's biggest arts festival is the outdoor art show held each June during the community's increasingly popular jazz festival, and in October, the civic center hosts another well-attended arts and fine crafts event.

What the Artist Says

Richard Swanson, an accomplished ceramicist whose interests extend both to fine art and the creation of multi-media projects, says the key to happiness in Helena is hard work. "It really helps to be a jack-of-all trades. The local market is much better now than in the past, but it's still concentrated on smaller ceramic pieces and paintings. My sculptural work usually heads to galleries outside Montana.

"We didn't have a college in Helena to give young people a reason to move in—the kind of person who lives here has some ties to state government, is in their 30s or 40s, and has an appreciation for art of all kinds. The town draws big-name performers at the Civic Center, and they usually stay on to conduct workshops at the Myrna Loy (a converted jailhouse that serves as the town's more accessible performing arts center). The artists here are just starting to get organized: They want to coordinate some sort of community art shows, something that goes beyond an arts and crafts fair in a city park. The jazz festival each June has turned into a big, city-wide arts event."

Kalispell, Montana

Location

The Flathead Valley, a broad expanse of land in the northwest corner of Montana, is named after the area's indigenous Native American people who reside on reservation lands spreading out across the valley's southwest corner. Kalispell, the region's largest population center, has 15,000 residents.

Climate

Nine months of winter and two brief shoulder seasons are followed by a summer so spectacular and warm that the region is one of the nation's premier cherry-growing areas. Deep freezes, with temperatures well below zero, are common winter weather patterns and tend to be a rude awakening for the town's newer, star-struck residents.

Living

An outdoors paradise, this section of Montana has some of the nation's most spectacular areas for fishing, hunting, hiking, and wilderness camping. A couple of nearby ski areas give Kalispell residents plenty of opportunities for downhill skiing, while large expanses of open land offer cross-country skiers an unspoiled paradise. Flathead Lake freezes over in winter, giving local residents a playground for ice fishing and ice boating, and this is the same lake that turns into a water skiing and sailing mecca during the year's warmer months. There's a community college in Kalispell, and a number of local artists have found part-time employment at the college, teaching everything from painting to ceramics.

Out On the Town

Summers here have started to resemble those in the Grand Canyon and Yellowstone National Park areas, which means they're overcrowded and too busy for local comfort levels. Kalispell has a lot of good press and word-of-mouth about the wonderful life that awaits those who sell their homes and move into the Flathead Valley. As a result, a number of talented, entrepreneurial individuals have decided to do just that.

Several great restaurants, and a number of bed and breakfast inns have come on line recently, and while there still isn't a Thai dining spot, several Italian restaurants and even a French café have opened their doors. For decades, locals and visitors have headed over to the legendary Moose's Saloon for an afternoon of elbow-bending, and this part of Kalispell culture hasn't changed—although now there is an abundance of newly arrived Californians hanging around, dressed up in their fresh cowboy clothes, trying to casually (but unsuccessfully) blend in with the crowd.

There are a few places to perform ritualistic leg shakin' on Saturday nights, with the bars at the Outlaw Inn and Bigfork Inn especially worth checking out. The Blue Moon on Main Street is a long-standing favorite any time of year. The Bigfork Summer Playhouse has a full run of plays at the Bigfork Center for Performing Arts, while each July's run of the Flathead Festival brings classical, folk, and jazz music performances to venues all over town. During winter, the Glacier Orchestra performs regular concerts.

Economic Impact of the Arts

What usually draws people into this area is the region's environment, which acts as a gateway into Glacier National Park. A short drive north from the 20-mile expanse of Flathead Lake, Kalispell has successfully parlayed its proximity to the park (and a recent surge in national magazine stories) into a magnetic sort of charisma. Once the non-outdoors oriented tourists get here, they find there's not much to do besides go shopping or take a lake cruise, so there's been a recent jump in the number of art galleries and fine craft stores, and most local residents expect even more new galleries in the coming years.

Local Art Agency

Flathead Arts Council, Hockaday Center for the Arts, P.O. Box 83, Kalispell, MT 59903, (406) 755-5268.

"We've got a very active center that serves as a major focus for most of what goes on in town," says director Magee Nelson. "Here, artists aren't very active politically, but they're well respected in the community and have their own support system. The local art patrons aren't concerned about snobbism, nor is our arts scene a provincial sort of creation. The town pitches in with lots of corporate sponsorship for what happens at the center. We have a continuing artist-in-residency program through local schools, and school groups are always coming through to look at the visual art exhibits and attend performances and workshops."

Galleries and Arts Festivals

Locals point to the existence of 40 craft and art galleries in Kalispell (many of which sell prints of western, cowboy, and southwestern scenes, with a few offering originals of both oil paintings and bronze sculpture) as evidence of the health of the area's arts community. The Hockaday Center's visual arts orientation leans toward displaying contemporary work created by the area's other-directed artists and the Native American artists from the Flathead Reservation in its nonprofit gallery. There's another nearby nonprofit exhibition space at the Bigfork Cultural Center in Bigfork. "We also present a diverse range of international cultural exhibits and historical shows," says Nelson. The year's largest art bash is Art in the Park, held the last weekend in July in Depot Park, attracting 65 exhibiting artists.

What the Artist Says

Landscape painter Mark Ogle, an artist whose originals and prints sell well in the Kalispell art market, works from his downtown studio/gallery space. "I'm seeing people moving here who want art work of the area in their homes—they're moneyed, mostly retired, and I see them as a plus for the community. I share space with a sculptor; both of us work in the studio and sell our work there, it's very informal. Here, artists aren't the organizing type—we may share secrets with each other, but there's not that inclination to work together in a group."

Livingston, Montana

Location

Stretching from the north boundary of Yellowstone National Park in a 30-mile zigzag pointing roughly toward the northeast, the valley that's home to Livingston's 9,000 residents is bisected by the Yellowstone River. Bozeman, the closest population center, is a half hour away.

Climate

Brace yourself . . . local residents refer to their corner of south-central Montana as being in the state's banana belt. All things being relative, this doesn't mean Livingston's artists wear their Hawaiian print shirts from St. Patrick's Day to Columbus Day. It does, however, mean that on many occasions the town gets less snowfall, and tends to be anywhere from 10 to 20 degrees warmer than other nearby regions.

Living

If you have seen the recent Robert Redford movie, *A River Runs Through It,* then you've glimpsed a major aspect of what draws artists and others into Livingston: the unparalleled fly fishing in local rivers and streams. Mountain waters pour into the Yellowstone River from snowmelt in both the Absaroka Range and the Madison Range, sheltering some of the nation's premier sites for anglers. Hip-waders and a fly rod are an absolute must for everyone living in this part of the country, and even for those just dropping by for a visit.

The valley has a remarkably long growing season (considering its northerly locale), and once summer loosens its grip, the area slides into an autumn hunting season that brings out the mountain-man best in many of Livingston's male and female outdoors-persons. Several ski areas are within an easy drive of town, and snowmobiling is popular in winter months.

Studio space is usually available upstairs in downtown businesses, with the average space renting for $200 per month. Housing prices have been rising steadily, with the average 3-bedroom home now selling in the $65,000 range.

Out On the Town

The authentic, small-town Montana atmosphere of the Stockman's Bar, as well as its burgers, steaks, and drinks, is a year-round favorite of local residents. But if you ask anyone in town for a lead on vegetarian food, expect a cross-eyed reply (this is, after all, cattle country). Livingston has a couple of organizations staging live theater, and if you're here when the Blue Slipper or the Firehouse 5 are in full swing, be sure to buy a ticket and enjoy. Down at the Murray Hotel you'll be able, every now and again, to catch live music of the leg shakin' variety, and don't forget to stop in at Mark's In and Out for a feed that'll stick to your ribs.

Economic Impact of the Arts

The art economy is good and getting better, but Livingston needs more places selling fine art, even though it already has nine galleries. This is a town with an interesting artistic reputation, mostly based on its being the home of Russell Chatham, one of the nation's most prominent regionalist painters. His presence lends a bankable identity to the Livingston area, attracting other artists and visitors who stop in at his gallery, and helping its reputation as a town where quality art work is created by the many artists exhibited in local galleries.

Local Arts Agency

Livingston Gallery Association, Rt. 62, Box 3229, Livingston, MT 59047, (406) 222-2740.

Working with the Park County Friends of the Arts, the association coordinates Livingston schools' artist-in-residence programs, as well as working with the town's nonprofit groups to address certain aspects of the community's art and cultural life. The Depot Arts Center, Livingston's historical art and artifact exhibition space, also stages occasional arts events.

Galleries and Arts Festivals

Nine galleries compete for visitor attention in Livingston, and while there's some pandering to the tastes of those just-passin'-thru types, here only due to the town's position as a getaway community for Yellowstone, a number of folks are pulled in by the community's artistic reputation. During the summer months, the Depot Art Festival (held in Depot Park on July 4th weekend) draws slightly more than a hundred exhibiting artists.

What the Artist Says

Rosalyn Mina, who has lived in the area for ten years, is a textiles artist who creates painted silk wearable art, canvasses, and room screens. "Here, the artists are appreciative of the local market, but it's really not enough to survive on, so we've got to do the crafts shows outside the state or find galleries in Seattle and Jackson. If you can get into the wholesale and retail markets, you can do it.

"Livingston is life in a small community that's affordable, with a support system for its artists," Mina continues. "We're surrounded by mountains and you can find peace here. Our social scene used to center around church meetings and tupperware parties, but now we've got these Seattle-style coffee bars. Livingston isn't changing as much as it's just getting larger, and the artists who have been here a while are getting a chance to grow with the town.

"Newcomers should just try to blend into the environment: Don't try to stand out, take the approach of being low-key, and eventually people will start including you in things. The most difficult thing for the locals to accept about development is its visual impact—when you can actually see the new homes, when things start standing out, there's talk of a sort of backlash."

Virginia City, Nevada

Location
A historic mining town within a 30-minute drive of Lake Tahoe, Virginia City with its 850 men and women, 243 dogs, and 176 cats thrive in a picturesque, Sierra Nevada Mountains setting just 20 miles southeast of Reno.

Climate
Characteristic of high desert regions, Virginia City's winters are typically filled with cold (sometimes snowy) nights and crystal-clear days with temperatures in the 50s. Summers are not as brutally hot as elsewhere in Nevada, but days in the low 90s aren't unusual, and it's extremely dry.

Living
Typical of most old mining towns, Virginia City's housing stock tends to be either of the carefully restored, turn-of-the-century Victorian type, or a dilapidated version of the same. If you're handy with a hammer and band saw, this could be the opportunity you've been looking for. An average 3-bedroom home in good condition sells in the neighborhood of $100,000. Lots of creative types call this town home, and your neighbors may be as diverse as a blackjack dealer from the local casino to a theater professional who splits time between gigs in Southern California and Reno. Some artists say that Virginia City's most popular creative medium is roulette, with drinking a close second, but that just applies to weekends.

Out On the Town
Even Hoss Cartwright couldn't keep his ten-gallon hat away from Virginia City's casinos, and today's artists can't be held accountable if, every now and again, they sidle up to the craps table and bet a month's rent on the luck of the dice. Of course, these days, Virginia City's surviving artists tend to be a bit more level-headed than that. Nonetheless, the town's several casinos beckon visitors with the lure of a 24-hour siren's call. The Gold Hill Hotel is one place where local artsy types feel welcome. The Great Room at the Gold Hill manages to have the best all-round bands from one weekend to the next. When it comes time for a bite to eat, from a burger and fries to prime rib, the local favorites are Solid Muldoon's and the Brass Rail Saloon. If your taste runs toward vegetarian or ethnic, it's best to make the short drive to Reno, and not bother the local folks with your exotic demands.

Economic Impact of the Arts
Big bucks are perpetually gambled away in Virginia City's casinos, and the savvy managers of these establishments are beginning to see that if they do a good enough job of encouraging artists to flourish in the community, it gives them an advantage over Carson City, Tahoe City, and Reno in attracting gambling tourists. The good news is that things are starting to be perceived this way; the bad news is that it's only just beginning to make an impression. Stay tuned!

Local Arts Agency

Comstock Arts Council, P.O. Box 81, Virginia City, NV 89440, (702) 847-0989. Publishes the *Comstock Arts Council Newsletter*.

"Our emphasis was on the performing arts," says council director William Beeson, "but now we've started bringing visual arts into the mix—we're finding places to have visual art exhibits and we've started funding visual arts programs in the local schools. Our performances are staged in the high school theater, which seats 200, but our dance programs are held in the old gym of the middle school. Our art teacher is a professional artist, and the state has a very active artist-in-residence program. Our level of community and state support far outstrips what a local arts organization in a town this size would normally get. The casinos are good about allowing us to do our fundraising at the hotels, and we do get some sponsorship from them, but in a way we're just starting to be seen as a part of Virginia City's business community."

Galleries and Arts Festivals

The three Virginia City galleries selling original works of art range from two representing the area's more traditional western realist painters to a newer gallery specializing in contemporary paintings primarily by Nevada artists as well as artists living elsewhere. There are a couple of notable local events that bring a flood of business into the arts community, including the Annual Camel Race in September (attracting over a hundred riders and several dozen musicians, artists, and assorted counter-cultural types), and the Historic Preservation Weekend in May (a house tour of Virginia City's old Victorian residences involving dozens of actors and musicians).

What the Artist Says

Tom Gilbertson, a painter who has lived in Virginia City since 1987, says the town's artists are supportive of each other. "Because of the casinos, tourists don't tend to mingle too well with the artists. They're more interested in conversing with slot machines. That makes the artists sort of stick to themselves. We turn out for each other's openings. I think all of us would be happy to see new artists and galleries come into town, especially things that may be innovative . . . anything to help it grow. What Virginia City needs is a good coffeehouse . . . that would be nice.

"There are some local shops exhibiting work that I'd consider more in the art guild category. The serious artists have to keep themselves on the art fair circuit or find the galleries they need in other areas. I'm always surprised when a tourist buys one of my paintings—it's usually someone who is in the area for a conference or just happens to be driving through. The state's artist-in-residence program is a great place for artists to find work. It's a good source of income and a great way to build your network of contacts."

Keene, New Hampshire

Location
In the southwest corner the state, Keene's 22,000 residents live within easy reach of the music center of Brattleboro, Vermont.

Climate
This part of New Hampshire has a milder winter than other parts of the state, along with a substantially longer growing season. Stock up on insect repellent in late spring, as the first weeks of New Hampshire's summer bring out the dive-bombing best in the region's legendary black flies.

Living
Far enough south to be within an easy, 4-hour drive of New York City, Keene's real estate values were bumped upward by a combination of weekending Manhattanites and, several years back, the price increases resulting from Boston's now faded high tech boom. An extraordinarily scenic community, still very desirable for relocating urbanites, Keene's average 3-bedroom home sells in the range of $175,000.

Very outdoors-oriented, Keene is a picturesque, safe community, frequently cited as one of the country's most desirable small towns for urban refugees. Autumn seems to last just a couple of weeks longer than in the rest of the state, and there's easy access to nearby lakes for anyone whose idea of fun ranges from sailing to ice fishing. Boston (for those who need a mall trip or want to take advantage of the city's cultural offerings) is only two hours away.

Out On the Town
The home of both a state-supported and a private college, Keene benefits from cultural programs presented at these institutions. There's lots of locally produced theater, along with a low-key, yet vibrant, music scene that supports jazz, blues, and folk music performances at several venues. Mocha Joe's and the Bagel Works are two places where locals enjoy get-togethers over lunch and evening activities. The Bench Cafe is Keene's best place for a burger and fries, while vegetarians flock down to the Bagel Works or Country Life Natural for their culinary fixes.

Economic Impact of the Arts
If all the pieces fall into place, Keene will soon have a new performing arts center located in the renovated quarters of the Colonial Theater downtown. This would be a major boost to the town's performing and visual arts scene, as it would focus local residents' attention away from what happens on the college campuses and toward the community's home-grown talent. That's not to say there's been any conflict within the diversified arts scene in Keene so far, but it would be an important step in solidifying the community's identity as a broad-based independent arts center.

Local Arts Agency

Grand Manadnock Arts Council, 31 Central Square, Keene, NH 03431, (603) 357-3906.

"The town's overall cultural atmosphere is a real drawing card," says Maureen Ahern, director of the Thorne-Sagendorph Gallery at Keene State University. "The gallery is supported by both the community and the college. We've built a new addition and are showing art work that's quite contemporary. We've found that the community is very much behind us: school teachers bring their classes in for tours, the people who live in town stop by and take a look at what's on the walls, and even if some don't understand the values expressed in contemporary art, they're still curious enough to take the time to investigate what's here. Keene is becoming the kind of arts-oriented community that's willing to take a chance on something new, and the arts scene is growing to meet that challenge."

Galleries and Arts Festivals

With only three commercial art galleries in town, it would seem that there's room for more exhibition space in the community's business district, especially now that there's a performing arts center on the way. The college's Thorne-Sagendorph Gallery serves as Keene's nonprofit art exhibition space, showing the contemporary work that would otherwise not find a prominent local venue. Several arts and crafts festivals dot the local calendar, a reflection of the community's historic attractiveness to tourists from across the Northeast. Each season has its big arts bash, with the Spring Festival of the Arts, Chinese New Year, and the Historic Summer Festival being amongst the most popular.

What the Artist Says

Printmaker and pastels artist Erika Radich has lived in Keene for 14 years, and finds the community's spirit to be an important aspect of its creative lifeblood. "Artists move here from all parts of the country: Some have New York connections, some are just getting started, and others are making their living on the road at craft fairs. You can always count on the artists being available to participate in what's going on in town—there's always an event being organized or some sort of plan being discussed. One of our recent big accomplishments was the Art Walk weekend in May.

"Tourists come into town for a short time, stay at one of the inns, and want to buy work that's produced locally. It's wonderful to have a market like that, and it's something the town has worked really hard to develop in recent years.

"To survive full-time as an artist it's important to sell outside the area. The best thing that could happen for the arts in Keene is for the Colonial Theater project to become fully funded. The town needs its own performing arts center and classroom space for art instruction. Right now there's an abundance of studio space for rent downtown where artists can find a large, sunny place for under $300 per month."

Lebanon, New Hampshire

Location
A few miles removed from the Connecticut River Valley, coursing along New Hampshire's western border, Lebanon's 12,500 residents live within a few minutes drive of several colleges and ski areas. Concord, the state capital, is a 90-minute drive southeast.

Climate
Far enough south to receive a share of all four seasons, Lebanon's splendid, lengthy autumn is followed by a winter whose grip tightens in early November, not letting up until Easter Sunday. Expect some hot days during summer, always followed by a return to the moderate warmth more in keeping with the area's usual weather.

Living
The cost of living tends to be on the moderately expensive side for this part of the state, primarily because of Lebanon's proximity to the large academic staff at Dartmouth College in Hanover. Some 3-bedroom homes in the $90,000 range are available for the handyman types, but in the town's more desirable northern end, expect prices to run $150,000 and up. Artists are generally able to find studio space in Lebanon's business district at a cost of $200 per month, but there are also studio rentals available at the arts center. The area's main summer outdoor recreation spot is Lake Sunapee, while Lebanon has a year-round public recreation center, and great terrain for everything from bicycling to cross-country skiing and ice skating.

Out On the Town
A strong tradition of community and campus theater gives this area an abundance of actors and playhouses in towns such as Hanover, White River Junction, and Woodstock, Vermont. A theater festival held annually in White River Junction is one of the Northeast's premier stage events. Those interested in classical and chamber music will be pleased to know that Dartmouth's music department schedules concerts throughout the year at Hopkins Center. Having historically drawn sophisticated tourists and well-educated individuals into the area, Lebanon (and its environs) are filled with great choices when it comes to the question of dining. Lou's, a traditional favorite, is the town's most popular place for the burger-and-shake crowd, while vegetarians have their needs served through the Co-op Food Store in Hanover. Sweet Tomatoes Trattoria is the place to head for an enjoyable dinner, and for nighttime dancing, it's Cactus Jack's, across the river in White River Junction.

Economic Impact of the Arts
One of the first parts of the country to have a year-round tourist business and a strong local economy, the Lebanon region is filled with small shops and galleries selling anything from original art by local painters and craftspeople to canvasses from established New York art-world types who maintain weekend homes in the area. The arts and spectacular scenery are the main draws everywhere in the area, along with the sports and cultural activities taking place at the colleges.

Local Arts Agency

Alliance for Visual Arts, 11 Bank Street, Lebanon, NH 03766, (603) 448-3117.

"From our offices in what once was an industrial building, the emphasis is on film, art exhibitions, and occasional performance programs," says Alliance executive director Bente Torjusen. "We're able to concentrate on our specialties because there's a strong museum outreach program and a very active performing arts focus at Dartmouth. Our AVA Gallery shows art created by students from the area high schools and elementary schools, and we use the teaching facilities in the art center to hold studio classes for children and adults. We also administer scholarships for those who are especially promising. The art center is in what was an overalls factory: We have 1,900 square feet of exhibition space spread out over three floors. Local businesses, for the most part, are supportive of what we're trying to do, and the area's tourism board is good about using regional arts as a way to promote business."

Galleries and Arts Festivals

In this part of the country, the nonprofit art exhibition spaces are just as important to the health of the arts scene as the commercial galleries. Besides the AVA space, there are organization-run galleries in Hanover and Newport, along with museum and college galleries in both Hanover and New London. The area's highest concentration of commercial galleries is in Woodstock, Vermont, while Lebanon has a single gallery, with two existing in Hanover. The year's largest arts festival is the League of New Hampshire Craftsmen's Fair, held each August at Lake Sunapee State Park in nearby New London.

What the Artist Says

"It's an invigorating place to live, not jaded and filled with stores selling junk," says filmmaker and painter Clifford West. "I'm continually surprised at the sophisticated art coming from this area, particularly in the fine crafts. We've got a few sculptors sprinkled around, but there are a lot of painters and woodworkers. The emphasis is on landscape painting, especially the cows-and-barns scenes people never seem to get tired of buying.

"We're getting an influx of people who, if they wanted to, could become a whole new generation of local art patrons, but there's still that mindset about going to New York or Boston for the large art purchases. If the local nonprofit galleries can continue showing the area's contemporary painters, that sort of thing may change in the coming years—at least it would help to create an interest in what these artists are doing.

"The natural beauty of the area is what makes it attractive to artists—it's just so damn green around here that you wonder how people can keep painting it. It would help the area's artists if the college would take a more active interest in things out in the community, away from campus. We could use more participation in that sense."

Portsmouth, New Hampshire

Location
An hour north of Boston is the brief stretch of New Hampshire's seacoast. While all of 10 miles in length, the region is packed with historic old forts, restored fishing villages, and some of the nicest beaches to be found anywhere on the East Coast. Portsmouth, a community of 26,000, is the area's art and cultural center.

Climate
During the summer, you'd swear this had to be Florida: Ocean breezes roll in off the Atlantic, sandy beaches beckon sunbathers and sailors, and the hot dog becomes a major part of the local diet. Autumn is similarly wonderful, balancing the colors of New England with the gradual shifting of the maritime climate. Winter is moderated by Portsmouth's proximity to the sea.

Living
The influx of urbanites seeking a way to live far enough from Boston so they wouldn't feel the need to escape the suburbs on weekends have upped real estate prices in the Portsmouth area far past its reasonable value. But in recent years, the cost of living has fallen back into a more earthbound pattern, with a 3-bedroon home readily available in the $110,000 range. Public schools, while experiencing budget cut backs, are still very strong in the area, which is loaded with small towns and tree-lined residential neighborhoods.

With the New Hampshire seacoast offering many arts and cultural (not to mention recreational) opportunities during its warmer months, local residents have to work hard to get their fill of festivals, art fairs, musical events, and beach time. Once winter's darkness and windy chill sets in, people in this part of the state turn to local theater and arts institutions for a creative life—or they just drive to Boston for a peek at museums, galleries, theaters, and the like.

Out On the Town
Seafood restaurants are something of an institution around Portsmouth, and on most weeknights, the family-style places down by the waterfronts are filled with local residents cracking lobster. Portsmouth itself is an historic community with an architectural legacy extending through several centuries—it's loaded with great places to eat, drink, and be merry. The town has a wide selection of ethnic restaurants, and is especially strong in regard to Italian dining spots (be sure to check Emilio's). The Rusty Hammer and Poco Diablo's are favorite places for lunch or meeting friends for drinks. If it's time for tofu burgers, local vegetarians head over to the Stockpot. As is the case in other parts of New Hampshire, this corner of the coast is loaded with community theaters and repertory troupes. The area's leading place for live theater is the Seacoast Repertory Company in Portsmouth. Look for blues, jazz, and folk music at the Press Room and at Rosa's Restaurant.

Economic Impact of the Arts

Since experiencing an economic downturn a few years ago, this area was forced to do an exhaustive evaluation of how to resurrect itself. Interestingly, the arts was seen as one of the more important aspects of community life, holding long range economic promise. Since then, Portsmouth business, arts, and tourism organizations have worked in synch to find ways to bring money-spending tourists back into town.

Local Arts Agency

Seacoast Arts and Cultural Allliance, P.O. Box 835, Portsmouth, NH 03802, (603) 433-8634. Publishes the *SACA Newsletter*.

"We're the umbrella organization for the region's many arts groups," says past president Janet Scarponi. "It's an attempt to pool resources—to keep focused on the larger question of how to promote the area's arts and cultural programs without any overlap. We put together conferences on things like grant-writing and legal issues for artists, work with municipal government to develop plans for art districts and artist studio spaces, coordinate community-wide events placing art in downtown storefronts, and publish an artist and arts organization directory."

Galleries and Arts Festivals

Portsmouth's twisting, cobblestone streets are home to 16 art galleries and craft stores. The most popular local art style is coastal scenes from the region, followed by traditional crafts based on the area's maritime heritage. Interestingly, Portsmouth is also a music center, serving as the home base and recording center for dozens of folk and traditional musicians. The year's most popular arts event takes place during the last weekend in July, when a large group of painters and craftspeople fill Prescott Park for its annual arts festival. Market Square Weekend in mid-June and the Portsmouth Jazz Festival in late June, are two other popular get togethers for the region's arts professionals.

What the Artist Says

Ceramicist Peter Lochtefeld, who creates functional, high-fire ceramics from white stoneware clay, says the local arts and craft market is surprisingly strong. "Most of the people I work with at the Button Factory (a complex of artist studios) are able to do well with the galleries and stores in town, but they're also aware of the need to sell 50 percent or more of their work outside Portsmouth. Personally, I have galleries in Nantucket and Boston, and occasionally do an art fair somewhere close by. Here, the arts community has a real sense of cooperation, which reflects the small size of the town. We're informal, neighborly, and enjoy each other's company."

Tom Daly, a songwriter and recording studio owner, says that Portsmouth is a good place for musicians seeking a place to make a living. "We've got a lot of professionals who gig around the area and get into their own independent album projects. There are lots of jazz groups here, some traditional country music, and a number of performing songwriters who are inspired by the history of the area. I like it here because people are honest and they do what they say they're going to do. All we need is people with more money to spend!"

Cape May, New Jersey

Location
The southernmost point in New Jersey, Cape May (pop. 5,000) is in an environment more similar to the Outer Banks of North Carolina than the seacoast of the Northeast. It's a 3-hour drive from Cape May to New York, but Washington, D.C. is closer, if you correctly time the ferry ride across the Delaware Bay.

Climate
Winter isn't unknown in this part of the state, and a heavy snowfall or two can be counted upon each year. Warmed by ocean currents and semi-tropical breezes pushing in from the South Atlantic, Cape May's spring arrives early—a precursor to what's always a busy and somewhat crowded summer tourist season. Summer temperatures are generally warmer by a few degrees compared to nearby areas, yet moderated by ocean breezes.

Living
Outside the summer tourist season, Cape May enjoys a wonderful slice of the American pie, slipping into its workaday life as a small community filled with historic, oceanfront homes in a region characterized by a succession of small towns. Because of its desirable location, real estate in Cape May is somewhat pricey, with the average 3-bedroom residence selling for $150,000. Plenty of rental housing is available.

Off-season, Cape May becomes a most livable small community, with parks, a small zoo, and endless miles of ocean views. Summer brings out the beachtime best in this area, especially for ocean fishing of the striped bass variety.

Out On the Town
A busy summer vacation town, Cape May comes into full bloom each Memorial Day and stays in its hectic, mid-year mode until late August. The community may lack a vegetarian restaurant, but Wildwood is an Asian dinner spot popular with the tastes of ethnic restaurant seekers. For real nightlife, local residents make the 50-minute drive up the coast to Atlantic City, but if you're seeking a spot for lunch or a place to meet friends, Season Restaurant is a local favorite.

Economic Impact of the Arts
There are three good reasons to visit this area: to enjoy its splendid beaches, to catch the ferry across Delaware Bay to Lewes, Delaware, and to explore its arts scene. Long a favorite of painters, actors, and musicians who preferred summering here as opposed to hunkering down in New York, Trenton, or Philadelphia, the Cape May area has a history of being the sort of area artists have turned into a vibrant, if temporary, center of creative thought and pursuits. In recent years, the seasonal nature of Cape May's arts scene has moderated, with an active local theater community, a regular slate of music performances, and several art galleries staying

very much alive from the time tourists leave until school kids break for vacation. The way things are going, Cape May's prospects for developing into a strong, year-round arts center look good.

Local Arts Agency
Cape May Culture & Heritage Department, 4 Moore Road, Cape May, NJ 08210, (609) 465-1005.

"In this part of the state there are organizations in each town along the coast, which are doing something specific for their community," says Jennie Ayres, director of this county agency. "Our focus is as an organizational services group—we put on symphony performances and are in the planning stages of doing our first big, regional arts fair—so whenever we program an event it's for the entire county. In Cape May and Ocean City (30 miles north) there's a great deal of community-wide support for the arts, and in both towns businesses work with the art groups to improve tourism. The health of the arts economy in this area could improve if the smaller municipalities became more conscious and supportive of what's possible through the arts."

Galleries and Arts Festivals
While there are several art galleries in Cape May, the surrounding county region is also well-represented, selling paintings and crafts by local and regional artists. As you would expect in a town with a strong summer tourist trade based on its oceanfront attributes, the streets of Cape May are loaded with artists standing by their easels, painting the boardwalks, beaches, and sea gulls. Toward the end of summer, the area throws its largest arts bash of the year, the Wings & Water Festival in nearby Stone Harbor.

What the Artist Says
Edward Scattergood, a landscape painter who has made his home in Cape May since 1972, says that local sales of art are surprisingly good. "There are a couple of galleries that have clients who buy originals, and the print exhibitions at the Art League are another good way for artists to find buyers, but like any tourist town, the biggest volume of sales are in the print area. If you want to do well from the standpoint of sales, you've got to get into what I call 'Victorian art,' which is paintings of Cape May homes, the flowers in people's yards, and folks walking on the beach.

"Newer families are moving in, and they seem to be the most interested in what the local artists are doing. Of course, the artists who can stand out in the sun and do their work in public also do very well, as do the artists selling at the street fairs during the summer. Cape May has a short season, but if you have a way with capturing the objective sense of what goes on in front of you, and get the area's wonderful natural light into your paintings, then you'll do quite well."

Clinton, New Jersey

Location

An hour's drive from both New York and Philadelphia, Clinton (pop. 3,000) is in a part of western New Jersey characterized by wooded, rolling hillsides and a feeling of being out in the country.

Climate

Each of the four seasons is given center stage in this part of the country, with springtime always coming in as a florid wonder leading into a humid, moderately hot summer. This part of the state receives considerably more snowfall than do other areas, and it's not unusual for winter to be somewhat of an ordeal.

Living

Close to both the natural wonders of the Delaware Water Gap and the metropolitan delights of New York, local residents are never at a loss for finding something to do on a three-day weekend. There's good fishing and fresh water sailing at Round Valley State Park, and the Atlantic Beaches around Asbury Park are within easy reach. Because it's so close to population centers, 3-bedroom homes in the Clinton area can easily sell for $225,000 and more, depending on the sort of property you need. But for that price, you'll be living in an area where the streets are safe, neighbors participate in community politics, and the fly fishing on local streams can be downright outrageous.

Out On the Town

Given how small it is, it's no surprise that Clinton is short on ethnic and vegetarian dining options. You can find basic Chinese just about anywhere, and like the rest of New Jersey, great Italian places abound, but local residents are good-spirited about driving to New Hope or Allentown (both in neighboring Pennsylvania) for anything stretching the culinary imagination. The local nightspot is a country and western dance hall called Yellow Rose, while one of the favorite places for lunch is the Towne Restaurant. Culturally aware, this area has a number of local theater groups and music organizations. Folk music is also very popular, as is the cultural programming available through nearby Princeton University.

Economic Impact of the Arts

Close enough to metropolitan galleries to be within an easy drive for deliveries of art, meetings with collectors, etc., Clinton has for a number of years been a favorite retreat of arts professionals. It's more of a living and working place—a sort of town that matters much to cultural tourists—with a Main Street that has everything from a pharmacy to a shoe repair shop. The center of Clinton's art community is the Hunterdon Art Center, a multi-use facility that serves many aspects of the town's cultural needs.

Local Arts Agency

Hunterdon Art Center, 7 Lower Center Street, Clinton, NJ 08809, (908) 735-8415. Publishes the newsletter *Sketches*.

"Our building is part of the old Victorian-era mill town that's been preserved from Clinton's past. We're in a three-story, restored stone gristmill that was originally built in the mid-1800s," says center director Ellen Siegel. "Our crafts shop has a resident artist program that brings someone new in every month or so, we've got a full schedule of arts classes for children and adults, and exhibition spaces on all three floors (connected by an elevator). For artists in this area, the most popular medium is painting. I'd estimate there are more than a hundred artists living in the area, and most are doing life drawings and landscapes. We also see a lot of collage work and printmaking. Studio spaces are located mostly within artists' homes."

Galleries and Arts Festivals

The arts center serves as Clinton's only exhibition space for original art work, according to Ellen Siegel. "The first floor gallery has young artists, mostly school kids; the second floor has regional artists; and the third floor gallery has our main exhibition space featuring shows by national and international artists in areas such as surrealism, outsider art, fine crafts, figurative painting, and Japanese papermaking. The shows are planned by a panel of local artists working with a part-time curator." The year's most popular arts event takes place during the summer months, when Main Street closes for the Children's Arts Festival and the business district is filled with performers and crafts booths. There are several professional crafts fairs in Flemington throughout the summer.

What the Artist Says

Nancy Sylvia, a painter of oil-on-canvas landscapes, finds Clinton to be a good market for her work. "I've always done well by selling to the businesses and corporations in the area. My collectors tend to be from this part of the country, especially here in New Jersey, so when they find my work in a gallery they can recognize what it's about. I consider Clinton to be an affluent area, a place that's attracting people with the resources to buy and collect art. My work is strongly influenced by the Delaware River and the soft landscape of this part of the state.

"Hunterdon Center is a wonderful facility, but here people are concerned about the way it will be hurt by state budget cutbacks. The levels of funding are too cyclical. If more funding were channeled into the arts, I think you'd see some incredible things start to happen around here. The artists who live here have connections to all the major arts markets."

Dixon, New Mexico

Location
Wedged into a wide spot along the Rio Grande Valley, about midway between Santa Fe and Taos, the 1,000 residents of Dixon live a bucolic existence that's a throwback to New Mexico of the 1950s.

Climate
Hemmed in by steep canyon walls on one end and opening out into farms and orchards on the other, the best thing that can be said about Dixon's high-mountain valley climate is that it's a creature of its own making. Deep winter snows are not uncommon in Dixon, courtesy of its surrounding Sangre de Cristo mountain range. Summer tends to be a bit cooler than those in nearby Española and Santa Fe, and autumn's characteristically early arrival heralds the start of the community's apple harvest.

Living
Considered to be a more rural and affordable alternative to northern New Mexico's tourist-conscious communities, Dixon offers small town living in a pastoral, if somewhat shabby, setting. Funny thing about this part of New Mexico (and others) is that its adobe homes (of mud and straw construction) need constant upkeep, from patching their flat roofs to plastering their fractured exterior walls. Still, people are willing to shell out $120,000 for a 3-bedroom home in Dixon.

School services are minimal, with high schoolers bused to Española. But on the recreational scale, Dixon rates mightily. Its easy access to the Rio Grande River's stretches of challenging white water makes this a hotbed of river runners from mid-April through June. Ski areas in Taos and Santa Fe are practically at the town's doorstep, and there are ancient Anasazi Indian civilization areas stretching out in nearly every direction, not to mention many small communities inhabited for hundreds of years by New Mexico's present-day descendents of Spanish colonist settlers and conquistadores.

Out On the Town
New Mexico's finest micro-brewery is the one run by Preston and Sandy Cox a few miles away at Embudo Station, a speck on the road map, but nonetheless the region's only restaurant or bar with a waterfront. The one here has a view of the Rio Grande as it rushes south toward the Gulf of Mexico (a somewhat scary thought, but regardless, it all starts right here in northern New Mexico and southern Colorado). Embudo Station is open from Easter through Thanksgiving, when its two owners fly south and turn into sea gulls for a few months. Ethnic foods from Asia, Europe, and even Africa are readily available in Taos or Santa Fe, but most visitors consider the regionalized ethnicity of northern New Mexico cuisine to be an exotic creature in its own right, and need go no further than Española for a taste of a different culture. However, if you're in Dixon and need a burger, feel free to join the locals at one of the four outdoor tables at LovatoBurger, and be sure to ask for lots of green chile.

Economic Impact of the Arts

This part of the state has traditionally been home to many talented folk artists—so talented, in fact, that it's not at all unusual to run into a Hispanic family whose parents, grandparents, or maybe both, have their work included in one of the Smithsonian Institution's museum collections. The area's most prominent traditional art forms are Rio Grande-style rug weaving, colcha embroidery, silversmithing, and the school of religious woodcarving pursued by craftsmen known as Santeros. In the past several years, a number of non-Hispanic artists have moved into the area, to take advantage of the community's proximity to the vibrant arts markets in Taos and Santa Fe, while also enjoying the rural lifestyle.

Local Arts Agency

There is no local arts agency in Dixon. Still an arts community in an early stage of development, the emphasis is on smoothing out any rough edges that may pop up between the town's traditional residents and its more recent arrivals. The good news is that so far, everything seems to be working, and it's to the credit of the town's newer residents that they've made, both individually and collectively, the effort to bring all of Dixon's artists a fair share of the economic benefits that flow through the arts economy. With continued effort and economic success, this town could turn into one of the West's most exemplary small art community success stories.

Galleries and Arts Festivals

So far, one cooperative gallery selling an eclectic mix of traditional and contemporary art works has opened in Dixon on a part-time basis, but the biggest arts impact felt here is in October, when the community organizes its annual open studio tour. A wildly popular event that draws thousands of visitors from as far away as Utah and Oklahoma, the open studio tour features somewhere in the neighborhood of 50 artists selling and exhibiting their art work in their home studios. It's a warm, fun-filled community event, well worth planning a trip around.

What the Artist Says

Gayle Fulwyler Smith, a realist/expressionist painter whose work is sold in galleries in four states, says Dixon's attraction is its artists. "In Dixon, you get the feeling that people honor the field of work you're in—there's serious support among the artists, and they really work hard to organize the studio tour. This is a traditional, Hispanic community and it doesn't need to become a popular place. Those of us who live here have come because it's sleepy and off the main highway. The biggest issue in town right now concerns the integrity of the community's ditch irrigation system which is hundreds of years old, yet still functioning as an important component of the area's agricultural economy—that's what I mean by traditional."

Las Vegas, New Mexico

Location
Plopped down at the edge of the Great Plains, where the eastern flank of the Rocky Mountains takes a sharp turn west before petering out somewhere south of Albuquerque, Las Vegas is a community (of 15,000) in northeastern New Mexico that looks as if it stepped right out of the pages of an 1800s guidebook.

Climate
Different from other parts of New Mexico in that it's often absurdly windy here on the edge of the Great Plains, Las Vegas has weather more like Denver's than Albuquerque's. The transition seasons of spring and fall tend to zoom past like a rush hour freight train, but Las Vegas usually gets an extended period when winter's grip alternates with blasts of warm air spilling over the Sangre de Cristo Mountains, resulting in the onset of a hot, dry summer.

Living
Once an important commercial center with fast rail service into the Midwestern cities, Las Vegas has lots of housing and commercial buildings left over from the years its economy boomed. Today, it's attracting an increasing number of artists who are feeling priced out of the Santa Fe area or turned off by the glitzy group of New York and California newcomers who have turned that city into a parody of itself.

Las Vegas has a number of large city parks, a golf course, a four-year college, and easy access into some of the West's best hunting and fishing grounds (Storrie Lake is a favorite). Schools could use some improvement (a common New Mexico lament), but with a 3-bedroom home selling in the neighborhood of $60,000, most artists with young children simply turn to home schooling.

Out On the Town
Nobody complains about the prices in local restaurants, because unlike Santa Fe, where suckers are reeled in for the privilege of paying $22.50 for a plate of black beans and a glorified chile relleno, any restaurant that tried to do that in Las Vegas would be hooted out of town. Las Vegas is been blessed with Pulcini's, a genuine, first-rate Italian restaurant in the classic east coast style, so don't hassle anyone in town about Thai restaurants (just go to Santa Fe and you'll find several). Here, artists love to hang out, drink coffee, and flip through the art book section at Bridge Street Books. But if it's breakfast or lunch you're seeking, the answer is at the Spic and Span.

Things are refreshingly inexpensive and unpretentious here, and that applies to the great art work created by Las Vegas's talented fine arts community. The theater department at New Mexico Highlands University stages an active slate of dramatic productions throughout the school year, and also presents a strong program of recitals, jazz performances, and chamber music events.

Economic Impact of the Arts

Las Vegas's arts community suffered a severe setback recently when its nearly-completed performing and visual arts center was destroyed by fire. Now, the several arts organizations that once thought they would be sharing space in their renovated, downtown building have scattered to the four corners of Las Vegas, attempting to regroup. On the other hand, things have never been better for the town's commercial galleries. There's much hope that plans for an arts center will be redrawn, money will be found to fund the project, and the town's arts community will be able to move ahead as originally planned.

Local Arts Agency

Las Vegas Arts Council, P.O. Box 2603, Las Vegas, NM 87701, (505) 425-1085.

"In the past, the town's galleries have tended to come and go, so there hasn't been an opportunity to form a strong bond between the downtown business community and the artists or galleries," says council director Cindy Montoya. "We have an orientation toward both the performing and visual arts, and we're very strong in presenting specifically targeted educational programs aimed at helping artists, writers, actors, and musicians find ways to advance their careers. We present programs on how to write a good resume, put together a strong portfolio, and target art galleries and art fairs. Our population is growing, and if the people relocating from the East and West Coasts start buying the work of local artists, it will be a very positive development. Las Vegas needs to support the families who have lived here for many generations—it would be wonderful if these people didn't have to struggle so hard to get by."

Galleries and Arts Festivals

Las Vegas has eight commercial art galleries and an occasional nonprofit exhibition space at the local college. The year's most popular arts event is the People's Fair, a weekend-long affair the last weekend in August at Carnegie Park.

What the Artist Says

Janet Stein-Romero, a printmaker and painter whose work is sold at several galleries in the state, coordinates a state-funded artist-in-residence program at four sites in the region. "Las Vegas is the kind of place where the dream can still come true," she says, "Artists want that small-town environment and something affordable. They're turned off by the Santa Fe mystique thing . . . that's over."

Paula Geisler, a sculptor and gallery owner, says that the town's arts awareness needs to expand. "The traditional landscape painters and folk artists have had their way here for years, and it's come at the expense of many contemporary artists who are still seen as outsiders. I like it here because it has the energy of the Wild West—we get the good, the bad, and the ugly. It's one of the Southwest's best-kept secrets."

Ruidoso, New Mexico

Location
Would you believe there's a ski area within a 2-hour drive of Ciudad Juarez, Mexico? Yep, there sure is, and it's right outside the southern New Mexico mountain town of Ruidoso. The Sierra Blanca range includes not only Ruidoso (pop. 5,000) and Ski Apache (on Mescalero Apache lands), but also the 12,000-foot peak of Mt. Sierra Blanca.

Climate
For decades, the Ruidoso area has been a refuge of cool summer relief for desert-dwelling Texans and New Mexicans. Afternoon thundershowers are an almost daily occurrence from July 4th through Labor Day, giving this area a lush carpet of pine forests and alfalfa fields. Autumn is brief, but spectacular. Spring comes in very subtly, with summer arriving several weeks prior to its arrival in Santa Fe and Taos.

Living
Set up like a vacation paradise, Ruidoso is a community wrapped around the bowl of an alpine valley—there are views galore and recreational opportunities abound. Down the road there's a thoroughbred racetrack, and there are lakes for water skiing, mountain trails for horseback riding, and a winter sports scene that's a blast (if somewhat brief). Three-bedroom homes sell in the neighborhood of $90,000. Ruidoso is a safe, somewhat conservative community with lots of retirees, and lots of opportunities to enjoy the outdoors.

Out On the Town
There are a couple of good reasons to take a close look at Ruidoso's dining and night life. First, there's a thoroughbred race track in town, and where you find gamblers, you'll find lots of opportunities for late night fun. Second, this is a vacation area, a place where Texans, Oklahomans, and New Mexicans have been coming for years expecting to have a good time. Catch a great meal during racing season at the Turf Club, and if it's lunch you're after, try the Texas Club. Nighttime at the Winner's Circle usually entails a good deal of fun, but there are lots of smaller, country and western honky-tonks scattered throughout Ruidoso. The best burger in town is at Mr. Burger, but if you're not a meat eater, Ruidoso could be somewhat problematic in regard to dining out. Try going Chinese. The Ruidoso Little Theater stages plays year-round in its facility, and there are occasional recitals and chamber performances programmed by the Community Concert Association.

Economic Impact of the Arts
While the community's arts scene was once mostly geared toward western realism, the past couple of years have seen an increasing interest both in regional landscapes and contemporary art work—two developments tied into the expansion of the town's gallery scene. There isn't yet the sort of

reputation for local art in Ruidoso that there is in Santa Fe, but as more artists start moving into the area (especially with the sculptural arts community that's starting to take shape) that's going to change.

Local Arts Agency

Ruidoso's greatest drawback is the lack of organization amongst its galleries and artists, perhaps due in part to a certain pride local artists and gallery owners take in being individualstic rather than joiners. In any case, the bottom line in a town like Ruidoso is that galleries and artists are frequently dealt hands from the bottom of the political deck. The failure to organize not only hurts the arts education propsects for local children, but robs Ruidoso of the opportunity to seriously address economic issues of concern to the arts community.

Galleries and Arts Festivals

Reflecting both the concentration of local artists in Ruidoso and the traditional interest tourists have had for the area's arts, there are 17 art galleries and fine craft stores in town . . . one of the highest concentrations to be found anywhere. An improvement in this community would be the establishment of an arts center that could be used for art classes, lectures by professional artists, children's classroom space, performing arts studios, and a nonprofit exhibition area for the town's (if not the state's) many fine artists. The year's busiest tourist season falls between July and October, and Ruidoso's most popular arts bash is the Ruidoso Arts Festival, held during the last weekend in July, attracting nearly 125 exhibiting artists and craftspeople.

What the Artist Says

Tom Knapp, a sculptor of wildlife forms, points to the region's natural beauty as a primary inducement to artists moving in. "In a way we get the best of both worlds: a relaxing, unspoiled environment in the Hondo Valley, and tourists coming in from San Antonio, Dallas, Tulsa, and El Paso. We're getting to be better known as an arts town, and I say the more artists who move in here the merrier. I'd like to see more shows and art fairs—it would help some artists out with their income. Still, anyone moving here had better have their galleries set up before they get into town—sales are good here, but not enough to survive on."

Teri Sodd, a pastels painter and gallery owner, would like to see more local organization. "It would be wonderful if the business community could work with the artists and galleries to have some sort of joint council—a group that would work together to organize art shows and get the collectors coming in more frequently. The opening receptions at galleries are about the only chance the artists have to see and visit with each other as a group. Right now it's our schools that could use the artists' help."

Silver City, New Mexico

Location

Along the Black Range foothills of New Mexico's Mogollon Mountains, about halfway between El Paso and Tucson, Silver City's 11,000 residents live in high-altitude bliss, roughly a 2-hour drive to the closest shopping mall in Las Cruces.

Climate

Moderated by its mountain setting, Silver City's climate isn't as hot and dry as one would expect to find in a western community that's further south than Phoenix and Dallas. Winter is cold enough to bring occasional snows, while summertime is cool enough to attract many second-home owners from the lower elevation cities in Arizona's broiling desert. Autumn is particularly spectacular in this region, bringing in a strong tourist trade for the colorful foliage and annual apple harvest festivals.

Living

Still very affordable, Silver City is attracting two types of newcomers: retirees who build small homes in outlying areas or drag in a prefab residence-on-wheels, and artists who are moving in from big cities on the coasts as well as places like Bisbee and Santa Fe, looking to escape the tide of California refugees. The artists tend to live in one of the town's neighborhoods, and many are beginning to open galleries or other stores.

An average 3-bedroom home in an older neighborhood sells in the range of $60,000, while a new place on the outskirts of town runs as high as $90,000. Silver City is home to Western New Mexico University, a college with an active fine arts program and a performing arts auditorium. The town is able to benefit from the school's arts program, both in terms of visual arts exhibitions held occasionally on campus, and for its more comprehensive programming in the areas of film and performance, such as theater and classical music.

A historic mining town, Silver City's largest employer is still the Phelps Dodge Corporation. Local outdoor pursuits include fishing at Lake Roberts, sailing at Elephant Butte Reservoir, visiting the ancient civilization sites left by the Mimbreno Indians, and driving into Tucson for Grateful Dead shows at the University of Arizona.

Out On the Town

Reflecting more of its good-old-boy past than its budding art community future, Silver City's dining scene nonetheless changing to adjust to the times. It's the kind of place where Pizza Hut is considered by some locals a vegetarian restaurant and chop suey is the most popular dish at the local Chinese restaurant. Artist types, and a good mix of the town's residents, tend to congregate down at the Corner Cafe, which serves the best burger and breakfast in these parts. Lunch and dinner at the Black Cactus Cafe (great name!) are popular with the town's visitors and artists who appreciate innovative cuisine. Nighttime action in Silver City tends to split up according to music preferences: If boot scootin' and two-steppin' are your pleasure, the place to be found is the Drifter Lounge, but if your passions run more toward Bob Seeger and Concrete Blonde, head for the Buffalo Bar. Look for occasional theater and musical performances at the college's fine arts auditorium.

Economic Impact of the Arts

Up until a few of years ago, there was little in Silver City that could have seriously been considered an art gallery. Now, however, there are nine such establishments and more are rumored to be on the way. What the town really needs is an arts center like dynamic local and state government bodies have funded in many of the states surrounding New Mexico, which could lead to a solidifying of the community's arts scene (and subsequently result in boosting the economic position of the arts and concurrent job opportunities for locals). It remains to be seen whether local politicians will have the foresight to plan for the future, or whether they'll slide back into figuring out innovative ways to fund questionable highway construction projects and protect ranching and mining interests.

Local Arts Agency

Mimbres Region Arts Council, P.O. Box 1830, Silver City, NM 88062, (505) 538-2505.

"We're a multi-disciplinary group," says council director Manuel Fred Barraza, "with an emphasis on performances and staging visual arts programs. One of our goals is to improve the ways we can work with local schools. The kids here get little opportunity to do art projects and there's hardly any instruction below the high school level. We have some artists going into the schools to do art workshops, but funding is so limited the programs we put together are uneven."

Galleries and Arts Festivals

Once the artists started moving into Silver City, the town began shaking its image as a dusty place where miners fell in and out of employment, and started looking more attractive to cultural tourists. The artists, most of whom arrived with their careers already well under way, began opening galleries, and that lured other businesses (such as craft stores and frame shops) into setting up shop. Those who had seen Bisbee and Santa Fe grow into odd versions of their former selves seem determined not to allow the same thing to happen to Silver City. One area that needs to be immediately addressed is Silver City's lack of a community-wide arts festival. There once was such an event, but petty bickering amongst some artists led to the suspension of what had been a popular summer weekend event. It's time for the new and old talent in town to show what organizing an event that benefits the whole community is all about.

What the Artist Says

Boleslaw Peplowski, a painter and gallery owner whose Silver City gallery exhibits the work of national artists working in contemporary imagery, says he's been surprised by the reaction to his gallery. "People here want to see paintings other than what's usually considered to be gallery art in this part of the country. The local artists have a professional point of view and an eclectic approach to their own art. There's artistic freedom and an encouragement for younger artists—it's a harmonious, bi-cultural community that feels very cohesive. My buyers come in from El Paso, Tucson, and Albuquerque. You'd be surprised at the kinds of people who are taking a close look at Silver City."

Truth or Consequences, New Mexico

Location
As the state with the least amount of surface water, New Mexico isn't exactly a beachcomber's paradise. Unless, that is, you're talking about the landlocked wonder of Elephant Butte Lake, a 10-mile stretch of warm, Rio Grande River that's backed up behind an enormous dam. Truth or Consequences, a town of 5,500 residents, sits below the dam overlooking the river. From here, it's more than a 2-hour drive to Albuquerque.

Climate
Light touches of winter chill ride in every now and again on stiff winds, giving Truth or Consequences a mild semblance of winter, but almost never threatening the town's bucolic, edge-of-the-desert ambiance. Even though it has easy access to the state's only respectable water recreation area, the town itself lacks vegetation, so autumn is barely perceptible. Summer is uniformly hot and dry.

Living
Named after a 1950s television game show, Truth or Consequences was once called Hot Springs, a reference to the many mineral spring-fed bath houses and ponds that once were the town's premier tourist attraction. Unfortunately, after having changed its name, the popularity of the bath house business dried up, so to speak, as the town's best free advertising vehicle (its name) was obliterated. Which explains why quite a few local residents are seriously considering the idea of changing the town's name back to Hot Springs (which is the name still used by the local high school).

What Truth or Consequences has going for it these days is its wonderfully mild winter climate and ridiculously low real estate prices: A 3-bedroom home sells somewhere in the range of $30,000. For that, you buy into a well-respected local school system, instant access to a large body of water, and a stretch of local bath houses that are both clean and cheap.

Anyone tiring of the town during winter months makes the looping, 2-hour drive to Ruidoso's ski area, or goes to Cuidad Juarez, Mexico, for some cross-border fun. Fishing on the lake is legendarily great, and the town's hunters have but a short drive to the east slopes of the Mimbres Mountains in nearby Hillsboro.

Out On the Town
As isolated as it is, Truth or Consequences has a surprising number of good restaurants and bars, most of which are a result of its strong summer tourism business from the lake. Of course, there are limits to the attractiveness of the bar scene, and anyone with the desire to catch a movie or take in a play (not to mention NCAA basketball) is obligated to make the hour-long drive south to Las Cruces, home of New Mexico State University and a bonanza of loose, wild college bars serving slightly deranged individuals of all ages. Of course, for those who have yet to experience the won-

derful pleasure of keeping a T or C bar stool occupied for several hours, there's always the Pine Knot Bar—a place that's both friendly and full of locals (definitely a rarity in New Mexico). The only burger place worth stopping in at is Big-A-Burger, and don't even think about finding ethnic or vegetarian food. But don't miss Planet Pizza, which is where all the cool people go, and the Turtleback Grill, an outpost of urbanesque chic.

What the Artist Says

Susan Reynolds, a painter and ceramicist, says the reason artists are moving to Truth or Consequences is twofold. "They want to live in a little town where nobody is going to bother them, and they want to be able to afford living and studio space. I own the only fine art gallery in town, and I'm always surprised at the number of European and Japanese tourists who come here—it's not like we have anything to attract them, so I guess it's just the idea of visiting this weird little place nobody's heard of that brings them in. Twenty New Mexico artists are represented in the gallery. Visitors come in here thinking we'll cut them a deal for the art. Local businesses will put art in their windows or inside restaurants—it's very informal, very small-town. Some artists volunteer to go into the schools to do art instruction, or to help out with special events the teachers need assistance with."

Nick Dodd, a furniture craftsman, works from his own gallery, a business that also carries work by local craftspeople. "Here, artists don't have big pipe dreams about making a lot of money and retiring, but we do have access into some good markets, and we can live here comfortably. There's little stress, little pollution, and you know your neighbors well. As long as you're careful not to step on anyone's toes, you'll do well here. The key is to be versatile—artists have to have their markets well-developed before getting here, and you need to figure out what it takes to make a decent income."

Andover, New York

Location

Upstate New York's Allegany County fits the ideal of small-town, rural living to a T. Picturesque as can be, artists live in a friendly and supportive environment that's just over an hour's drive from both Rochester and Buffalo. Andover, a community of 2,000, has an especially high concentration of artists, but each town in the region is loaded with creative talents.

Climate

Winter weather patterns in this northerly locale fall somewhere between Ice Station Zebra and tolerable. Just put it this way: buy a snowmobile for both fun and transportation (and pray for summer). Autumn brings out hordes of "leafers," a regionally significant tourist population whose pursuit of colorful leaf configurations knows no bounds. Summer is glorious and almost never humid enough to be uncomfortable. Expect to find streams and lakes everywhere, along with many parks and nature preserves.

Living

Here's where you can find the 3-bedroom, two-story home of your dreams—the entire area is filled with classic, wood-frame houses that look as if they were plucked right off a Hollywood set. Best news of all is their astoundingly low cost: $35,000 for a place with a garage, maple trees, and room for a monumentally large garden. Artists who want to keep their work spaces removed from their home quarters can readily find studio or gallery space in the business districts of any small town in the region. And for a clean, street-level space with lots of windows the average monthly rent of $200 seems like a too-good-to-be-true dream, but it's not!

Schools in the area are very good. This is a part of the country that respects its teachers and works hard to make sure its kids have the best possible learning environment. The area is so crime-free that high school pranks are among the authorities' biggest worries. Access to the great outdoors is a simple matter of walking down any street and finding a hiking or bicycling trail leading into the woods. Autumn hunting season provides an important economic boost for the area, and helps keep the deer population manageable.

Out On the Town

You've got to be willing to drive a bit, but once you get over that barrier, you'll find this area loaded with good, affordable restaurants and a surprising variety of ethnic dining options. The nearby college town of Alfred, home of Alfred State University, probably has the widest range of restaurants, with the usual stable of great pizza joints, Greek diners, and coffee houses you expect around a campus. If you're in Wellsville, a great bet for burgers and barbecue is Texas Hot or Karen's Country Kitchen. The South Main Deli has some vegetarian specialties, and the Beef Haus is a favorite for its lounge. For something to do at night, most people in the area head to Alfred, where the college stages regular theater, dance, and musical performances. Gentleman Jim's is a favorite place for dancing.

Economic Impact of the Arts

Alfred's college curriculum includes a specialized and well-funded program in the study of ceramics: a department that's drawn a number of talented artists into the area for teaching positions, many of whom quickly sink their roots into this wonderful region. There's a great deal of respect accorded to artists in all the area's small towns, which is partly due to the local awareness of the economic potential of the arts, and partly due to the general attitude that the arts are an important part of everyday life. Here, artists are perceived as the owners of cottage industries, and as such are given a place at the political round table.

Local Arts Agency

Allegany Arts Association, 84 Schuyler St., Belmont, NY 14806, (716) 268-5078. Publishes the newsletter *Allegany Arts News*.

"One of the best things that could happen to the Allegany County arts community would be getting an arts center—a place that would allow us to do both indoor exhibitions and outdoor performances, as well as holding arts classes," says Association executive director Wilhelmina Allen. "As it is now, we try to hit the entire arts spectrum: We have school children attend things like string quartet performances, we work with the college to get local art exhibitions on campus, and we produce the Art Fair in spring. Artists like living here because it's affordable and you're within a day's drive of all the major markets in the Northeast."

Galleries and Arts Festivals

While most towns in the area have at least one place that does double duty as an art gallery and fine crafts store (Alfred has a few), the real action takes place at artists' studios—places where their entrepreneurial best comes out, and visitors are welcome (pick up a map and artist phone number list at any chamber of commerce office). The year's biggest arts bash is the annual Allegany Artisans Studio Tour, an early November weekend coordinating dozens of open artist studios with gallery shows and a crafts fair. Hope Zaccagni, an Alfred pastels artist, advises tourists to schedule time for late April's Hot Dog Day, a community event where kids and professional artists alike show their work on downtown streets.

What the Artist Says

Stephen Walker, a contemporary jeweler who travels the high-end craft show circuit, says the Allegany County region is underrated. "We've had a loss of medium-size manufacturing in the area, and that's hurt everyone. Our taxes went up and government regulation increased, but the cost of living is still so low that artists want to make this their base. The business community understands what the artists need and it promotes our existence in the area. We're seen as small business incubators. The historic preservation movement was a big help to us in getting the ball rolling. Arts are seen as bringing in fresh dollars from other places, and as providing an environment conducive to making art-related things happen. This is a great place to live if you want to get on with the business of producing your work."

Corning, New York

Location

In upstate New York, about halfway between Albany and Buffalo, the 12,000 residents of Corning live in a rolling, green landscape that's within easy reach of the Finger Lakes region.

Climate

Expect winter, and lots of it. This part of the state may not exactly be in the middle of what's referred to as the "snow belt," but it's close enough not to mistake the December landscape around Corning for any place south of Detroit. Despite this drawback, the region's climate during the rest of the year is delightful. Spring floats in smoothly and causes the hillsides around Corning to bloom into a sea of cherry, apple, and dogwood petals. Summer is moderately warm and nowhere near as humid and sticky as elsewhere in the state's southern reaches. Autumn is glorious by anyone's standards, if somewhat brief.

Living

There aren't all that many people living in this part of the state, which means that uninterrupted stretches of wooded forest lands abound—as do medium-size family farms and a succession of small towns, each of which seems to have its own town square and historic church. While many artists have been attracted to Corning simply because of the strength of the local arts community, others arrived by the more roundabout path of having been affiliated with the town's largest employer, Corning, Incorporated (formerly Corning Glass Works). These artists, including some who are highly educated experts in the technical aspects of glass and ceramics, tend to have blended into the community as fine craftsmen. Those who were not drawn to Corning by opportunities with the company, tend to be the town's painters, textile artists, and sculptors.

Affordable living is a big draw, with an average, 3-bedroom home selling in the neighborhood of $70,000. Schools are uniformly excellent, which is not surprising, considering the high standards that scientists and corporate executives working in the town would likely apply to their own kids' education. A good-sized studio space (on the second story of an historic building in Corning's five-block business district) rents anywhere from $250 to $350 per month.

Out On the Town

Because it's within a 20-minute drive of Elmira, a larger community with a couple of colleges, artists living in Corning have a tendency to drive out of town to find their entertainment, be it movies, theater, or music. One sure-fire place to find an artist or two passing the time is Corning's Book Exchange, the sort of sit-down-and-sip-coffee bookstore most communities would give an arm and a leg for. In keeping with this part of the country's rich heritage of Italian culture, everyone in Corning has their own opinion about where the town's best pizza is served, and more often than not, the likely choice would be Aniello's. The downtown business crowd likes to lunch at T.J. Watson's, which is also a favorite watering hole, and those with a burger urge can get fast relief at the London Underground. For great cuisine in a romantic setting, try the newly-opened Upstate Tuna in Corning. But if you must drive into Elmira, the choice there is Moretti's.

Economic Impact of the Arts

The most wonderful thing about being an artist in Corning is that you're in a place that has an historic appreciation and financial commitment to all the arts. Being an artist, arts administrator, or gallery owner in Corning has its advantages: from the type of civic funding Corning, Incorporated provides for specific arts infrastructure and organization needs in the community to the individual pieces of art bought and collected by the company's arts-savvy executives and technical people.

Local Arts Agency

The ARTS of the Southern Finger Lakes, 1 Baron Steuben Place, #8, Corning, NY 14830, (607) 962-5871.

"We're involved in the performing arts and the visual arts—our mission has no bounds," says council director Kevin Geoghan. "Corning has around 45 cultural organizations that are our members—everything from an art museum to literary programs—and one of the main things we're trying to do is update the region's art facilities. I'd consider the community's support for the arts to be extraordinarily strong. The businesses understand that arts are an important part of this community's life and whenever we need their support, it's there. One area that can use improvement is the approach our local schools take toward the arts. We have artist-in-residency programs and an arts-in-education program, but the teacher-to-student ratio is too high."

Galleries and Arts Festivals

Corning's small, five-block downtown area has three galleries and a nonprofit art exhibition space at the 171 Cedar Arts Center. The quality of work shown in these galleries is very strong . . . a reflection of the seriousness with which local artists regard their careers. The year's biggest arts bash is the Market Street Festival of the Arts, a two-day celebration the third weekend of August in downtown Corning, featuring 125 artist exhibitors and numerous performers.

What the Artist Says

Tom Gardner, a landscape painter and gallery owner, says the local art market is surprisingly good. "I have to keep my pencil sharp and make sure the work in here is affordable, but people are responsive, and do buy art. Artists in Corning have lived in large cities, so they know what it takes to reach out and get their work into people's hands. Our sales are building in two ways: from collectors across the country and from local collectors in Corning. The physical beauty of this area is spectacular. It's an environment that becomes more intimate or more expansive, depending on how you respond to it. Here, artists like to get together and keep themselves entertained. We even organize our own black tie affairs, just keep things in perspective."

Peekskill, New York

Location

A community of 20,000 in the Hudson River Valley, Peekskill is a former industrial town located an hour's drive north of New York City and across the Hudson River from West Point.

Climate

A spectacular autumn, with changes in the nature of the reflective light of the Hudson River, is followed by a somewhat lengthy, bitterly windy winter that is occasionally broken up by stretches of rain and fog. Summer is moderately hot and humid, with some relief offered by winds blowing in off the river. Expect a soft, wonderful spring.

Living

Close enough to Manhattan for many local wage slaves to commute to the city by train, the charm of living in Peekskill lies both in its proximity to and its psychic distance from the hubbub of the metropolis. Until recently, as the town's industrial base slowly deteriorated and died, Peekskill's shabby downtown was never considered to be a serious alternative to city living. But when downtown Peekskill was vacant and run-down, city and regional government authorities started considering the options available to them, and lo and behold, someone hit on the idea of developing the place as a sort of Soho North.

Consultant Ralph DiBart (who in years past had been in charge of New York City's program to promote lower Manhattan as a haven for artists' studios and converted loft living spaces) was brought in to oversee the Peekskill project—and, voilà, Soho North is now a reality.

Today, a renovated 1,000-seat theater serves as the city's performing arts center. There is a rejuvenated downtown district with eight new galleries, a dozen restaurants, an art supply store, a bookstore, and even an authentic Seattle-style coffee bistro. While most artists prefer renting studio space at $200 to $500 per month in the converted downtown industrial buildings and living in one of the town's more ordinary neighborhoods (a 3-bedroom home lists around $175,000), others want to recreate the New York City experience, opting for the retro-urban appeal of both living and working, 1970s-style, in downtown Peekskill. Be sure to bring your leather jackets and Ramones albums. For the privilege of living this bit of the region's nostalgic past, artists pay anywhere from $700 to $1,400 per month for a converted studio and living space.

Out On the Town

One of the country's strongholds of first-rate, unpretentious ethnic restaurants, Peekskill is a town where the artists don't feel starved for affordable culinary inspiration. The Italian restaurants range from basic, wonderful pizza joints to fancier spots serving Northern Italian fare. The Greek and Latin American restaurants are legendary. The best place for coffee and casual conversation is the Bruised Apple Bookstore, and vegetarians find welcoming arms at Offenbacher's and at Jasmine's Marketplace. The burgers are great at Elmer Suds, the Monhegan Diner, and Connolly's Pub (which does double-duty as Peekskill's jazz club). Two-steppers and leg-shakers shimmy on down to the Country Kitchen, and if it's raining cats and dogs, howl on over to Bad Bills Bar. Nobody around here is hurting for things to do at night, either. The Paramount Center for the Arts presents an extremely ambitious and well-attended schedule of events: from documentary and European films and top-name concerts cutting across all musical preferences to national dance companies and outstanding off-off Broadway theater. There's also a range of performance art programs offered at both the Paramount East Performance Space and at the One Station Plaza Performance Space.

Economic Impact of the Arts

The arts, in all forms, have turned Peekskill's economic outlook from moribund to unbridled optimism. It's no exaggeration to say that hundreds of new jobs in this community are in some way dependent upon Peekskill's art-generated economic revival.

Local Arts Agency

Paramount Center for the Arts, 1008 Brown St., Peekskill, NY 10566, (914) 736-9585.

"Everything's in place for Peekskill's emergence as an arts center," says center trustee Andrea Jeffries. "We've got the loft spaces artists need, a river front that's being renovated, and an arts center that's starting to attract the very best names in their fields." Her husband, artist Paul Jeffries, said that not only is the center the town's performing arts focal point, but its visual arts programs and classroom instruction facilities keep it in use year-round. "Arts are seen as having an integral role in the way this community can thrive. As the arts become more commercially viable, the town government, businesses, and schools direct more of their attention to the arts. Everyone around here has become a 'true believer'."

Galleries and Arts Festivals

Indicative of the seriousness with which Peekskill's artists approach their profession, the quality of locally created work exhibited in the town's eight galleries is uniformly high, which explains why the area lures in so many arts-conscious buyers from the nearby metropolis. There are non profit exhibition spaces at both the Paramount Center and at 44 North, a cooperative gallery. While the annual crafts fair in Lindenhurst remains a very popular event, Peekskill's artists have successfully organized a Christmas arts and craft exhibition in a downtown arts space, and are publishing a mail-order catalog of artists' creations. Plans are underway to produce annual arts and music festivals.

What the Artist Says

Jo Ann Brody, a multi-disciplinary artist, enjoys the arts community's cohesiveness. "It seems like what happened took place in the last three years, with artists coming in for various reasons. Then one day we all figured out what was taking shape in Peekskill. Now, we've got a creative intensity and an affordability, which we need to protect. But we also need to continue to develop our reputation. I enjoy the area's music scene—there are serious professionals who play mostly in the city, but find spare moments to do things around here. Here, artists can develop a New York clientele and regional gallery contacts, just by showing locally. We're starting to make sales, and need to keep the art affordable. That's what will keep people coming back here to spend money on art."

Asheville, North Carolina

Location
Unless you've visited Asheville, you'd never believe North Carolina would be the place to find a sophisticated, growing arts community in a university town built on a mountaintop. At 60,000 residents, Asheville is more a small city than a town. And as an arts center, its magnetism and vitality are exceptional.

Climate
This is the part of North Carolina where winter roars in like a lion and hangs on like a pit bull. Local residents have the usual array of four-wheel drive vehicles and cross-country skis found in the high country. Downhill ski areas near Boone are just a short drive away. On the bright side, autumn is so singularly spectacular that for almost the entire month of October the region experiences a near-gridlock from out-of-state tourist "leaf-mobiles." Summer is much cooler and more tolerable than in the rest of the state, while spring is a four-star wonder of dogwood blooms and flowering everythings!

Living
The secret of Asheville's model lifestyle escaped several years ago, and the town is still struggling to keep up with the influx of newcomers. This is the sort of low-crime town where downtown streets are safe to walk at all hours, tree-lined neighborhoods boast parks filled with kids playing baseball, the public golf course is friendly (and it's easy to get a tee time), and community pride is much more than an abstract concept batted about in city council meetings. The local college has a graduate program in education, which means Asheville's schools are full of teachers who utilize the latest ideas and learning concepts in their field. In this overwhelmingly Democratic community, a 3-bedroom home in a quiet neighborhood lists in the $100,000 range. Many residents are able to walk or bicycle to their downtown jobs from Asheville's tidy neighborhoods.

Out On the Town
Sophistication has hit this furthest corner of the Tarheel State, as the first Thai restaurant (Siam Palace) has begun a busy trade in South Asheville. Of course, Asheville has long drawn tourists to its verdant, cool climes, and as a result this town has traditionally been blessed with great places to eat, from pit-cooked barbecue to coq au vin. Two of the town's most popular places to linger over drinks and dinner are Magnolia's and Boston Pizza. The best burger in town, bar none, is the slab of sizzlin' ground beef served at McGuffey's. Vegetarians, and right-minded individuals of all backgrounds, have long made Asheville a favorite stop on the counter-cultural trail, and a pair of eateries, Laughing Seed and Stone Soup, have catered to their special culinary needs. There's even a bit of nightlife, with Be Here Now drawing in an eclectic crowd.

Economic Impact of the Arts

Asheville is attractive to a well-heeled type of tourist, and the community's artists, arts presenters, and galleries have taken their own initiative in providing these individuals (and the many thousands of arts-conscious Asheville residents) with an arts scene as vibrant as any in cities five or ten times its size. From rock concerts that tap into the local student population to string quartet concerts geared to the town's many retirees from large metropolitan areas, there's a whole range of options year-round. The town's visual arts scene is also quite strong, with hundreds of professional artists. Many elect to continue selling their work through out-of-area galleries and live in Asheville because it's an arts-conscious town with a kind soul.

Local Arts Agency

Arts Alliance, P.O. Box 507, Asheville, NC 28802, (704) 258-0710.

"We're working to convince Asheville's business people that artists are serious entrepreneurial types," says executive director Linda Wilkerson. "One program that's gone a long way toward opening this door is the joint effort of the Arts Alliance and the Chamber of Commerce to establish Asheville as the center of "Handmade in America," which acknowledges the community's large number of fine craftspeople, some of the best in their fields. We're a niche organization, one that's trying to bring more cultural resources to bear in Asheville. We do some presenting, but we search for more appropriate agencies to come in and pick up that function. We're housed in a cultural facility (Pack Place) with a 520-seat theater, so Asheville has a first-rate venue for all types of performance arts."

Galleries and Arts Festivals

There are nearly 20 commercial art galleries in Asheville, ranging from a retro-60s clothing store with a cutting-edge gallery in back to a coffeehouse/arthouse with a flair for contemporary work to a serious first-rate gallery run by a New York art dealer. The community has three nonprofit art exhibition spaces and a center for folk arts. Asheville's biggest arts bash is the Belle Chere entertainment fest at the end of July, but First Night on New Year's Eve is also very popular, drawing in 350 artists and craftspeople.

What the Artist Says

Tucker Cooke, painter and chairman of the art department of the University of North Carolina at Asheville, says there's a strong emphasis in local art in the town's galleries. "There are some sophisticated exhibition spaces and not much evidence of trendiness. People are concerned about price, so artists keep their work affordable—those who feel otherwise send their work elsewhere to be sold. Our folk art center has strong exhibitions of work that ranges from functional to kitschy. I see students in the arts department from age 17 to 70, so that tells me the community has a healthy mix of art-interested individuals. There's a lot of diversity in Asheville, and the artists need to decide how they're going to harness that in improving the town's arts awareness."

Penland, North Carolina

Location

Spreading out from the northern flanks of Mt. Mitchell, the 6,600-foot peak that is North Carolina's highest, the Toe Valley (pop. 5,000) has for years successfully attracted a highly talented group of artists and fine craftspeople. The region is slightly less than an hour's drive from Asheville. Penland is one of the valley's larger communities.

Climate

A top reason many artists prefer to live and work in the Toe Valley is its location: mountainous and isolated, offering few distractions. Winter is long and frequently harsh, with snowfall totals that seem more like those found in Vermont rather than 1,000 miles south of the Canadian border. Surrounded by high mountains, the valley's summer climate is more moderate than elsewhere in the region. Autumn is spectacular for several weeks, and spring marks a gradual transition from winter's grip.

Living

The many small towns that comprise the valley's arts community are dotted along several two-lane country roads. It's a very rural area, one where the indigenous residents are somewhat wary of outsiders and take plenty of time getting to know people. Penland, which is the location of one of the country's most respected craft schools, has proved itself to be a welcome bright spot in the regional economy, and the area's residents have been quick to realize that the arts are an expanding sector of the valley's economic base.

There's lots of land around the homes in Toe Valley, and the usual set-up for an artist encompasses a home studio (usually in a separate structure), a few acres of wooded land, and a 3-bedroom, wood frame residence. The average cost: $60,000, which is one of the main reasons artists and craftspeople are compelled to stay in the area after completing their studies at the Penland school, one of the nation's most respected art training centers.

Another reason artists stick around is that over the past several decades the Toe Valley's reputation as a hotbed for artwork that is superb in both the technical and creative senses has spread to galley owners up and down the East Coast. It's not unusual for local artists to be called by metropolitan area gallery owners who are visiting the area and want to stop in at a few studios—which explains why the work of Penland craftspeople and artists can be found from Maine to Miami.

Out On the Town

Sure, there's plenty of great, Carolina-style barbecue (the shredded pork variety that's served with a red pepper and vinegar sauce), and yes, there's even a fish camp or two (casual joints serving fried catfish, flounder, stuffed crab, and popcorn shrimp). Burnsville, the largest town (pop. 1,400) in the valley, has a Chinese restaurant, as does nearby Spruce Pine. Vegetarians need to drive to Asheville for their afternoon snacks, but if it's time for a non-veggie lunch or dinner, try the Cedarcrest Restaurant in Spruce Pine for its burgers. Recently, the valley has successfully attracted a growing community of talented music professionals, and every weekend there's at least one noteworthy act, if not several, gigging at Young's Mountain Music. There's a summer chamber music series in Spruce Pine, an annual folk music festival in Yancey County, outdoor music during summer evenings on the Burnsville town square, and special musical performances produced throughout the year by the valley's arts council. At the Parkway Playhouse in Burnsville, visitors can join local residents for live theater.

Economic Impact of the Arts

Without much in the way of manufacturing employment, the local economy is largely reliant on the many national and state parks surrounding Toe Valley for jobs. Fine crafts and arts, while not large employers, are seen as having a positive ripple effect for the entire region, especially in terms of their capacity to attract fairly well-off visitors to the valley's restaurants and country inns.

Local Arts Agency

Toe River Arts Council, P.O. Box 882, Burnsville, NC 28714, (704) 682-7215. Publishes the newsletter *TRAC Record*.

"Our reach extends into two counties, so our activities vary depending on where we're operating," says council executive director Denise Cook. "One county will ask us for assistance on their recycling program's street signage, and another county will ask us to help with grant proposals for their plans to build an animal welfare facility. We're always glad to pitch in wherever we can, and the artists enjoy their contact with the valley's residents. If an artist chooses to get involved in local government, their views are taken seriously, which is why there are some surprisingly progressive approaches to problem-solving around the valley. Artists are also involved in the education process at local schools. There are lots of volunteer programs and one-on-one instruction taking place inside the studios."

Galleries and Arts Festivals

While many artists regularly receive collectors and gallery owners in the privacy of their studios, there are several commercial galleries in the valley that represent the extremely sophisticated work created by the area's artists and craftspeople. Two nonprofit exhibition spaces at the Toe River Craft Shop and at the Penland School Gallery stage rotating exhibits of art and fine crafts. The year's two largest arts bashes are the Mt. Mitchell Crafts Fair during the first weekend in August, and the fall Celebration of the Arts in Spruce Pine during mid-October.

What the Artist Says

Kate Vogel, a glass artist whose work is represented in many galleries around the country, says that rural lifestyle is the area's big draw. "We're not about fancy cars and dress-up for the galleries. Here, artists like to work in their gardens or go white water canoeing. We help each other as much as we can, and have several local organizations aimed at keeping the arts vibrant and alive. I can pick up the phone and get 20 professional opinions about how to solve problems in my work. We're all delighted when another valley artist starts doing very well. Our summer market is becoming extraordinarily strong . . . it's a phenomenon!"

Washington, North Carolina

Location

The eastern end of North Carolina embraces some of the nation's finest seashore, tidal regions, and water foul sanctuaries. Washington, a historic community of 10,000, was founded along the banks of the Pamlico River and sits in the heart of a fisherman's paradise.

Climate

Summertime can be counted on to deliver a seemingly endless succession of hot and humid days, but the good news is that Washington is within a short jaunt of the Cape Hatteras National Seashore's white sand beaches. Autumn tends to be a bit on the forgettable side, primarily due to the region's dominance of pine forests. Spring starts creeping in around the last week in February, and by late March the entire area is aflame with blossoms on everything rooted into the red, Carolina clay soil. Winter is mild, with insignificant amounts of snow.

Living

Small town life in eastern North Carolina is a luscious step back in time, to the days when neighbors watched out for each other, kids in class called their teachers "ma'am" and "sir," town cops could be engaged in casual talk about the high school basketball team, and senior citizens were respected for what they had achieved during their lives.

North Carolina is a state with one of the nation's most dynamic and well-funded school systems, so education at all levels of the community's schools is exemplary. A 3-bedroom home on several quiet, pine-shaded acres of land runs in the neighborhood of $100,000, slightly more for waterfront property. For an artist, one of the more attractive aspects of this community is its proximity to the larger town of Greenville, which is home to Eastern Carolina University, a large, state-supported university with active departments in both fine arts and literature. The college offers a number of regional artists the opportunity to teach a class or two, or to take classes aimed at improving their own skills.

Out On the Town

With a college town (10,000 students strong) only a 20-minute drive away, residents of Washington have more than just a few places to choose from when it comes time for movies, live theater, classical music, jazz, and dining. Nightlife isn't much of a problem, either, with college bars galore and a wide range of typical, Carolina coast oyster bars like the Riverside in Greenville, one of the country's premier places for frozen mugs of tap beer and ice-cold platters of plump oysters. Washington's favorite place for dinner and drinks is the Riverfront Restaurant, and ethnic food is something folks around here will travel at least to Greenville for, and possibly as far as Raleigh. Washington's arts council produces an active, year-round slate of concerts at the Washington Civic Center, free to local residents.

Economic Impact of the Arts

This is the sort of place where artists and other arts professionals have chosen to blend in with the community, rather than define themselves as a special group. Many are connected with the college, and so their preference is to work quietly when at home, expressing themselves more fully in an academic setting. Others have chosen the natural beauty of the Washington area as the perfect place to create their art, while electing to market it outside the region. The highest profile the Washington arts community achieves is through arts festivals and public musical performances.

Local Arts Agency

Beaufort County Arts Council, P.O. Box 634, Washington, NC 27889, (919) 946-2504.

"When we first started, our orientation was strictly toward the visual arts," says council director Judy Meier Jennette, "but now we're split about 50/50 between programming for the visual and performing arts. We've even started getting involved in literary arts, which is a different emphasis for us. A lot of our energy goes toward cultural programming in our schools. We're aiming to institute artist-in-residency programs using some of the wonderful artists living in the area, and whenever we program a performing arts event we always have the musicians do workshops in the schools. We have a large African American population and work hard at including that community's input into everything we do. Our local governments have an understanding of the economic impact of the arts. We get as much support as we need, including free office space and access to a first-rate civic center."

Galleries and Arts Festivals

While Washington itself does not have a commercial art gallery, it does have a nonprofit exhibition space inside its arts center, located in the town's renovated railroad station. North Carolina is a state with a rich history of traditional craft—everything from woodwork to quilting, furniture making, ceramic dolls, and basketry. The arts council strives to balance its exhibitions between both the contemporary and the traditional arts being created in the Washington area. There's a cooperative art gallery in nearby Orient, and several galleries and craft stores are located in Greenville. The biggest arts bash of the year is the Summer Festival, held during the last weekend in July on Washington's historic waterfront, featuring hundreds of artists, craftspeople, and performers.

What the Artist Says

Sam Wall, a painter and furniture craftsman, says the Washington environment is an important influence for local artists. "It's the marshes, the river, and the light around here that's so inspiring. It just gets you excited about doing work that's able to express the feeling of being around so much water. It's an inexpensive place to live, and very safe. Artists come out for each other's shows, and you run into a lot of artists whenever something happens in Greenville. Many hold down teaching jobs. The galleries you need to get into are in Raleigh, Pinehurst, and Wilmington. We need to stay active in the juried show circuit in order to survive."

Athens, Ohio

Location
Set amidst the bucolic, rolling hills of southeast Ohio, the 22,000 residents of the university town of Athens live on the edge of Wayne National Forest. The closest art museum is in Columbus, an hour's drive northwest.

Climate
Far enough south to duck many of the winter snowstorms that blitz the state from November through March, Athens enjoys one of the longest, loveliest spring seasons anywhere. Autumn tends not to be as colorful as elsewhere in the state, but summer is a long, very warm affair that lasts through early October.

Living
Pretty enough to be the location for several movies set in small-town America, Athens is the home of Ohio University, a state college with a fine journalism program, a large agricultural department, and a school of homeopathic medicine. The community was founded well over a hundred years ago, has cobblestone streets, is divided by the Hocking River, and has an outstanding school system. For decades Athens has been known as a stop on the counter-cultural circuit, and the community's composition reflects an interesting balance of farmers, aging hippies, academicians, students, and businessmen. The average cost of a 3-bedroom home on one of the town's tree-shaded streets is an affordable $70,000, which explains why many professional crafts artists choose to live here and use the town as a base to easily travel to art fairs in the East and Midwest.

Out On the Town
With a college in town to keep things interesting, Athens gets more than its normal share of rock concerts, football Saturdays, and cutting-edge clothing shops. The college can also be counted upon to produce a number of theater and music programs throughout the year. Dining and entertainment options in Columbus are much more diverse than in Athens, but there are still places here to see foreign films, catch a jazz act at a nightclub, and enjoy a night on the town. One of the most popular hangouts (and a sure-fire bet for bumping into an artist or two) is Casà Nueva, but Another Fool's Cafe also ranks high, presenting music in the evening. For years, the famous darts bar, O'Hooley's, has served Ohio University students needing anything from a shoulder to cry on to a hot date. For burgers and shakes, a booth at the Pub will do just fine, while vegetarians head over to the Farmacy for their tofu infusions.

Economic Impact of the Arts
While Athens is certainly attractive to creative individuals, the visible economic impact of the arts community is somewhat subdued, a likely reaction to the overwhelming presence of the town's university and the strength of its student-based economy. Open-minded and progressive in most

ways that artists would find important, it seems that life in Athens is good enough for the arts community to be comfortable with its low local profile.

Local Arts Agency

Dairy Barn Cultural Arts Center, P.O. Box 747, Athens, OH 45701, (614) 592-4981. Publishes the newsletter *Dairy Barn News*.

"Our emphasis is on the visual arts," says center executive director Susan Urano, "with some statewide and national exhibit organizing. Every year we organize a touring quilt exhibition—quilts are an important traditional craft in southeastern Ohio. The university handles the performing arts so well that we only do a musical program twice each year. We're located in an historic landmark: a 1919 dairy barn located right outside of town. There's a great deal of interest from the business community in what we're doing. School children come in all the time to tour our exhibits. We've served the community as a sort of arts museum, but now that the university is building the Kennedy Museum we'll go back to our regular presentations of visual arts exhibitions and arts classes for adults and kids. The area is also getting a new crafts school, which should go a long way toward preserving the region's strong crafts tradition."

Galleries and Arts Festivals

Athens has three galleries selling locally created art and fine crafts, and once the Kennedy Museum is completed there will be two nonprofit exhibition spaces in town—one at the museum, and the other at the Dairy Barn. Being a college town, Athens does not lack for a regular series of arts festivals, some which serve as excuses for wild, uninhibited partying for everyone from frat rats to retired Weathermen radicals. Each September marks the annual Barn Raisin' Festival in downtown Athens. Later in the fall, there is the Foothills Arts and Crafts Festival and the town's annual Halloween madhouse (an occasion that forces cops to block off Athens streets as thousands of college kids pour into town from all directions). The spring music festival on the Athens river front is another crazed blowout.

What the Artist Says

David Hostetler, a contemporary sculptor who owns a gallery in Nantucket, Massachusetts, says Athens is a great place to live. "Here, an artist can own his home, live in a place that's very safe and friendly, and have things like land and independence. Athens is similar to towns like Boulder and Ann Arbor, just done on a smaller scale. We're seeing collectors coming into Athens from all over the East Coast, sort of like they know there's something going on here—a renaissance. It's got great music and a strong feeling of personal support. An artist has to be versatile and hard-working to survive—discipline, and the ability to connect with other people, is important. There are a lot of mature artists who are willing to help the younger ones, but their advice has to be sought out. Nobody here is going to hand you something like that."

Peninsula, Ohio

Location
In the middle of a wooded, national recreation area about halfway between Cleveland and Akron (less than an hour's drive to either city), Peninsula's residents are surrounded on three sides by forests, with the Cuyahoga River cutting through the middle of town.

Climate
Winter sets in for a lengthy spell of freezing temperatures with intermittent snowfalls, and blizzards are a common occurrence in town. There are two nearby ski areas (the Ohio version). With its wooded setting, Peninsula's autumn is a major draw for tourists. Summer is more moderate than elsewhere in the region, with daytime highs rarely pushing into the 90s.

Living
Peninsula is in danger of becoming too enchanted with its own success. Once a rural alternative to life in the not-too-distant cities, in recent years this community has been discovered by the regional travel media—and also by corporate executives commuting into nearby Akron and Cleveland who seek a more desirable place to live. As a result, what was once viewed as eccentric small-town living (i.e., scraggly yards and several inoperative cars parked in a neighbor's backyard) is often deemed unacceptable by upscale newcomers. Prices of 3-bedroom homes have reached the $150,000 range for a stylish Victorian or Greek Revival residence. Peninsula's public library is an 80,000-volume facility with a video library of 2,000 titles. Local recreation includes bicycling on the 19th-century railway path paralleling the Cuyahoga River and swimming in the sandstone quarry on the edge of town.

Out On the Town
A great place to dine, Peninsula has lots of restaurants catering to the appetites of its nearly year-round tourist trade. Fisher's is acclaimed as the best place to spend a rainy afternoon munching down a burger and fries, while the Winking Lizard is another fine spot to catch up on local chit-chat, or even go dancing at night. Close as it is to the city, anyone who desires Thai food or vegetarian fare simply takes the 15-minute drive to a neighboring town. The Blossom Music Center, summer home of the Cleveland Symphony and the site of a packed summer schedule of musical performances, is nearby. The National Park Service stages an ambitious summer music program that covers everything from Irish folk groups to blues bands, and there's usually jazz being played at the local library.

Economic Impact of the Arts
While many of the community's residents are professional artists, writers, actors, and musicians, the town's retail sector is on the verge of being overrun by T-shirt and souvenir shops. Increasingly, the folks running Peninsula's half-dozen quality art galleries and craft stores are feeling sur-

rounded by such transient merchants, but unfortunately, the local business community has never rebelled in an organized manner against this trend and the problem remains unaddressed.

Local Arts Agency

The library serves as an informal arts center, but Peninsula still lacks a local arts agency. With nearly a hundred retail stores, Peninsula is one of those places where the voice of the professional arts community needs to be organized and heard. The local artists, musicians, craftspeople, etc., have started distancing themselves from the town's problems rather than banding together to promote their own interests. Mercantilism's mentality is threatening to turn Peninsula into another Dollywood. Someone needs to turn this town upside down before it's too late.

Galleries and Arts Festivals

The town has a half-dozen galleries and fine crafts stores representing the work of regional artists. True to its sell, sell, sell mindset, the town has yet to dedicate any space to the nonprofit exhibition of work by the many fine talents who live and create in Peninsula, but elect to opt out of the local commercial gallery scene. The year's two largest arts bashes take place during summer—Boston Mills Arts & Craft Festival and the Valley Festival—each of which draws in over a hundred exhibiting artists and craftspeople.

What the Artist Says

Walter Herip, a graphic designer who has lived here for 20 years, says things are quickly changing in town. "Some people would like to see everything gentrified and for everyone who isn't wealthy to leave, but there's a group of us who have lived here a while who are resisting, who want to see the community's diversity maintained, and who want to stabilize our population. The original attraction of Peninsula is still its beauty. The community has a great regard for its artists, and there's a lot of community cooperation on certain activities . . . people don't hold grudges."

Douglas Unger, an artist, craftsman, and arts educator, is an 18-year resident. "It's our eclectic nature as a community of artists that's giving us problems. We're not using our strength as a group. The newer people don't understand artists, and they have a limited understanding of the arts. Even the local schools don't see art as an educational priority. Peninsula's artists get more respect outside the community than they do inside it. Still, it's a great place to raise kids."

Astoria, Oregon

Location

Astoria's 10,000 residents live on the storm-raked northwest tip of Oregon, at the mouth of the Columbia River. The swirling waters of the Columbia are five miles wide at this point, and have historically been a graveyard for ships of all kinds. Astoria is a 90-minute drive from Portland.

Climate

Temperatures are moderated by Pacific Ocean currents, which means that snowfalls of more than an inch or two are rare (but winter ice storms aren't unusual). Spring and autumn have the potential to be quite picturesque, depending upon the lack of what is usually lots of rainfall. Summer is glorious . . . a time when sunlight and warmth break through for days, and sometimes weeks, on end.

Living

If pure air, stormy skies, whitecapped waters, and an old, falling-down seaport sound romantic, then pack your bags and move to Astoria. In the past several years, as the town's fishing and logging industries have fallen onto increasingly difficult times, artists from all over the country have started moving in, snapping up Victorian homes for a mere pittance. Most artists don't concern themselves with selling locally, they just want a fantastic, end-of-the-world sort of place to live . . . and Astoria is it. Yes, there's a decrepit side to Astoria's attraction, but that's more a matter of the lack of repairs and renovations made to the town's commercial and residential structures than a criminal element you'd have to be concerned about.

Here, artists have it very easy . . . studio spaces on the upstairs floors of downtown brick mercantile buildings rent for as little as $75 per month, and a really nice studio can be had for far less than $200 per month. Astoria is also filled with quaint, cobblestone-street neighborhoods. A large, 3-bedroom home sells in the $80,000 range, but there are hundreds of fixer-uppers available for much less than that. The community has two theater companies and a concert hall presenting a year-round program of classical, jazz, and chamber music performances.

Out On the Town

Whatever Astoria lacks in the dining possibilities can easily be found in nearby Cannon Beach and Seaside. As for cultural entertainment, the vibrant arts scene of Portland is within easy reach. Still, the town has started to reflect its influx of creative professionals in the establishment of Ricciardi's Espresso and Gallery, one of those laid-back, quality hangouts that art towns around the country would kill for. From morning till night, this is Astoria's place to see and be seen . . . what an asset! Nighttime fun means staying clear of the bars packed with unemployed loggers, and heading over to the Hong Kong Lounge, home of stiff drinks with colorful parasols and waiters named Tommy. Those with a burger urge can find relief at the Pig'n Pancake. Vegetarians do their grazing down at the Columbian Cafe.

Economic Impact of the Arts

The arts are starting to make an impact on the city's fathers, who have finally given up on the idea of luring another lumber mill, fishing fleet, or auto transmission plant to Astoria. One of the largest local employers is the Job Corps, so you know this is a town in deep economic trouble. The trouble is, though, that the local business community held on far too long to the faint hopes for a revival of the old industrial base Astoria knew best, and has only now started seeing the economic sense in turning to the arts as a way to resurrect the town's economy. If it plays its cards right, Astoria has the potential to turn itself into another Eureka, California, or Port Townsend, Washington.

Local Arts Agency

Columbia Pacific Arts Forum, P.O. Box 586, Seaside, OR 97138, (503) 738-3628.

"Astoria has started getting some performance arts programs, but there's not yet an appropriate space," says Susan Brewer of the Forum. "We've been able to do a lot more with films and visual arts exhibitions in Cannon Beach, but Astoria is just starting. The public schools aren't yet emphasizing the arts in their curriculum, but our approach is to work with certain schools individually. It takes a strong nonprofit group to be able to convince the schools to be innovative, and that usually takes a number of professional artists getting interested. Astoria's business community is just starting to work with the artists and galleries in town to have coordinated opening nights . . . it has a lot of potential."

Galleries and Arts Festivals

Astoria has no history of tourist traffic, so its several art galleries are practically devoid of the cliched, seaside watercolor scenes that clog the walls of gallery spaces in nearby Cannon Beach. Instead, you'll find lots of contemporary artwork in Astoria, which is somehow fitting because of the town's vaguely urban context. There's one nonprofit exhibition space at the local community college. The year's most popular arts event is the Astoria Arts Celebration on the waterfront in mid-September.

What the Artist Says

Harry Bennett, an expressionistic oil painter who draws his creative inspiration from the Astoria environment, has lived here for three years. "I'm surprised that the people living around Astoria actually buy art work. My paintings are largely of the area, but they're not straight realism and take some getting used to. There's a great feeling here: The artists moving in have a sense of adventure, that something very good is starting to happen. The town's architecture is frozen in 1922, that era of old-fashioned America. The galleries are opening, and they're taking on new talent. Somehow or another, it's all coming together. You'll be happy if you come!"

Joseph, Oregon

Location

Folks in Joseph like to say that their town is "at the end of the road." And from this far corner of northeast Oregon you can't go anywhere except back out the same way you came in. Hemmed in by Hell's Canyon on one side and the Wallowa Mountains on the other, Joseph's 1,100 residents enjoy a quiet, isolated existence in a place of great natural beauty.

Climate

Don't forget to bring your Sorel boots, as winter weather is far from being a stranger to this land-locked quarter of the Pacific Northwest. Spring gyrates between the rainy, overcast muck blowing in from the coast, and surprisingly warm periods of sunny skies poking northward from central Oregon's drier, desert-like moonscape. Autumn isn't much to get concerned about, but summer is so hot and dry that the Cowboy Bar has shakers of rock salt set out on table tops, so the locals can replenish while they refresh.

Living

If you can tolerate the climactic extremes, Joseph (and the entire Wallowa Valley) is somewhat like a land of its own: far removed from even the smaller population centers in western Oregon, and located at the end of a two-lane highway that leads into the valley. One of the more unspoiled and underpopulated parts of the state, Joseph got its start as an art town due to the presence of a community of sculptors drawn here after a bronze foundry started doing business several years back.

One sculptor led to another, and pretty soon the place developed one of those reputations that acts like a magnet for artists looking for a way out. Now, three foundries and a number of painters and jewelers have packed their trucks and headed to the Wallowa Valley, forming a bona fide arts scene in this unlikely town.

Things are truly wonderful . . . right now. But there could be problems on the horizon, as a wave of commercialization has started taking root, primarily in the form of T-shirt shops, and the like, run by re-located Californians. Joseph, and the neighboring community of Enterprise, should take a hard look at what's happened to Sedona, Jackson, and Ketchum after the outsiders swarmed in. There needs to be zoning, planning, and stiff tax penalties (call them gifts to the community from the newcomers who will find a way to cough up the cash) applied on any new development . . . and fast!

Still, the schools are quite good, even as Oregon goes through a revenue shakeout that's caus-ing cutbacks in state services. A 3-bedroom home on one of the quiet streets in the valley runs any-where from $80,000 to $110,000, depending on the views. Local theater groups stage a year-round slate of productions, with the summertime outdoor melodrama in Joseph being especially popular. Musical performances take place both at the Joseph Community Center and at the restored O.K. Theater in Enterprise. There's a ski area in the state park right outside Joseph, and Wallowa Lake, the area's biggest summer recreational draw, is several miles long and lies at the base of a 10,000-foot mountain. White water rafting and trout fishing are superb at dozens of sites in the region.

Out On the Town

Ethnic food-wise, this area is still playing catch-up—you've got to drive an hour-and-a-half to LaGrande to even find a Chinese restaurant! Thankfully for Joseph visitors, the Wagon Wheel Cafe has just opened as a comfortable alternative to the valley's traditional hash houses, and the Old Town Cafe is still a great place for burgers. Artsy types like hanging out at the Book Loft in Enterprise, while local folks with a hankering for pool tables and beer mugs skedaddle over to the Cowboy Bar. Vegetarians graze on down at the Common Ground.

Economic Impact of the Arts

As the area's lumber industry continues its decline, the importance of the arts to the valley's economy can't be understated—tourism, especially arts-related tourism, is about all that's left, outside of the marginally profitable fields of agriculture and ranching. In the near future, local business types may want to give up their dreams of attracting the next Japanese computer chip plant and instead help the arts flourish.

Local Arts Agency

Wallowa Valley Arts Council, P.O. Box 306, Enterprise, OR 97828, (503) 432-2361.

"I'd consider the strength of the area to be its cooperation between different groups," says foundry owner Shelley Curtiss. "The merchants are doing well from our arts festivals, there's an arts consciousness in the community, local schools have well-developed visual arts programs, and we're trying to add sculpture to the arts education curriculum. We've tried to use the arts fairs as a way to tie together all the region's constituencies."

Galleries and Arts Festivals

Joseph's Main Street now has eight art galleries, most of which include locally-created bronze sculpture. Enterprise has a half-dozen galleries, but the art tends to not be as strong as what's found in Joseph. The year's biggest arts bash is the Wallowa Valley Arts Festival in Joseph, attracting 75 or so exhibitors each summer.

What the Artist Says

"Here, you've got nothing to interfere with your concentration," says sculpter Ramon Parmenter. "The foundries are great, but we need more business and less rhetoric. Lots of sculptors do western realism—it's no-nonsense, hard work. We know what garbage art is."

Painter and gallery owner Mark Kortnik says, "Sales are improving each year and people have started buying original bronzes and paintings from the galleries, which is a sign the collectors with money are taking us more seriously. There's a development issue that's of concern to a lot of people. We don't want big resorts, but there are developers with their eyes on this area."

Neskowin, Oregon

Location
Along an isolated stretch of Oregon's Pacific coastline, Neskowin's 500 residents live slightly more than an hour's drive southwest of Portland.

Climate
Neskowin has typical Pacific Northwest overcast skies and drizzle for a good part of the year, punctuated by regular hellacious storms and unexpected breaks of sunlight. Summer is characterized by stretches of sunny warmth lasting anywhere from several days to a few weeks.

Living
Very rural and outside the mainstream of coastal tourism patterns, Neskowin's artists have chosen to live in an ideal place for both concentrating on their art work and raising their families in a safe, small-town environment. Artists have home studios on several acres of land, and live within an easy drive of stores and services in Salem, the state capital. An average 3-bedroom home sells somewhere in the range of $95,000, but that includes a good-size patch of land for gardening, horses, and detached studio structures. Beachcombing in the tidal flat areas, windsurfing, and the area's excellent salmon and steelhead fishing are favorite leisure time pursuits of local residents.

Out On the Town
Surprisingly, this area's remoteness hasn't been a deterrent to the establishment of several fine dining and drinking spots, which is a reflection on both the creative, can-do nature of those who live here and the urbane restaurant-going patterns of locals. There's a four-star restaurant at the Salishan Resort, in the nearby community of Gleneden Beach, for special nights out. The Otis Cafe is dishing up grits, gravy, and chicken fried steak year-round, and Kyllo's Seafood restaurant is a favorite retreat for everything from salmon to squid. Burgers and micro-brewed beers are the specialties of the house at the Lighthouse Brewpub. Breakfast, lunch, and pizza are great at Hawk Creek Cafe. Nearby Lincoln City (15 miles away) has both community theater and regular programs in classical music and jazz.

Economic Impact of the Arts
Here, the arts community keeps a low profile, yet there's an unmistakable presence from arts-related endeavors at the Sitka Center for Art and Ecology, a teaching and research institution in Neskowin. Visiting artist programs bring experienced professionals in many visual arts fields to the Sitka Center for months at a time. Artists receive classroom instruction, as well as access to a quiet, well-equipped working facility for career advancement.

Local Arts Agency

Neskowin Coast Foundation, P.O. Box 65, Otis, OR 97368, (503) 994-5485. Publishes the newsletter *Cascade Headlines*.

"We've made our impact on the local business community," says Sitka Center director Randall Koch. "It's a matter of being seen as bringing along our share of the local economy, but not many realize the full potential of what a facility like this can do for the region. We utilize our artists-in-residence for teacher-in-residence programs of up to six weeks at local schools. It's a matter of combining our initiative with the school's own perceived needs. Artist perspectives are listened to closely in this community. People look at things in the long-term perspective and hold back on quick judgments about what artists say. There are opportunities for artist involvement at all levels of government, from city councils to school boards. Artists are willing to receive visitors in their studios, providing people call to make appointments, but be prepared to travel some rough roads getting to people's property."

Galleries and Arts Festivals

There are two commercial galleries in the area: the Maveety Gallery in Gleneden Beach (which exhibits sophisticated ceramics and original paintings) and the Salishan Resort Gallery (with regional crafts and a mixture of original paintings and reproductions). There's a cooperative gallery space in nearby Pacific City. Things pick up around here in the months between July and September. The busiest arts fairs in the region are the Art Harvest in McMinnville each April, and the Salem Arts Festival each July, with 250 exhibiting artists.

What the Artist Says

Judith Lehrman, ceramicist, has lived in the area for six years. "The artists who live here year-round have a wonderful sense of community—our kids go to school in a converted barn. It's not unusual for the artists to get together and organize the things they want to see happen, like dance classes and poetry readings. This is one of those places where life can be lived in a much simpler way, and many people take advantage of that option. There's [something] about Neskowin that artists are drawn toward. Lots of artists come in and find part-time jobs while they're waiting for their careers to develop. Our Friday evening volleyball game is a great place to get caught up on what everyone is doing. We're starting to see some growth and I think most of us feel that is inevitable, but anything that looks like yuppification is something to be avoided. Artists cooperate on scheduling open house weekends, which are good events for bringing more collectors into our studios. But around here people don't readily come out to see your work . . . you've got to be willing to get out there and promote it yourself."

Newport, Oregon

Location

The historic fishing community of Newport (pop. 9,000) is located on the Yaquina Bay, along the Pacific coast, about a 2-hour drive from Portland.

Climate

Ocean breezes are the region's most characteristic climactic feature, bringing rainy and overcast skies for much of the year, but breaking out into warm, beach type weather during the relatively brief stretch of summer. Even though it rains quite a bit, Newport has a surprisingly mild climate, with an outstanding growing season and thousands of serious, almost competitive gardeners.

Living

One of the Pacific Northwest's best places to either raise a family or retire to is Newport, Oregon. Life in this growing, yet safe, town can best be described as wholesome and entertaining. Miles of sparkling Pacific beaches await strollers and beach-casting fishermen. The community's school system is one of the best in the state, even in the face of budgetary cutbacks. There's a strong sense of integrity in the locally defined architectural style, and an aesthetic continuity to much of Newport's residential and business districts. Most artists have home studios, but those who prefer an in-town studio can rent suitable space for $200 per month, or less. Newport has hundreds of painters, writers, dancers, craftspeople, and actors, as well as a surprising number of low-profile Hollywood types who maintain their second homes in the region. An average 3-bedroom home in one of Newport's quiet, safe neighborhoods lists in the $70,000 range, while property with ocean views run considerably more.

Out On the Town

The bad news is that there's not yet a Thai restaurant in Newport (opportunity knocks), but the good news is that the area's Japanese restaurant in nearby Seal Rock is one of the best in the Pacific Northwest. Three great places to hang your hat and knock back a few brews are the Cosmos Cafe, Whales Tales, and Canyonway. Burgermaniacs get their buns and fries fix at Danny's Tavern, while the veggie crowd gets plenty of rabbit food down at the Boardwalk. Nighttime movers and (booty) shakers gyrate at Riptide's and at Bay Haven. The area's performing arts community is especially strong in theater and music. Newport's Performing Arts Center is home to five very active theater companies, staging a year-round calendar of plays ranging from musicals to experimental theater. Classical, chamber, folk, and jazz music performances are also regularly produced at the Center.

Economic Impact of the Arts

Newport has a strong tourism economy, so there is a constant call for the type of artwork that's evocative of seacoast beauty. Some artists see this as a great way to make a living, while others see it as pandering. In any case, the market for affordable, recognizable visual work is strong. Many galleries also do well with fine crafts, and Newport is loaded with individuals creating everything from seashell bracelets to weather-proof deck chairs. The Sylvia Beach Hotel, an eclectic place with oceanfront views, has each of its rooms named after certain famous writers, decorated in a manner that would be most suitable for that individual (were he or she to show up and ask for the room key). I'll take the Alfred Hitchcock attic, please!

Local Arts Agency
Oregon Coast Council for the Arts, P.O. Box 1315, Newport, OR 97365, (503) 265-9231. Publishes the newsletter *Newport News Times*.

"We're the umbrella organization for many individual groups in the region," says council executive director Sharon Morgan. "Our local audience is very receptive to new experiences, which is why our arts center is able to do a lot of research and development on theater, music, and visual arts programs. We don't have the big corporate sponsors some areas have, so we depend on local support, and fortunately, everyone seems to understand that by supporting the arts they are in effect supporting Newport's surprisingly strong economy. Our schools have a mutual use agreement with the arts center: we place artists-in-residences and we've funded a theater arts teacher position. Our long-range plan is to develop a magnet school for the arts. Kids attend all our performances at reduced rates. Our arts center is truly a community resource—it's not about getting dressed up in furs and diamonds to see great music, theater, or dance . . . but we have all of that, without making a big fuss of things."

Galleries and Arts Festivals
Newport's market for locally created art work of all types is very strong, which explains why 20 commercial galleries manage to do well in this town. There are three nonprofit exhibition spaces at the Visual Arts Center, the Backporch Gallery, and at Casbah. In mid-July, the community's largest arts event is the Ernest Bloch Music Festival, a curated musical festival that includes new works, symposia, orchestral performances, classes, and arts exhibitions.

What the Artist Says
Michael Gibbons, a renowned regionalist landscape painter, says it's visitors who keep the local visual art market strong. "We're not a very wealthy community, but we get a lot of tourists who buy things here and ship them out-of-state. Some high-powered artists are moving in, some are moving to Toledo (5 miles from Newport), and starting to create an arts district. It's not a destination, just a place where artists live and have their studios. The light here is wonderful. I'd like to see more plein-air painters move in and try their hands at restoring these old homes, using the local subject matter in their work. The big social gatherings for artists are the gallery openings. Toledo is a real do-it-yourself sort of place. If an artist is willing to work hard and open their own gallery, they have a chance at finding a niche for themselves where they can control the bucks, but nothing in this place is easy, and you've got to be able to hang in through the slow periods."

Sandy, Oregon

Location
In the foothills of the Cascade Range, Sandy is a community of 4,500 residents snuggled up against the base of Mt. Hood (11,000 feet) and within a 30-minute drive of downtown Portland.

Climate
With its altitude being much higher than most of metropolitan Portland, Sandy gets winter snows, while the communities nearby receive rain. Overcast skies are the predominant weather pattern for most of the year, with summer bringing stretches of hot days broken up by occasional periods of liquid sunshine. Spring and fall are usually rained out, but every few years there's an exceptional transition season.

Living
Though becoming more crowded as the rootless herds migrate in from southern California, Sandy is still an area of great scenic beauty, with homes built deep into a wooded landscape carpeted with fir trees. Living here is sometimes like being inside a terrarium, with periods of rain that seem to stretch on forever rolling in anytime from early October through early May. Certainly, skies clear up and the sun breaks through every now and again, but the chance of that happening for more than a day or two during the colder months is so remote, locals resign themselves to indoor activities. One way to escape the clouds is by skiing at nearby Mt. Hood, or by taking a drive across the Cascades to eastern Oregon. Shopping malls, bowling alleys, movie theaters, and coffee houses are also popular diversions. Those with an orientation toward the great outdoors manage to find gore-tex raingear, and carry onward with their running, bicycling, and hiking pursuits. The average cost of a 3-bedroom spread in Sandy, or nearby Estacada, is $90,000.

Out On the Town
With a city of 450,000 right at its doorstep, folks around here aren't lacking access to cultural events ranging from art museums and foreign films to jazz clubs and professional theater. Sandy itself has a local theater troupe that stages plays at the high school auditorium. A great local lunch spot (and one of the region's best watering holes) is the Elusive Trout. It's Calamity Jane's for burgers and shakes, and the Good Earth for vegetarian fare. Anyone who doesn't want to drive down to Portland for an evening of hip-shaking, usually makes it over to the Resort at the Mountain in nearby Welches.

Economic Impact of the Arts
Sandy is a community that's emerging as an affordable and attractive rural alternative for artists in the Portland area. What seems to have brought artists into town is a reaction to the California migration that's crowding and pricing artists away from areas closer to the city. There has not yet been an opportunity to organize the voices of the area's creative professionals, and as a result, there's nothing resembling an arts center, or even an arts block, in Sandy's small business district.

On the other hand, the artists moving in know a trick or two about how to get things done, and it would appear that this is a community with a solid potential to emerge with an arts town identity—a region-wide reputation as a place to find art and artists.

Local Arts Agency

Sandy Arts Society, P.O. Box 1298, Sandy, OR 97055, no phone.

"Right now we're doing a number of arts projects that are extensions of those that were started in the schools," says society director Meri Lynn Ealy. "We've managed to complete one downtown mural and have just been funded to do another. If our three-year plan moves along, we'll receive funding for things like outdoor sculpture and a performing arts program. Our dream of dreams is to one day have a community arts center with classroom space for school kids and adults, exhibition space for visual art, and a performing arts auditorium. People in Sandy are just beginning to embrace the visual arts. We're not yet considered a part of the business community, but our weekend arts festivals bring more business into this town than anything else. Private support for the arts has started to increase, and the school system is finally starting to give arts in the classroom some serious consideration."

Galleries and Arts Festivals

There are three commercial galleries in the Sandy area, with the emphasis being on locally made craft items and some original paintings. Maiden Bronze, a foundry used by many artists in the Oregon and Washington region, is also in Sandy. There is no nonprofit gallery, but the local library has a rotating exhibition space for visual work. The year's biggest arts bash is the Sandy Mountain Festival, an event with 180 performers and artists taking place in mid-July. The Arts Society Annual Exhibition in October is also very popular.

What the Artist Says

Marj Gordon, textile artist, says that establishing an arts community in Sandy is going to take hard work. "There's a rural nature to the way Sandy sees itself, and not all the local people appreciate the artists who are starting to move here. The trick for most of us is to sell our work out-of-state, and use the Portland art museums and galleries as a resource. There are some good places to sell your work in Portland, but galleries are slow to take on new talent. Sandy is also known as a town with good antique shops, and I think the downtown murals project will help people understand a little about what artists can do for a town. The new people moving to the area and building homes are the ones buying art, but we need to draw more interest from the people who have always lived in Sandy. The artists need to be better organized if they're going to pull it off."

Easton, Pennsylvania

Location
At the confluence of the Lehigh and Delaware rivers, Easton is a community with a glorious industrial past, and a future which will be determined by its transition from an industrial to arts-based economy. Philadelphia is an hour's drive south.

Climate
Typically cold in winter, Easton can get pounded with snow one season and drenched with gloomy rain showers the next. Summer tends to be hot and humid affairs, while the area has a spectacular autumn and a long, gentle spring.

Living
When its economic base went south several years ago, Easton was left with a downtown business district in relatively good condition, and an enormous amount of vacant space that needed to be filled. A forward-looking group of local political leaders called upon planning consultant John Shapiro to come up with a plan for switching the local economy towards that of a historic, regional arts and retail center.

What followed was nothing less than a complete turnaround from the past, as a river front park and a renovated downtown theater project helped Easton to make a startling leap forward. Brick commercial buildings, with high-ceilings and wood-planked floors, were renovated into artists' living and working spaces; the Crayola crayon people, a large local employer, began building a children's museum on the town square; private retailers and restaurateurs took their own entrepreneurial initiatives and established new businesses, and . . . voila!

Today, Easton's once-empty downtown is alive with visitors on weekends, bar-hopping students from the region's colleges on weeknights, and the hum of commerce during the days. While a 3-bedroom home in an Easton neighborhood lists in the $100,000 range, there's comparable spaces available in the downtown artists' loft district for far less (sans vegetable gardens, of course).

Out On the Town
The downtown arts district's entertainment anchor is the restored, historic State Theater, a facility that functions not just as a center for the performing arts, but also contains a visual arts gallery. While the theater may not have the financial stability and concurrent program flexibility that the Paramount Theater in downtown Peekskill enjoys, it still pulls in a regular schedule of theater, film, and music performances. As the downtown's economic strength increases, so will the State Theater's. One of the favorite places locals head to for a lunch break is Shorts Pub, but the Ferry Street Cafe is also a popular spot to pass a few leisurely weekend hours. Josie's New York Deli has the best ham-and-cheese subs in town, and vegetarian's have it their way at Nature's Way.

Economic Impact of the Arts

Increasingly, Easton's regional reputation is developing as a place where artists live, along with a number of galleries and craft stores selling locally-created work. It's still a transitional process, but one which has the promise of growing, as visitors return and word-of-mouth spreads. You could look at downtown Easton and say the area's very survival depends upon the economy generated either directly from or ancillary to the arts, but that would be jumping the gun a bit.

Local Arts Agency

Lehigh Valley Arts Council, P.O. Box 20591, Lehigh Valley, PA 18002, (215) 967-4343. Publishes the newsletter *Inside the Arts*.

"Easton could use more galleries to attract more buyers into town," says sculptor Patricia Meyerowitz, who sold her lower Manhattan loft to move here several years ago. "The artists here have lots of New York connections, which are essential because there's still a limited local market for original work. But when the area's art museum moves downtown later this year, that should really help things. We're only 80 miles from New York City, and a town that actually wants artists to move in. You can find living and working space here for a fraction of what it costs in the city. There are local colleges with wonderful music programs, and the State Theater puts on some great plays."

Galleries and Arts Festivals

There are three commercial art galleries in Easton's downtown arts district, one of which specializes in locally made fine crafts. The community's nonprofit art exhibition space is at the State Theater, and it's open year-round. The year's two most popular arts and craft events are the Heritage Days Festival in July, and the Musikfest in autumn.

What the Artist Says

Karl Stirner, a contemporary sculptor, moved to Easton after spending most of his career in New York. "Downtown is really getting its act together—once the children's museum and the art museum are opened, these abandoned industrial buildings will start attracting a lot more interest from artists. This is a city that's on the right track. There is still a small town atmosphere, and it's an arts community that hardly needs to look to the east for inspiration. We're hooked into the idea of working with the arts as a way of turning the city around, even though the local politicians don't fully understand the concept. The city sees a direct connection between the health of the arts community in Easton and its own economy's health. Our State Theater has 1,500 seats and is benefiting from a $3 million restoration project—it's bringing in theater, dance, and music—it's cranking right along."

New Hope, Pennsylvania

Location
A Delaware River community in Bucks County, New Hope is a town of 1,400. Across the river is Lambertville, New Jersey, a town of 4,000 residents. Philadelphia is a 30-minute drive south.

Climate
Wooded and rural, the countryside around New Hope is blanketed with many of autumn's most colorful tree species. From early October through almost Halloween, weekend "leafers" provide the community with a late-season tourism boost. Summer can be hot and humid, while winter has the potential to turn nasty, but rarely does.

Living
Because it's within easy commuting distance of Philadelphia, New Hope's artists share their town with a battalion of suburbanite professionals. An historic community (founded during the 1700s), New Hope has as many landmark buildings as it does artists (well into the hundreds on both counts). During weekdays, when the careerists and tourists are kept off the town's streets, New Hope actually looks like a bit of paradise: quaint shops, first-rate restaurants, orderly streets, and a populous that smiles and says "hello" to each other. Average home costs are high, with a 3-bedroom residence selling in the $200,000 range. Fortunately, there's Lambertville, the New Jersey manufacturing center right across the river from New Hope. Less chic than a New Hope address, and unthinkable as a mailing address for the green-turtlenecked social climbers, it remains a more affordable refuge for artists and many of the area's more interesting individuals.

Out On the Town
With the Bucks County Playhouse stuck on a cycle of safe, mainstream musicals, New Hope's stage activity is limited to community theater groups, and the summer staging of a new and experimental group of plays. When it comes to big-name concerts and opera, music performance tends to bow in Philadelphia's direction, while New Hope's cabaret scene flourishes with two hot spots specializing in both the new and the tried-and-true. When it comes to booking new acts, whether they be rock, blues bands, or folkies, John & Peter's has a reputation as one of the East Coast's most innovative clubs. Odette's is more of a smoke-filled hangout for the piano bar and cabaret crowd, while on weekends, the jazz band at Havana's is always hot to samba. Because of its suburban location, New Hope is within easy reach of any imaginable style of ethnic food. Needless to say, the Italian restaurants are first-rate anywhere near Philadelphia, but if you're after Thai food, you'll need to cross over to Lambertville for satisfaction. The Raven is a great place to hang your hat on a rainy afternoon, while Havana's Cuban delicacies are a vegetarian's best bet.

Economic Impact of the Arts
The community's reputation was built on the presence of a strong artists community dating back to pre-World War II days. From the European-trained modernists who settled in during the 1920s to

the highly skilled fine craft artists who now make their homes in the area, New Hope's historic attraction for creative professionals is the root of its present success as a tourist destination. The town's business community, from restaurant owners to dentists, has a tradition of accepting art work in trade for merchandise and services, but the most disturbing recent trend is the overpricing of local real estate and the overcrowding of local streets. Many artists are considering heading to Lambertville, or points in Lehigh County, to escape the crush of weekend tourists.

Local Arts Agency

New Hope Arts Commission, 41 N. Main St., New Hope, PA 18938, (215) 862-2060. Publishes the newsletter *State of the Arts*.

"We're oriented toward both the visual and performing arts," says commission executive director Robin Larsen. "There are arts education programs that we coordinate in local schools, productions of the New Hope Performing Arts Festival each summer, art exhibits at donated commercial space in town, and musical concerts in the schools. Business here is very supportive of the arts—they have a sense that whatever is good for us is going to somehow be beneficial to them. The arts programs in local schools are very strong, helping us to develop new audiences for the arts. Some of our new plays have gone to off-Broadway, and we're given a lot of attention by the New York and Philadelphia press."

Galleries and Arts Festivals

With its long-standing tradition in the arts, you would rightly expect New Hope's galleries to be filled with great work, and that is indeed the case. With seventeen serious galleries in town (and a number of minor ones), there's room for most of New Hope's visual and fine crafts artists who want to reach the town's bustling, arts-buying tourist market. The one surprising absence is a non-profit exhibition space for visual and craft work, which is probably a reflection of the town's proximity to state and private museums and college art galleries. The year's biggest arts bash is the New Hope Performing Arts Festival, a month-long event taking place in July and August on the grounds of the Solebury School Theater.

What the Artist Says

Bob Griffiths, a playwright, stage performer, and educator, has lived in New Hope for five years. "The town is loaded with talented people. If you live here, you can see the town's creative side, but if you're just visiting you'll probably miss it. Weekends just swarm with tourists. Until a few years ago the arts community went its own way, but now we've got an active arts commission, and that's led to a lot more interaction among the artists, writers, and actors. If the town can get an arts center built, it would help a great deal to preserve what's here. We're becoming too expensive, and a lot of artists are starting to walk across the bridge (to Lambertville)."

McCormick, South Carolina

Location
A community of 2,000 in the southwest corner of the state, McCormick is an hour's drive west of Columbia, the state capital.

Climate
Summer settles into this region toward the end of April and refuses to leave until nearly Halloween—and it's a hot, sticky summer to boot. Fortunately, there's relief nearby in the form of Strom Thurmond Lake, a 30-mile reservoir attracting most of the local population during the year's uncomfortable months. Autumn comes and goes without much fanfare, winter is always mild with occasional dustings of snow, and spring is lovely while it lasts.

Living
Once a gold-mining boom town, most of McCormick has the restored appearance of an 1800s frontier village. Today it's the sort of small town where the local drug store has a lunch counter and you can still order a fountain coke with a grilled cheese sandwich. Kudzu vines are the region's most dominant living organism, followed in descending order by pine trees, livestock, wide-mouth bass, and finally, the residents of McCormick.

Long a favorite wide spot in the road for those seeking hand-crafted furniture, antiques, and locally created traditional crafts, McCormick has started to attract a mixed group of artists who are either potters with an abiding interest in the region's indigenous Edgefield style of pottery, or older, more established painters who are moving into the planned communities springing up along the area's miles of lake shore. Artists are finding solace in both the area's low cost of living and its increasingly successful position as an arts community. The local arts council provides free working quarters to any artist who needs studio space. An average 3-bedroom home along one of McCormick's many tree-shaded streets lists in the $40,000 range, while lake front spreads cost upwards of $150,000.

Out On the Town
The nearby town of Augusta, Georgia, offers just about any of the dining and entertainment options you would expect from a town with a major military base and one of the nation's most renowned golf clubs (Augusta National). There are several public and privately supported organizations in the McCormick area that are focused on the preservation and recreation of the area's historic legacy, and one long-standing local favorite is the Stevens Creek Heritage Preserve. Lunch and dinner options in this area include Migs Pizza and the Sugar Shack, but if your entertainment needs go further than simply a good meal, it means driving to Augusta.

Economic Impact of the Arts
It's taken a little more than ten years for McCormick to shake the image it once had as a backwater ghost town. The turnaround was accomplished through a community-wide effort to work with the

existing downtown structures in a renovation program that has brought newcomers, tourists, and even real estate developers into the region. Today the challenge for McCormick is to maintain the momentum of being a small town on the comeback trail. Hopefully, the town's business community will find this task compatible with supporting both the area's traditional craft forms and the new group of artists and gallery owners eager to contribute to the town's revitalization.

Local Arts Agency

McCormick Arts Council at the Keturah, 115 S. Main Street, McCormick, SC 29835, (803) 465-3216. Publishes the newsletter *Horizons*.

"We try to do as much as we can with our limited facilities," says council director Laura Talbott, "but because we don't have access to a theater, we're prevented from staging plays or dance programs. We do have a well-equipped arts center that can be used for classroom instruction in music, painting, photography, pottery, and dance. Our visual art exhibitions are targeted toward the work of the area's craft artists and painters. Local membership funds are very important to what we're doing, because business isn't yet at the stage of supporting us financially. There's tourism promotion that mentions the arts that are here, but we still haven't established the connection in business owner's minds that what's good for the arts is also going to be very good for the economy. Our local schools have had art instruction for several years—there are regular programs with visiting artists in the schools, and the state's been taking a strong interest in promoting the case for rural arts."

Galleries and Arts Festivals

While there are a couple of stores in town where visitors can spot a painting or two and find strong examples of Edgefield-style pottery and local craft, most of the visual art is exhibited at the arts council's nonprofit gallery. The year's largest arts event is held in May, when downtown Main Street is blocked off for the Spider Lilly Festival.

What the Artist Says

Steven Ferrell, a ceramicist and historian, says the national interest in the region's indigenous style of pottery is increasing. "I think the popularity has something to do with Edgefield's being the first truly American school of pottery, a British form that used Chinese techniques and was made by African slaves. Museum curators are down here all the time looking for originals, and there are a number of potters doing reproductions."

Ingrid Hofer, an established painter who moved here a year ago, says McCormick's attraction is in its climate. "The town tries very hard to preserve what's still standing, but there's a lot that remains to be renovated. The art center is really coming into its own, it's been a magnet for the new people. We're seeing lots of young families who are interested in doing whatever they can to build up the town's arts programs."

Deadwood, South Dakota

Location
Set amidst the 7,000-foot mountains in the Black Hills Range, the 2,000 residents of Deadwood are at the far western edge of South Dakota, an hour's drive from Rapid City.

Climate
During the hot, dry, and unrelentingly bright skies of summer, this corner of South Dakota takes on the desert-like conditions more commonly associated with places like Tucson and El Paso. Autumn brings out thousands of tourists who drive through the region's many high-country roads. Winter is a serious affair that drops temperatures well below zero, locking the landscape in a shroud of ice and snow. Spring tends to be warm and muddy.

Living
Things used to be pretty quiet in this part of the state until South Dakota legalized a limited form of casino gambling (bets are held to $100). Today, millions of dollars are being poured into the area, both in terms of development funds for casinos (like the $90-million Dunbar Resort being built by Kevin Costner) and from gamblers who make the trek in from Canada, Montana, Wyoming, Nebraska, and the Dakotas. Suddenly, Deadwood isn't dead any more, and neither, for that matter, are nearby Sturgis (home of the summer Harley-Davidson convention) and Spearfish. Local residents have jobs as blackjack dealers, high-rollers are keeping hotels and restaurants filled, and there's plenty of tax revenue for school and highway construction projects.

Deadwood is a mostly Republican town, with around 20 or so professional artists, craftspeople, writers, and musicians. But if you drew in the creative professionals who live within the Black Hills region, that number rises into the 75 to 100 range. A 3-bedroom home in Deadwood is difficult to find, but is still very affordable at $45,000. Studio space on the second floor of a downtown building rents for $150 per month.

Out On the Town
Just a few years ago, a night on the town in Deadwood meant driving into Rapid City for chicken-fried steak and a few hours at a rugged country and western bar. Now, with gambling tables, showgirls, nightclub entertainers, and French restaurants all having crammed into the area over the past few years, the traffic flow on I-90 is reversed, and it's the rest of the state that's pouring into Deadwood every weekend.

The casinos lining downtown Deadwood's streets are located in historic, three-story, turn-of-the-century mercantile structures (almost all of which are 25 feet wide and 100 feet long) and are limited to having 30 gaming stations per business. That has resulted in each casino having its own restaurant and nightclub. Miss Kitty's casino has the popular Chinatown restaurant, while the Italian cuisine at Mama Leone's (inside the Lucky Wrangler) is first-rate. The best steaks in town are served at the restaurant inside the Depot casino.

Those with a nightclub urge can have their musical tastes catered to at a number of places, from rock to jazz and country music. The town even has an Elvis impersonator in one casino lounge, and the Bullock Hotel hosts a musical comedy troupe. Kevin Costner owns the Midnight Star Casino in downtown Deadwood.

Economic Impact of the Arts

There have always been a number of artists, writers, and craftspeople living in the Black Hills region, and most of them have successfully sold their work through the many small town galleries scattered about the countryside. Musicians are moving here in droves, drawn by the steady employment at casino lounges and nightclubs. One problem is that as the profile of the gaming industry rises, local arts groups are going to have to struggle to maintain their place at the table.

Local Arts Agency

South Dakotans for the Arts, P.O. Box 472, Deadwood, SD 57732, (605) 578-1783.

"We're an area made up of lots of small communities, so individual organizations are still convincing the businesses that there's an economic impact to the work they do," says Janet Brown, the group's executive director. "There's a lot of interrelating between the arts groups and the local Chambers of Commerce, but no direct ties in terms of funding. Deadwood has entertainers who are brought into town by the casinos, but we still don't have an arts center or some sort of a place where local residents can go for dance, visual arts programs, or recitals. Our schools have a very progressive attitude toward the arts—the arts councils support artist-in-residency programs, and most schools have a visual arts teacher on staff. One of our main challenges is to try and convince people that there are artistic endeavors they don't normally think about when they consider the arts, and that those can be lots of fun."

Galleries and Arts Festivals

While there's a single art gallery in Deadwood and another twenty or so scattered around the Black Hills region, the town does not have a nonprofit art exhibition space. The year's biggest arts bash, Art in the Park, is held in nearby Spearfish in July, drawing over 150 exhibiting artists to town for a weekend.

What the Artist Says

Dick Termes, a visionary painter who creates environmental scenes painted on spheres, says the area's isolation is a large part of its attraction. "I'm like a lot of the artists here—I sell to galleries from Seattle to Santa Fe, and try to take full advantage of what comes by during the summer. It's a wonderful place to think and work—the Black Hills are quiet and inspirational. You have to be diligent about marketing outside the area in order to survive because the local market isn't strong enough yet. We're seeing an extraordinary number of very fine artists moving into the area, and development is going to be the big issue for the next few years. I'm not convinced that the casinos bring in the type of person who buys art."

Gatlinburg, Tennessee

Location

Deep in the eastern Tennessee end of Great Smoky National Park, the 3,500 residents of Gatlinburg, one of the nation's most prominent fine craft communities, are less than an hour's drive from Knoxville.

Climate

Sitting in the foothills of mountains soaring as high as 6,500 feet, Gatlinburg's summer climate is gently moderated from the oppressive heat and humidity afflicting the rest of Tennessee. By the same token (especially in light of the busy ski area that's just outside town), Gatlinburg has a winter snow-and-ice season that can turn downright nasty. Autumn is spectacular, bringing in tourists from across the mid-South, while springtime provides a gradual, gentle wind-up to the height of tourist season.

Living

Once upon a time this town was a cultural backwater, but the Gatlinburg of today is an economic dynamo that's built up a tourism industry reaching far beyond the community's original roots as a center of traditional crafts. The town's business district was once filled with artist-run shops and friendly cafes, but the past decade of escalating rents and a heated business climate have pushed just about every Gatlinburg craftsperson and artist out of the downtown area. What used to be a pleasant experience of wandering from one friendly studio gallery to another has turned into a tourism nightmare. T-shirt shops, ice cream parlors, franchise clothing stores, and fast-food restaurants now dominate what once was a quaint, attractive business district.

Fortunately, the talented individuals who comprise Gatlinburg's arts and crafts community haven't left town . . . yet. Instead, they've moved a few miles away from the center of town and have formed the Great Smoky Arts & Crafts Community, an enclave of nearly a hundred artist- and craftsperson-run studio/shops. For these professionals, Gatlinburg's adjacent setting to a national park is a primary reason for staying—along with the great hiking, fishing, and hunting. The average 3-bedroom home in one of the town's neighborhoods sells for $85,000.

Out On the Town

With Dollywood only a 5-minute drive away from Gatlinburg, it's hard to believe anyone wouldn't find everything their heart and soul desires in the fantasy land named after America's buxom sweetheart. Actually, if it's musical entertainment you're after, the chances of catching a big-name act from Nashville appearing on one of Dollywood's stages is fairly strong. And with performances taking place year-round, this gives local artists a nice entertainment option during the year's more relaxed months.

Locally, Gatlinburg has a great bluegrass music tradition, and one of the finest clubs around for this classic American music is the River's Edge. With so many of the downtown fast food and chain restaurants packed to their gills with tourists, local artists are careful to select a few calmer places for a quiet lunch or dinner. One favorite spot is the seasonally opened Wild Plum, while the pair of family-owned spots, Teague's Mill and Teague's Creekside, are also popular with local residents. The Greenbriar Lodge is a dependable spot for those with a late-night dancing urge.

Economic Impact of the Arts

Tourism got its start here for two reasons: Gatlinburg's strong craft tradition and the town's position as an entryway into one of the nation's most-visited national parks. The park survives, the town prospers, and the craftspeople, artists, and jewelers who got things started in the first place are left wondering if there will be room for them in the near future.

Local Arts Agency

Great Smoky Arts & Crafts Community, P.O. Box 807, Gatlinburg, TN 37738, (615) 436-3301.

"Each of the artists and craftspeople own or lease their individual shops and run it the way they want," says Susan McDonell, the group's president. "We're trying to preserve what's left of the original crafts community that made Gatlinburg a popular place for visitors, but it seems that we're always having to deal with some issue or another involving change and growth. Rents are becoming very expensive, and tourism continues to draw in more people, but they're not the type who are concerned about traditional crafts or art. One of the most important anchors we have is the Arrowmont Craft Center—it gives many artists employment opportunities and continually brings talented, dedicated individuals to town."

Galleries and Arts Festivals

Downtown Gatlinburg tries to put together an arts festival now and again, but with the low quality of what passes for art and craft in the downtown area, these so-called festivals have become something of an arts insider's joke. The only festivals worth taking a serious look at are the Christmas, Thanksgiving, and Easter shows held in the 90-artist compound of the arts and crafts community.

What the Artist Says

Betty Jane Posey, a painter working in both watercolor and oils, came here because of the area's crafts traditions. "The original crafts of the area were quilting, broom-making, wood carving, and pottery. Now, of course, we've taken in all types of art. To survive here you have to make a long-term, complete commitment to your work. We get lots of artists moving in who think they'll be overnight sensations, and they usually last a couple of years before moving somewhere else. Selling directly is what the arts and crafts community is all about—we're a pretty friendly bunch and enjoy having visitors in our studios. We get together for official things and just as friends. The town has to do something to stabilize rents in this area, or the artists will be forced to leave."

Alpine, Texas

Location

West Texas is, for the most part, a parched desert runway stretching hundreds of miles from Junction to El Paso. Except for the Davis Mountains, that is. This triangular-shaped range of 6,000-foot peaks is an oasis of wildlife, trout streams, and forested valleys. Alpine's 6,000 residents live a 3-hour drive southeast of El Paso, and a 7-hour drive west of San Antonio.

Climate

Moderated from the relentless heat of the nearby desert, Alpine's name is indicative of the town's comparatively cooler air and its access to mountain waters. Summer descends on this part of the state like an open oven door, and while Alpine may not get weather as severe as is found in other parts of west Texas, it's nonetheless hot as hell. Winter is very mild, with 70-degree days speckling the January calendar, giving spring's wildflowers a head start on their peak season.

Living

Quiet and relaxed, Alpine's way of life is a stress-free alternative for artists moving in from Houston, El Paso, and Santa Fe. There's a college in town, Sul Ross University, so for nine months of the year local housing rentals are tight. The school contributes a great deal to the community's cultural life and economy, giving Alpine a leg up on many larger Texas towns when it comes to entertainment and opportunity. "The kind of retiree we get is the educated city person who wants out from all the activity," says local Chamber of Commerce director David Busey. "The kind of younger person we get is either self-employed as an artist or a business owner working over a fax machine."

Mostly a Democratic area, Alpine's average 3-bedroom residence sells in the $45,000 range, while some newer places with hillside views bring closer to $100,000. Recreational activities in the area are centered around both Big Bend National Park, an hour's drive south, and the Ft. Davis Mountains, just a few minutes north. The closest lake suitable for sailing is a couple hours away in Del Rio, but Alpine residents are happy to take an occasional rafting trip down the national park's section of the Rio Grande River. Sul Ross University has a strong program in teacher development, which means that Alpine's schools are filled with educators who are up on the latest developments in their field.

Out On the Town

Because there's a college right in Alpine, local residents have access to performances in classical music, dance, film, and theater. Isolated as it is, Alpine's residents tend to keep their VCRs in tip-top condition. There's a good Chinese restaurant, the Golden China, in town, and surprisingly enough there's even a natural food selection at the Corner House. Alpine has a decidedly multi-cultural population, so there are several great Tex-Mex dining spots, the best probably being Alicia's Burrito Place. After sunset, Alpine's cowboys head over to the Crystal Bar for a few cold brews and an occasional brawl, while Cinnabar is the nightclub attracting a more sedate crowd, as well as visitors attracted by its restaurant's nouveau West Texas cuisine. In Alpine, Downtown Brown's is the place to go for live music and leg shakin', while down the road in Lajitas, there's the inimitable Starlight Theater, a hangout attracting a crowd of friendly loonies and river runners, as well as the Terlingua Cafe, a great place to see and be seen.

Economic Impact of the Arts

The economic base of this region relies on ranching and the tourism dollars generated by its proximity to Big Bend National Park, which means that the area's arts economy is seen in terms of the work sold to visitors through local galleries and gift shops. There still aren't many professional artists in the area, so the overall economic impact is perceived as being small.

Local Arts Agency

Davis Mountain Art League, 504 E. June, Alpine, TX 79830, no phone. Publishes the newsletter *The Palette*.

"We're not what you'd call a 'packaged' art community," says Alpine artist and gallery owner Barbara Jones. "We've got a museum, and the town has the makings of becoming an arts and fine crafts center, but if you want to find the artists who live around here, you've got to go out there and look for them yourself." One of the town's long-range goals is to spruce up and unify its historic downtown architecture, a program being addressed through local participation in a Main Street USA program, says Chamber of Commerce head David Busey. "Because we're so far off the main highways, Alpine's artists have to connect with the area's environment or heritage for inspiration. We've got a number of traditional craftsmen making spurs, saddles, and silverwork . . . some of the best anywhere. Any artist who wants studio space can rent it downtown for just about nothing."

Galleries and Arts Festivals

Alpine has several commercial galleries selling mostly local art, the majority of which is either western realism painting or traditional western and ranch craftwork. But there's an increasing number of contemporary artists coming into town and they're opening their own studio galleries. The college has its own art exhibition space. There are two main arts festivals in Alpine, the first being the annual April exhibition of the Davis Mountain Art League, while the Cowboy Poetry Gathering in March attracts visitors from around the state.

What the Artist Says

Charles Bell, a multi-media artist whose hand-made paper creations are both dimensional and representational. "I've gotten onto the art education circuit and am doing a lot of residency programs at schools. My work uses the fibrous plants and grasses you find in this area, so being at the source of my materials is an important part of my work. Alpine is the kind of place that forces you to be organized. Out here, you've got a sense of the vastness of the land. We've had a number of artists move in recently, but some just come and go. The ones who stay tend to be pretty isolated from each other. Here, kids grow up in a safe, neighborly environment, and that was a very important consideration for me."

Clifton, Texas

Location
Set amidst the agricultural lands of north-central Texas, Clifton is a community of 3,200 residents about a 90-minute drive southwest of Dallas.

Climate
Far enough north to experience bouts of freezing winter weather, Clifton is also well-removed from the oppressive humidity common to summer in more southerly parts of the state, keeping the weather mostly hot and dry. Spring's bloom of wildflowers starts in late February and continues through April, while autumn goes by in a flash.

Living
Clifton is a small, down-to-earth sort of town that has managed over the years to attract a surprising number of artists. Drawn here by both the presence of an active arts museum and the community's proximity to galleries in Dallas and Ft. Worth, this is the sort of town where the artists feel a living connection to the state's frontier past. Clifton is a hotbed of painters and sculptors working in the western realism genre, and those who come to town for art exhibitions (both galleries and collectors) expect to find strong art work being created by talented artists. A 3-bedroom residence sells anywhere from $60,000 to $125,000 for newer homes along the Bosque River. The pace of life is slow.

Out On the Town
With Dallas just an hour or so away, and Waco only a half-hour drive, residents of Clifton are within easy reach of everything from shopping malls to professional sports teams. Driving, in fact, is one of the main activities for anyone wanting a night out at a place serving margaritas, because Clifton and its surrounding county are "dry," meaning they prohibit sale of liquor by-the-drink. On the other hand, if you're looking for barbecue, there are places in just about every little town in the county serving sliced beef sandwiches. A good place for lunch or dinner is Two Amigos, a Tex-Mex restaurant serving great enchiladas and large glasses of ice tea. For burgers, local residents head over to Harmon's. Nearby Waco is the home of Baylor University, a college with one of the nation's strongest graduate music programs, and a favorite for music lovers from across the state. Community dinner theater and dance presentations are regularly staged at Clifton's Bosque County Conservatory of Fine Arts.

Economic Impact of the Arts
A ranching and farming area, Clifton's business relationship to the arts has yet to be defined. There are in the neighborhood of 25 professional artists living in the area, but because the area's ranching economy is quite healthy, the arts are seen by most local residents as something more closely connected with larger cities than their own community.

Local Arts Agency

Bosque County Conservatory of Fine Art, P.O. Box 373, Clifton, TX 76634, (817) 675-3724. Publishes the newsletter *ArtBeat*.

"The arts in Clifton have a larger impact than most people realize," says Mrs. Roland (Joyce) Jones Jr., president of the organization. "The conservatory brings in art shows, conferences, dinner theater and performances, which keep our bed and breakfast inns full, and help our restaurants to prosper. Our primary orientation is toward the visual arts. We're located in a three-story brick building that was once part of a college campus and could use a lot of repairs, and we put on our stage performances in a facility that was once used to manufacture oil field equipment. Art has just started to be seen in the school system as a vital part of education—we're still at the stage where we have five football coaches in our schools and only one person teaching art. We're still dealing with a lot of old attitudes towards the arts."

Galleries and Arts Festivals

There's one art gallery in Clifton primarily selling the original work of local artists and craftspeople, and a nonprofit exhibition space operated by the Bosque County Conservatory of Fine Art. The year's most important arts event is a juried exhibition called "Preview 94," which is this year's staging of an annual show taking place in September at the art conservatory. The show, which awards a grand prize of $5,000 (and several other awards ranging from a few thousand to a few hundred dollars), draws in 40 or so artists from across the Southwest, Louisiana, Kansas, Arkansas, and Missouri. It also attracts hundreds of collectors, and receives coverage in national art magazines.

What the Artist Says

Bruce R. Greene is a western realist painter who moved to Clifton four years ago. "A lot of what I paint has to do with the frontier women of the West. I need an inspirational landscape in which to work, and Clifton presented the artistic opportunities I was looking for—it's beautiful here, month in and month out. A lot of the artists have elements of this environment in their work—the hills, the oaks, the prickly pear cactus—it's good ranch country with lots of wildflowers in the spring.

"Clifton has a good little gallery in town that most of us put something in, mostly reproductions. Most of my work is sold in Scottsdale and Santa Fe. There's a good word-of-mouth in Texas about Clifton as an arts community, and I think that's because there are so many nationally recognized artists living in a small area. It's a supportive group of artists and a great place to raise your family—there's art instruction in the schools and at the art conservatory, but I'd like to see some improvement in the way the schools handle things. Whenever there's an art exhibition at the museum, you'll see the kids bussed in for tours of the show. Afterwards, they do a question-and-answer session and rate their favorite artists and paintings."

Fredericksburg, Texas

Location

In the heart of the Texas hill country, Fredericksburg is a charming community filled with historic buildings, country inns, and lots of reminders that the original European settlers in this part of the state were proud Germans. Fredericksburg's 7,000 residents live an hour's drive from both San Antonio to the south, and Austin to the east.

Climate

The region's hot and humid summer is moderated somewhat by Fredericksburg's westerly location, but every now and again you'd swear the Gulf of Mexico must be just a few hillsides away. Winter is very mild, with brief cold snaps. Spring and autumn are glorious seasons, changing the landscape's color into a spectacular palette of nature's most inventive glory.

Living

Fredericksburg has come into its own over the past decade, growing from a well-preserved backwater into one of the state's most desirable weekend vacation spots. The town's proximity to major population centers hasn't hurt, nor has its outstanding efforts to preserve and restore the dozens of mercantile buildings that line its main street. While there are several motels on the outskirts of town, the main attraction for overnighters in Fredricksburg is a stay at one of the town's bed and breakfast inns, then shopping in the many clothing stores, craft shops, and art galleries in the business district.

Artists come here for much the same reason visitors do: they are attracted by the historical beauty of the town. Once here, they find a large group of both fine craftsmen and visual artists living in a community with an arts market of its own, yet close enough to large city galleries for artists to maintain a high regional profile. Fredericksburg has an extraordinarily active music scene, starting with music instruction in the local schools and continuing with year-round performances of chamber, orchestral, and pop music at venues around town. A 3-bedroom home on one of the community's tree-shaded streets runs in the $90,000 range, but just outside of town there are small communities with much lower-priced places on large parcels of land.

Out On the Town

There's something for everyone in Fredericksburg, and if you can't find what you want in town then it's a short drive away in Austin. One of the best places to catch artists and gallery owners during daylight hours is at the Kaffee Klatch, while older folks prefer the Cookie Jar. Ranchers congregate at Andy's Diner, and teens hit one of the town's drive-ins. Being a tourism center, Fredericksburg has a number of great dining options, but when it comes to burgers and a shake, the concensus choice is the Plateau Restaurant. Nighttime action is to be found on the dance floor of the South Star, but with Austin just a short drive away, many prefer that city's hoppin' night clubs and incredibly diverse restaurants.

Economic Impact of the Arts

The community enjoys a broad-based economy, one in which the arts are recognized as an important component of what works in keeping local people employed and tourists making return trips into Fredericksburg to spend their money. The town has a large group of glass blowers, furniture makers, quilters, jewelers, blacksmiths, sculptors, and painters, many of whom are involved in local politics and nonprofit organizations.

Local Arts Agency

Pedernales Creative Arts Alliance, 108 N. Adams, Fredericksburg, TX 78624, (210) 997-4810. Publishes the *PCAA Newsletter*.

"We may not have an arts center or an arts museum, but we've still got a reputation as a community with a lot of artists," says Susan Rees, president of the town's music club. "There's a new concert hall being built and it might have some dedicated visual arts exhibition space. I'd say the community's emphasis is on performing arts, but the visual arts and fine crafts are also very important. Fredericksburg has a city sales tax and a lodgers tax, with most of the revenue going toward promoting the town and helping local arts groups. We're small, cultural, and historic, and that's what's attracting a lot of people to move here. There's something for everyone."

Galleries and Arts Festivals

There are eight galleries in the downtown area selling original paintings and prints, but Fredericksburg's surrounding countryside is loaded with craftspeople and artists who sell directly from their home studios. Trouble is, you've either got to know the artist, or try to wrangle a Fredericksburg local to point you in the direction of a studio or two. The year's biggest festival takes place in the fall, when Octoberfest has downtown streets blocked off for the thousands of beer lovers who pour into town.

What the Artist Says

Gerald Harvey, who paints under the moniker of G. Harvey, is one of the nation's foremost artists working in the western realist genre. "To me, Fredericksburg is like stepping back 25 years in time. Here, artists are just another one of the neighbors you meet on the street. It's an enjoyable place to paint and you don't have to feel like you're living in a fishbowl, even though there are tourists in town just about every weekend of the year.

"There are lots of great homes built by the German settlers, and a talented artist can come in here, buy a place and fix it up himself. What you end up with is a perfect place to come home to and just turn off the switch. I'm in favor of anyone who comes in here to help keep this area's historic qualities alive—you learn to appreciate the German culture. People move here and sacrifice in order to make it—you've got to work hard and be versatile, but it's a great community of people."

Kerrville, Texas

Location
Right where the green hills of Texas hill country flatten out into the dryland expanse of the west Texas desert, Kerrville's 17,000 residents live in a land of rivers, mesas, and pinon-covered rangelands.

Climate
Much less humid than the weather common in nearby San Antonio (an hour's drive southeast), Kerrville is the beneficiary of some of the rainstorms that sweep northward from the Gulf of Mexico. Yet, whenever that happens, there's always a warm, dry front that pushes in from the west, restoring the area's more typical sunny warmth. Summer is hot and almost always dry, while winter is mild and eminently tolerable, which explains the region's attraction as a retirement haven.

Living
While Kerrville's location in south-central Texas may seem isolated, it has actually worked as a powerful inducement for artists seeking both a stunning and inspirational desert landscape setting, as well as easy access to galleries in San Antonio, Houston, and Dallas. The community has one of the best managed and most influential art centers found in any small American town, and because of it Kerrville (and Ingram, 7 miles away) not only has a center for its artistic energies, but also an identity that gives the arts priority. A 3-bedroom home in one of Kerrville's neighborhoods lists in the $85,000 range, but in the smaller communities nearby, such as Comfort and Ingram, places cost considerably less. Local residents make regular shopping and entertainment trips into San Antonio, with the hour-long drive being considered about as inconvenient as would be a trip to a suburban mall for a city-dweller. Gulf Coast beaches are just a few hours away, but the favorite fishing and boating spot in Kerrville's corner of the state is the Guadalupe River.

Out On the Town
For a small town, Kerrville's commitment to activities involving both the visual arts and performing is impressive. Sure, the lure of San Antonio's art museums and galleries beckon, but Kerrville has an impressive museum of its own in the Cowboy Artists of America Museum, a facility holding a large annual arts bash and regular one-artist exhibitions throughout the year. The Kerrville Performing Arts Society presents an ambitious schedule of classical music and dance at the town's auditorium, while the Hill Country Arts Foundation, in nearby Ingram, produces a year-round slate of offbeat theater at its Smith-Ritch Point Theater, and in an open ampitheater along the Guadalupe River during summer. Dining out isn't a problem in this area. Local residents who want a great hamburger have about a zillion places to choose from, but the concensus for top honors goes to the Ranch House in Ingram. Another nearby town, Hunt, seems to be the best place to go both for dinner at the Hunt Store, and staying on for the nighttime fun at Crider's, a club featuring live music and boogie-woogie entertainment.

Economic Impact of the Arts

Kerrville is in a fortunate position these days: The local business economy is doing very well just trying to keep up with the recent influx of new residents to the area, the state's economy has been gaining momentum after a few lean years at the end of the 1980s, and the community is developing a broad reputation as an exciting place to visit for both visual arts and musical performance. There seems to be enough funding available to support the arts programming being brought into the area, and the commercial end of the area's arts scene also is doing surprisingly well. This is an exciting place to be right now. There seems to be a balanced approach to art and business . . . and it's working!

Local Arts Agency

Hill Country Arts Foundation, P.O. Box 176, Ingram, TX 78025, (210) 367-5120. Publishes the newsletter *Spotlight*.

"We don't really have a special emphasis, but it seems that it's our theater programming that gets the most attention," says foundation executive director Betty Vernon. "Our facilities are outstanding—we've got an 1,800-square-foot visual arts gallery, a 700-seat ampitheater on the river, three multi-purpose studios, and an art library. People say they move here because of the area's beauty and rich cultural life. Right now we're not officially involved in art education programs through the schools, but our location across the street from the high school gives us a constant flow of students. Working with a focus on youth is part of our long-range planning. We have an annual student art show, an annual art career day, and on occasion we have theater programs in the schools. One of our challenges is to continue working with the local business community in emphasizing that there's a broader economic impact from the arts in this area than they realize."

Galleries and Arts Festivals

Both the Hill Country Arts Foundation and the nearby Cowboy Artists of America museum have nonprofit exhibition spaces. There are ten commercial galleries in the Kerrville area, many of which exhibit western realism. One of the biggest arts bashes of the year is the Texas State Arts and Crafts Fair on Memorial Day and the following weekends, while the Kerrville Folk Music Festival in late May and early June attracts hundreds of musicians and craftspeople.

What the Artist Says

Dan Burt, a painter who works in a broken color, impressionistic style. "Artists have been drawn in by the Cowboy Artists Museum. It used to be a lot quieter around here than it is now, and it would be a shame if Kerrville lost its tranquility. This town is a good place for an artist to start—you've got places to sell and show your work, lots of art fairs and shows, and there are people in the little towns around here who buy art and have an intuitive feel for good art. Still, you've got to be careful about selling your work outside the area. There's some Sunday painter-style work in the galleries here, but there's also a lot of more professional, serious work in pastels and oil."

Round Top, Texas

Location

The pastoral splendor of Round Top is typical of the Texas Hill Country, a region of rolling hills, flowing springs, and oak forests. Round Top and its 200 or so full-time residents are an hour's drive southeast of Austin, the state capital.

Climate

Long considered a refuge from the intense heat and humidity of Houston (a 2-hour drive), Round Top is a summer retreat for city folks needing a weekend break. Of course, it's still hot and humid here in summer, just less so than in places closer to the Gulf of Mexico. Winter is quite mild, with occasional snatches of freezing temperatures, quickly followed by a return of the region's more characteristic gentle coolness. Spring arrives early, bringing out the blazing color of Texas' legendary wildflowers, while autumn is rather undistinguished.

Living

Settled by German farmers and ranchers, Round Top is still the small town it always was, except now there are hundreds of weekend homes spread throughout the region on anywhere from two to two hundred acres of land. While there's been a gradual rise in real estate prices, a 3-bedroom residence on a couple of acres can be purchased for $100,000. Some folks prefer buying raw land and moving a older home from elsewhere in the area onto their property. Schools in the area are considered quite good, if somewhat strict. There are a few state parks and lakes scattered throughout the area, but most local residents prefer driving a few hours to the Gulf Coast for relaxation over a three-day weekend. Austin's nightclubs and malls are within easy reach, as are the glitzier attractions of Houston.

Out On the Town

While the nearby community of Winedale hosts an annual Shakespeare festival, the unique music center of Festival Hill is what sets Round Top apart from other small art towns in the country. Established in 1973 by James Dick, an internationally famous concert pianist, Festival Hill and its reputation among classical music audiences has grown like Topsy over the past two decades. Today, it's the center of both a summer-long academic program for musically gifted students and the location of a year-round schedule of musical programs that range from simple recitals to full-scale orchestral extravaganzas in its 1,000-seat concert hall.

The grounds at Festival Hill are a wonder in their own right, combining European fountains and stone bridges with residences and administrative buildings strongly influenced by Russian and Germanic architectural aesthetics. Festival Hill provides this wonderful community with a year-round economic lifeblood, filling bed and breakfast inns, as well as the community's cafes, gift shops, and art gallery.

This being the Texas hill country, you can count on finding lots of restaurants (and some places that defy description) serving either German hofbrau-haus style food or the area's local favorite of barbecue beef. Trouble is, you've got to drive some distance to get anywhere and find anything, but that's not a complete drawback, since doing so takes you through other Hill Country communities, many of which are picture-postcard visions of small-town America.

Round Top has its own café (Royer's Round Top Cafe) on the town square, and if you want you can sit outside on one of the bales of hay stacked on the porch and have a great, liberally sized cheeseburger and a delightfully democratic strawberry shake, not to mention the yummy Jimmy Carter favorite peanut butter-and-jelly sandwich. On the other side of the square is Klump's Cafe, a long-standing local favorite for its Friday night fried catfish feeds. Hackemack's, a Bavarian-style restaurant just outside nearby Fayetteville, is one of the area's most popular places for dinner and a stein of lager.

Economic Impact of the Arts

By all means, the effect of the arts on the community is substantial. Not only does Round Top benefit from the financial ripple-effect associated with the concerts and programs at Festival Hill, it's also the headquarters for the enormous, twice-yearly antiques festivals organized by the state's antiques and traditional folk arts impresario, Emma Lee Turney. Held in early April and October, these events are among the nation's largest antiques shows, bringing thousands of buyers into the region for a three-day spending fest. Emma Lee's bashes are so successful that towns for miles around have organized similar events, but the originals at Round Top maintain the highest level of quality.

What the Artist Says

James Dick, concert pianist and founder of Festival Hill. "We're attracting visitors from the three major cities (Dallas, Houston, and Austin), as well as many local residents who are interested in what we're doing. Our interests are in education and performance. I see Festival Hill as a neutral base, a non-affiliated home to all organizations and groups who may want to use us as a conference or training center. The public is growing more aware of the value of having a place like Festival Hill."

William Anzalone, a landscape painter working in pastels, has this to say: "Round Top's location lets an artist stay in close touch with galleries in Texas, New Orleans, and Oklahoma, but it also allows you to live in a rural, relaxing environment. The town is becoming a retirement magnet and that's dictating some change. There's a shrinking of the family farms and a raising of taxes that's threatening a traditional way of life. Something has to be done to allow everyone who was raised in this area to continue living here and not be priced out. Round Top is a community with an arts awareness, but the people who come in here to buy art are from everywhere. If you want to live here and make a living as an artist you've got to have markets in other places."

Bluff, Utah

Location

At the northern edge of the Navajo Reservation, the southeastern Utah community of Bluff has 250 residents most of the year, but during the river rafting season that number easily triples. The closest city is Albuquerque, New Mexico, a 5-hour drive southeast.

Climate

At times you'd swear you were on Mars: The landscape is devoid of what most people would consider vegetation, there are flat-top mesas and steep arroyos everywhere you turn, the yearly rainfall totals can be measured in a juice glass, and it can get hot enough to melt a dashboard. Winter is windy and occasional snowstorms blow in from nearby mountains. But spring is always an early-arriving season, followed quickly by the river runners and busloads of European tourists searching for their own *Dances With Wolves* sort of experience with the local Utes and Navajos.

Living

As you would probably guess, the artists attracted to Bluff are here for only part of the year, choosing to live and work in the arid vastness of southern Utah while the weather is hot, then hightailing it back to the city when the cold winds start blowing. For some, summer rentals (as hard as they are to find) are the way to go, while others have built small residences on a few acres of land scattered around Bluff and are happy just to make their homes here during the warmer months. Homes rent in the $500-per-month range, and once in awhile a 2- or 3-bedroom home sells in the neighborhood of $65,000.

Surrounded by state parks, national parks, and the Navajo Nation, local residents are hardly at a loss for things to do. If sailing and water skiing on Lake Powell don't appeal to you, there's always great fishing in the Blue Mountains. Monument Valley's spectacular rock formations are just a short drive away, as is the Hopi Reservation. The closest ski areas are a couple hour's drive away in Colorado.

Out On the Town

Bluff has a Thai restaurant! Yes, that's right, this little town is the smallest community in the entire world (okay, Southeast Asia not included) with its own palace of fanciful, traditional Thai dining. Folks around here were pretty shocked, to say the least, when they found out that a new restaurant was being built in tiny Bluff a couple years ago. After all, Bluff's only other restaurant, the Sunbonnet Cafe, had been doing good business for years, serving everything from morning flapjacks and coffee for the town's two cops to flipping burgers for the local teenagers who stop by on weekends. Then, when the residents of Bluff found out that their new restaurant wasn't going to be serving T-bone steaks, fried fish, and apple pie . . . well, let's just say the whole town had something new to talk about over morning coffee.

Every once in a while a few local musicians will get together for an informal afternoon jam session, and there's a stage group up the road in Blanding that puts on drama and musical performances every so often. If your needs are more complicated than that, or if you want to go out and beat the living daylights out of a dance floor, the best thing to do is drive to nearby Farmington, New Mexico.

Economic Impact of the Arts
Visitors come into town, run a river, fawn over a Native American child, eat at one of the two restaurants (did I mention one is a Thai restaurant?), and then look for something to buy.

Local Arts Agency
Creative Freedom Alliance, P.O. Box 327, Bluff, UT 84512, (801) 672-2337.

"Here, art here isn't a highly visible presence, you've got to go out and look for it," says founder Margaret LaBounty. "The local business community is very supportive of the arts and sees much of its growth as directly tied into the health of Bluff's arts and artists. When we have an event in town, it's usually something sent in by the state arts council, and almost everybody attends and supports it with donations. We're very concerned about helping Utah's Navajo and Ute artists to enter the state's arts mainstream. We help with organizational and educational assistance. Our schools are very aware of the need for arts education—we have artists going into the schools for classes, and there are programs organized by the state arts council that make their way down here. Housing is very limited, so artists have to be flexible enough to make do with different living situations. Crime is very low, and any artist who has an opinion about the way things are run is listened to and respected."

Galleries and Arts Festivals
Bluff has two art galleries selling local, original work (unlike the garbage shown in Moab) and has three trading posts in its area (which are mercantile buildings selling everything from milk to hand-woven, Two Grey Hills rugs made by Navajo craftswomen). The year's largest arts festival is the Bluff Fair and Pow Wow, a 100-artist and performer affair taking place over a September weekend.

What the Artist Says
Howard Holiday, a landscape painter and jeweler whose imagery concerns traditional Navajo lands and communities. "We're able to sell lots of work in the gallery and the trading posts, but it's best to make your paintings small if the Europeans are going to buy them. I learned painting a long time ago, and this is the only area I've painted. Someday I'd like to try painting the Indian lands in Canada. I've seen photographs of their mountains and that's something I'd like to paint. Here, younger artists have a hard time making enough money to keep them happy—they go to Santa Fe or Phoenix to be closer to the galleries, or they stay here and have two occupations. In any case, the main thing for them to do is work hard on their art and not just talk about doing it—get out there and do it."

Moab, Utah

Location

Southeast Utah is a landscape of smooth (also called slick) rock formations that, in many instances, are mountainous hillsides coagulated into a continuous moonscape of red and yellow terrain ideally suited for mountain bikes. Moab's 5,000 residents live in a verdant canyon of the Colorado River, nearly a 4-hour drive southeast of Salt Lake City.

Climate

Dry as a bone, Moab gets its share of mid-winter blasts, but they're almost always brief affairs that are followed by spells of warmer air blowing in from the Arizona desert. Spring arrives early, bringing out desert wildflowers and heralding the start of Moab's river rafting and slick rock bicycling season. Both are major tourism attractions, along with the allure this former mining community holds for the summer hordes of Europeans and wandering midwesterners. Summer can get very hot in the desert areas outside Moab, but temperatures in the town itself are moderated somewhat by its canyon setting.

Living

The most pressing issue being dealt with locally is growth . . . and lots of it. From the crush of tourists lured here by Moab's proximity to Arches National Park and Canyonlands National Park to the newcomers building homes on the town's outskirts, the subject on everyone's mind is how to deal with Moab's success. Commercially, the downtown business folks spend most of their time and money building mini-malls filled with trinket shops, and too few people seem to care. The average tourist coming through Moab is so unfamiliar with the American Southwest that they often make the mistake of thinking they've stumbled onto the real thing.

Moab's residential areas, once crime-free and peaceful, are now on the receiving end of a troublesome string of burglaries. An average 3-bedroom home close to the business district sells in the $90,000 range, but there are farm homes in much quieter areas just a short drive from town selling for considerably less.

Out On the Town

From the dining perspective, Moab's growth has been a godsend. There's a brewpub in town, Eddie McStiff's, that's one of the Southwest's best watering holes. Creekside is a Szechuan restaurant that does a credible job with General Tso's chicken and the like, and Club Rio is a great spot for Tex-Mex dishes and margaritas, along with Moab's best nighttime scene. Don't miss the dance floor action at Sportsman's Lounge, which also has pool tables and dart boards. Eli's Branding Iron is the town's best bet for burgers, while Honest Ozzie's serves up vegetarian dishes for confirmed grazers. Music in Moab takes a couple of interesting forms, with folk music concerts and an occasional classical program being presented at Star Hall throughout the year. During summer, the Utah Symphony and Utah Ballet team up with one of the town's many river rafting companies in presenting performances along the Colorado River. The community has also started a week-long music festival covering contemporary and ethnic musical formats in mid-September.

Economic Impact of the Arts
The community's economic outlook is bright due to the popularity of river rafting and mountain biking tourism. Music performance is in better shape locally than the visual arts, primarily because local business types see a way to make a buck selling tickets to tourists. In other words, the entire arts scene here is money-driven, even though there are somewhere close to 60 serious, professional artists living in Moab.

Local Arts Agency
Canyonlands Arts Council, P.O. Box 1441, Moab, UT 84532, (801) 259-843. Publishes the *CAC Newsletter*.

"Galleries in Moab are struggling to duplicate the clichéd appearance of those in Santa Fe, and aren't overly concerned about the work of Moab's fine artists," says local photographer and mixed-media artist ViviAnn Rose. "There are lots of paintings by Anglo artists of corny, romanticized images of Native Americans, and that seems to be what sells to tourists and to the people who are buying artwork for their new homes around here. The schools coordinate programs with music performers, and the arts council has workshops for school kids—we're just starting to see the schools get interested in arts beyond simple painting classes. The arts council is dominated by advertising people and store owners who have no interest in fine art, and are just using the council as a way to protect their T-shirt shops."

Galleries and Arts Festivals
While there are six commercial galleries in Moab, only one, the bizarrely named Marc II Gallery, shows original work by the town's best painters, jewelers, and craftspeople. Two nonprofit exhibition spaces are also attractive to fine arts professionals: the Post Office Gallery, and the rotating gallery at the Dan O'Laurie Museum. The town's biggest arts bash is the Moab Arts Festival in late May at Moab City Park.

What the Artist Says
Sereena Supplee, watercolorist, has lived in Moab since 1980. "There's not much of a local market. Things in the galleries are kept low-end and anyone serious about their art sells outside the area in Santa Fe, Park City, or Aspen. The kind of tourist we get knows little and cares less about art. I love painting from the landscape here . . . I couldn't see leaving. My work is like a dream memory of having been somewhere in this area. Moab needs to put a greater emphasis on quality and good planning—it's a great place to live, but you've got to move your work in other areas. The galleries here just aren't interested in anything besides howling coyotes and junk that even the worst galleries in Santa Fe wouldn't touch with a ten-foot pole."

Park City, Utah

Location
So close to Salt Lake City that it could be considered a suburb, Park City (pop. 8,000) is a historic community that once owed its livelihood to mining, but is now known as a year-round resort area with one of the country's best ski areas, and one of its most prestigious film festivals.

Climate
Winter is snowy, long and cold, which is just the way ski-crazed locals like it, thank you. Summer has an unforgettable alpine accent, with frequent afternoon thundershowers breaking up day after day of spectacular weather. Autumn is breathtakingly beautiful as the Wasatch Mountains burst into life with golden aspen colors. Spring is muddy and windy.

Living
Remember, you're just an hour's drive outside a major city, so everything from an international airport to professional sports, rock concerts, and shopping malls are right at your doorstep. Meanwhile, you're in a community that occasionally realizes its best economic bets lie in preserving the local charm and keeping a year-round flow of visitors into Park City for weekend and weeklong stays.

Being both popular and convenient has its price, and in Park City that's meant the usual, Californicated housing market and an ever increasing number of newcomers. There are a lot of 3-bedroom homes available for $250,000, which means that native and long-time Utahans can't afford living in Park City. There's an inflow of Californians (usually not welcomed by locals), and an outflow of savvy locals (look for them in towns 30 miles away).

Out On the Town
Absolutely great restaurants, movie theaters, and live music—and anything you can't find here is less than an hour's drive away. There are local theater productions staged at the Egyptian Theater. The best local hangout is the Black Pearl Club on Main Street, a place to meet friends and pass the hours shooting a few racks. The local Thai diner is called Bangkok Thai, and burgers are fantastic at, of course, Burgie's. Vegetarians mow their favorite garden greens down at the Windy Ridge, and nightlife has lots of choices, but there are less puffed-up cowpokes at Cisero's, a popular place with locals.

Economic Impact of the Arts
Throughout the months that fall between April and November, the local tourism promotions and events have a decided arts component at their center—from film festivals to arts fairs to juried exhibitions, there's some connection to the community's arts scene made as part of the pitch. As a result, almost the entire community realizes that were it not for the arts, Park City's off-season tourism would be flat.

174

Local Arts Agency

Park City Arts Council, P.O. Box 4455, Park City, UT 84060, (801) 647-9747. Publishes the newsletter *Park City Cultural Arts Quarterly*.

"We emphasize performing arts programs aimed at children," says council executive director Joanna Charnes. "We regularly bring in children's theater, storytellers, dancers, and puppeteers, with performances held at the school auditoriums. We don't bring in touring plays because there's a private promoter already filling that need. The town is filled with too many nonprofits for local business to support all of them (Note: newcomers with no social contacts form nonprofit groups as a way of occupying their spare time). There's a lot of emphasis put on marketing golf courses, but there are far less golfers than people who come in for the arts festivals and shows. Schools are minimally involved in building arts into their educational curriculums—they're unaware of how to use local artists to shore up the shortcomings in their own staffs and programs."

Galleries and Arts Festivals

There are slightly more than a dozen commercial galleries in Park City: a couple of which are first-rate, and some that show locally created original paintings, photography, sculpture, and crafts. A few others emphasize western realism created by artists from around the region, and more than a few show the trite, commercialized images of Native American life. The year's best arts bash is the Park City Arts Festival, a weekend-long event in early August, with over 200 exhibitors.

What the Artist Says

David Whitten, photographer, has lived in Park City for 14 years. "The town is a good market for art, if you give people what they want. During winter you can sell just about anything, but it's more difficult in spring and fall. That's the time I'll do arts and craft fairs in California and Colorado. We're seeing some of the best open spaces get developed, and I hope that the people moving in here won't just turn around and trash Park City's environment the same way they trashed the last places they lived. It's a struggle trying to get local galleries to show serious photography, and the rents are so high downtown that there's a constant turnover of businesses forced out when their leases aren't renewed. There's a good market for locally-inspired art work, but there aren't enough artists here who are interested in doing it. People who are buying homes here want to find regional art, but they have a difficult time getting their hands on it."

Springville, Utah

Location
Less than an hour's drive from the shopping malls and professional sports arenas in Salt Lake City, Springville's 16,000 residents live in the shadow of the Wasatch Mountains, spread throughout a valley known as one of the state's premier fruit-growing regions.

Climate
Winter in the lowlands bordering the Wasatch range can be surprisingly mild one year and brutally difficult the next. One thing that's always dependable is the fabulous skiing in the nearby mountains. Local residents keep their fingers crossed whenever a big storm rolls through, hoping the worst weather stays in the hills. Summer is fairly hot and dry, while spring's arrival in March provides a gradual wind-up into the year's hotter months.

Living
Safe and committed to educational excellence, life in Utah is a family's dream. Each community seems to have public parks with youth recreation programs, not to mention senior citizen centers and local governments with a positive, can-do attitude. Springville, the state's most prominent arts community, has long been a magnet for artists of all media and imagery. From contemporary painters to western realist sculptors, this community has embraced its creative professionals and used its outstanding art museum as a showcase for the region's arts talents.

Recent years have seen a resurgence in the area's economy, with a concurrent rise in the numbers of out-of-state newcomers who are finding Springville a great place to live. Artists have no difficulty locating downtown studio space for $400 per month. The average 3-bedroom home in one of Springville's quiet neighborhoods sells for $70,000. Recreation opportunities are practically unlimited in this area, ranging from the winter sports in nearby mountains to freshwater lakes for fishing and sailing. Southern Utah, an area with a much warmer climate, is also a popular getaway for its national parks and extensive system of lakes.

Out On the Town
Just down the road from the college town of Provo, home of Brigham Young University, Springville has this larger city and its numerous cultural opportunities at its disposal. BYU has an extremely active performing arts school, especially in music and theater, which means that on any given weekend there's bound to be a play, recital, orchestral presentation, or opera underway somewhere in Provo. Springville's art museum presents an ambitious program of Sunday musical performances throughout the year, with a concert each month, ranging from woodwinds ensembles to classical guitar recitals. The school's visual arts department is also highly respected, and the art department's annual exhibitions are attended by gallery owners and artists from throughout Utah and its surrounding states.

Eating in Springville isn't quite as fulfilling an experience as it is in Provo, which has a broad selection of ethnic restaurants and dozens of the usual college hangouts for the pizza and submarine sandwich crowd. La Casita, owned by a Mexican family, is a Springville lunch and dinner favorite, as is Hoagie Yogi, a sandwich palace. Art City Trolley is a casual place for great burgers and salads. The best ice cream in the area is at Neilsen's Custard in Provo. Lemar's nightclub in Provo, and the Brass Bucket Lounge at the Provo Holiday Inn, are two favorite places for nighttime fun. Johnny B's Comedy Club is a Provo nightspot drawing national talent.

Economic Impact of the Arts

Springville has always promoted itself as the Art City, and to drive down its main street is to observe a number of ambitious public sculptural installations, along with several galleries and an active influential and broad-minded museum. The town's business community sees art as an important underpinning of the local economy—there's a large frame manufacturer in town, as well as a bronze foundry serving Springville's growing community of sculptors.

Local Arts Agency

Springville Arts Commission, 50 S. Main, Springville, UT 84663, (801) 489-2726.

"Our orientation is toward the arts and humanities," says Teddy Anderson, executive director of the commission. "We support theater, historical representations, literary programs, and musical performances at the museum. Local dance is covered by a person affiliated with BYU. Springfield businesses are involved, one way or another, in the arts. Private industry is an important funding source, now that the state arts council is under attack and having its budget cut. We'd like to see more of an emphasis on the arts in our local schools—the art teachers are good, but there needs to be a broader arts experience than simply bringing the kids through the museum."

Galleries and Arts Festivals

Downtown Springville has eight commercial galleries, most of which exhibit creations by the community's sculptors, painters, and traditional craft artists, while the community's nonprofit exhibition space is at the art museum. The notable arts festival held each year in Spring Acres Arts Park is the Springville World Folkfest in early July, a week-long celebration of international dance featuring performers from all over the globe. Each April, the Springville Museum of Art holds its Spring Salon Preview, an exhibition held in conjunction with a fundraising ball.

What the Artist Says

Gary Price, a realist sculptor whose figurative bronzes are sold at galleries in Santa Fe, Scottsdale, and elsewhere, says, "I don't mind the town growing, because now it's easier to find sponsors for our public art pieces. We're losing a lot of open space, but we'll always keep our small town atmosphere. Here, the arts are seen as something that's supposed to benefit the entire community. Our sculpture program is trying to place two public pieces each year in Springville—we've got seven pieces up now, and are about to install our first contemporary piece.

"If this community can attract 30 or so full-time sculptors, there's no telling what could happen in Springville. The town sees its art museum as a place to be used—there are lectures, wedding receptions, art auctions, and musical performances at the museum throughout the year. The new corporations that moved in are responsible for a lot of local art sales, both for the offices and by the executives who are acquiring locally made work."

Brattleboro, Vermont

Location

The southeast corner of Vermont is a landscape of low, rolling hills and medium-size farms carved from dense woodlands. Brattleboro (at 12,500, the region's largest population center) is slightly more than a 2-hour drive northwest of Boston.

Climate

Magnificent summers, though brief, were responsible for pulling the first Boston and New York tourists into Vermont, and Mother Nature's mid-year magic is still working. This part of the state tends to experience more heat and humidity than does the rest of Vermont, and autumn's arrival lags a couple of weeks behind as well, but that means the blinding colors of fall can be appreciated much later in the year in Brattleboro. Winter is almost always cold and snowy, but every few years there's a problem with El Niño and the local ski areas end up taking it in the shorts. Spring is a gorgeous season in its own right.

Living

A strongly artistic community, Brattleboro is unusual in that it has attracted large numbers of both visual artists and musicians. The visual artists are a mixed community of established names in the New York art world who maintain vacation homes and studios in the area, along with over a hundred local talents in painting, sculpture, and fine craft, who sell in the region's many galleries as well as market their creations outside Vermont.

The musicians, on the other hand, are drawn here by the powerhouse Brattleboro Music Center, an institution presenting a year-round program of classical, chamber, and orchestral music performance in classroom, festival, and concert settings. Due to the music center, Brattleboro has become a favored home base for an internationally respected community of musicians and arts administrators. The town is also the center for both the New England Bach Festival and the Marlboro Music Festival.

Brattleboro's past as a manufacturing town has given today's artists and musicians an abundance of studio rental sites, with the average rent in the $500-per-month range. There are several neighborhoods and a strong local school system. The average 3-bedroom home sells for $125,000. Outdoor recreation opportunities—from the many small trout streams meandering toward the Connecticut River to hiking and mountain biking trails in state parks—are just a few minute's drive from the town square. Winter turns the area into a cross-country skiing paradise, and some of the state's largest ski areas are within a half-hour drive.

Out On the Town

A number of venues around Brattleboro are pressed into service during the hectic summer music season, including churches, public auditoriums, college recital halls, and the center's own performing arts facilities. Two theater groups, the Vermont Theater Company and the Whetstone Theater Company, are active year-round in Brattleboro. The town has a first-rate East Indian restaurant and a number of fancier dinner spots ranging from Northern Italian to seafood. Popular places for musicians to knock off a few leisure hours are the Mole's Eye Cafe and Mocha Joe's. Latchis Bar & Grill has the town's best burgers. Vegetarian specialties are the order of the day at the Brattleboro Coop. The town's two-steppers prance over to the Common Ground for nighttime fun.

Economic Impact of the Arts

While most of Vermont has managed to identify itself strongly with the winter ski-oriented economy, summers have presented dilemmas of their own for resort operators, restaurateurs, and gallery owners. Brattleboro is very fortunate to have an economy that's founded on a firmer, more year-round range of attractions rather than having to place the lion's share of its hopes in the arms of Mother Nature and her bountiful snowfalls.

Local Arts Agency

Brattleboro Music Center, 15 Walnut Street, Brattleboro, VT 05301, (802) 257-4523. Publishes the newsletter *Grace Notes*.

"The kind of support we get from Brattleboro's business community is very strong," says Center publicist Virginia Fleet. "There are those in the area who consider what we do to be elitist, but they tend to be the people who have never been here to attend a performance, or taken the time to try and understand what we do. Our approach has been to provide a series of free concerts on the town square and to provide the elementary schools with free classroom lessons from our musicians. We also have a subsidized ticket program for music students who want to attend any of our performances, and we bring musical groups into the schools for free performances. The kind of attention we get from newspapers in Boston, New York, and Washington, D.C., brings in the type of tourist who has money to spend on hotels, restaurants, performance tickets, and art work."

Galleries and Arts Festivals

With the Music Center's performance schedules, the Marlboro Music Festival and New England Bach Festival attracting well-heeled visitors to Brattleboro, you might assume there would be lots of art galleries ready to expose these tourists to the talent of the region's artists, but that's not the case. Brattleboro has only one commercial gallery, and a few shops mixing craft into their retail displays. There is a nonprofit gallery, but in a community of this nature there needs to be a stronger emphasis placed on mainstream commercial art exhibition spaces. Each summer, the Stratton Arts Festival is the region's most popular visual arts event.

What the Artist Says

"One of the problems with keeping an art gallery open year-round in Brattleboro is that winter tourists tend to drive right past us and head north," says Norman Krampetz, director of the nonprofit Windham Gallery. "This is a great place for younger artists to start their careers—you can make good gallery connections outside Vermont by showing your work locally."

William Hayes, a painter and co-organizer of the Stratton Arts Festival, says the town is changing. "We're seeing more gentrification, but my hope is that there will be some new art galleries along with these changes. The visual arts need to be as well-organized as the music arts are if we're going to be successful at broadening the town's tourism appeal."

Johnson, Vermont

Location
About as far north as you can go in Vermont and not see road signs in both French and English, the community of Johnson has a number of resident artists, a state college, and a regional arts center serving its population of 2,500.

Climate
Bring your snowshoes in the winter and a fishing pole in summer. Winters are difficult and lengthy, an environment the artists in this part of the state find most conducive to concentrating on their studio work. Summers are marked by an intensely distracting insect season followed by three months of perfect weather, neither too warm nor too cool. Autumn arrives very early, which means the swivel-necked leaf addicts start showing up in mid-September for their yearly ritual of driving down local roads at dangerously slow speeds.

Living
Isolated and beautiful, Johnson appeals most to the painters who take their inspirational cues from the glory of Mother Nature. There are a number of contemporary artists living in Johnson and the surrounding terrain, along with many dozens of traditionalist painters. The area is an outdoors-man's paradise, attracting an economically important flood of hunters in late fall, and fly fishermen during the summer months.

Johnson State College has an active arts department with theater, dance, and film programs staged throughout the school year, serving as an important cultural anchor for local residents who prefer not to make the hour-long drive into Burlington. The Vermont Studio Center, a nationally known center for education in both visual arts and literature, provides a resource for artists that is practically unheard of in the normal context of rural communities. The Center pulls in artists and big-name instructors not just from the Northeast, but from the rest of the country, Europe, and Mexico as well. They stay for residency programs that combine quiet, studio work time with instructional sessions for mid-career painters and writers. The atmosphere is one of dedicated professionalism pursued in a setting of camaraderie, natural splendor, and serious work.

Out On the Town
A short drive from Johnson brings you into the resort community of Stowe, the center for a sophisticated summer music festival, as well as many great restaurants catering to the taste of well-heeled summer and winter visitors. Locally, the theater productions at Johnson State College and in Burlington, are quite popular. Johnson has several places to enjoy a fine meal, including the Plum & Maine Restaurant, a place that manages to serve both the area's best hamburger along with an extensive menu of vegetarian specialties. If it's raining on a Saturday, try knocking off a few spare hours at the Long Trail Tavern, while those with a burning desire for leg shakin' can try the dance floor at the Northern Lights Cafe in nearby Eden.

Economic Impact of the Arts

Johnson has retained its traditional economic base of textiles manufacturing, but its business community realizes that many of the folks packing local restaurants, buying clothes in downtown shops, and filling their gas tanks at the service station are drawn in by the Studio Center. It's a small town, but one with an interestingly well-rounded economy and an appreciative, supportive business and government structure.

Local Arts Agency

Vermont Studio Center, P.O. Box 613, Johnson, VT 05656, (802) 635-2727. Publishes the newsletter *Green Muse*.

"We try to have a positive influence on whatever parts of Johnson we come into contact with," says Center founder Jonathan Gregg. "We have our instructors spend time in the local schools, have adult classes on weekends, and do murals projects in nearby towns. We don't ask for a lot. Our approach has been to become well-integrated, to keep a low profile, and to be seen as part of the community."

Galleries and Arts Festivals

In a sense, almost all of the Studio Center is an art gallery, albeit one with wet paint on the canvasses and paintings hung a lot more casually than would normally be the case in an exhibition setting. There's a more typical, nonprofit art space inside the Red Mill, which is also part of the Center. Commercial galleries have yet to make a foray into Johnson, and who can blame them? This would be a mighty tough crowd to please, and if someone looking at a painting said, "I could do a better job than that in an afternoon," you'd know they probably weren't just making an idle threat.

What the Artist Says

Andrea Pearlman, abstract painter: "There's a visible impact from the Studio Center in the many downtown buildings that have been renovated into classrooms, studios, and living spaces. The town is very livable, with lots of new shops, but still very rural and friendly. A good bookstore and a cafe with pastries and espresso would be wonderful, though!

"It seems as if a good part of the New York art world finds its way into Johnson—you can always count on there being a lecture, a demonstration, or an exhibition of somebody's work. The artists who live in the area are very supportive of each other, socialize a great deal, and are quick to share information on galleries and marketing opportunities. There are galleries near the ski areas, and they seem like good places for artists who are selling traditional landscape work.

"If you're a contemporary artist like I am, then you live here, work here, and ship your paintings out every month or so. If you come to live here, you've got to be prepared for the climate and the isolation, but it's wonderful to live in a small town where you can walk down the street and people will say hello to you, yet you still feel connected in some way to the art world outside of Vermont."

Montpelier, Vermont

Location

The state capital of Vermont is a quiet community of 8,000 residents, three colleges, and many creative arts professionals. Boston is a 3-hour drive southeast.

Climate

North-central Vermont is on the receiving end of winter's full force blast—snow starts flying at Halloween and doesn't let up until Easter, which explains why some local artists pack their VW campers around Labor Day and head down to the Florida Keys until it's time for the busy summer art fair season. Summer temperatures rarely climb past the 80-degree range, and the season is a brief, but wonderfully clear, few months. Autumn is typically New England spectacular, and spring creeps in slowly, providing the region with a tantalizing lead-in to the year's warmest days.

Living

Because it's the state capital, Montpelier has ridden out the Northeast's recession in much better shape than other similarly sized or larger communities. Craft artists have the highest profile in town, along with several galleries exhibiting fine craft work created in both contemporary and traditional forms.

This is a town filled with historic, centuries-old structures, and its residential districts are characterized by large, clapboard homes with porches and roomy yards. Studio space is somewhat difficult to find, primarily because the small downtown's surplus commercial space is rented to businesses involved in government contract work. The average 3-bedroom home in Montpelier lists in the $90,000 range, and there's a lot of open land available within an easy drive of town.

Alpine skiing is just a half-hour drive away, but cross-country trails are everywhere. There are many running trails around town, and a large community park. The nearby Mad River is one of the country's premier white water rafting and canoeing sites, and during the river's warmer, slower summer runs it turns into one of New England's largest nude sunbathing refuges.

Out On the Town

Winter seems to bring out the best in this town's performing arts scene, with several theater groups staging plays both at the colleges and in public venues such as the Pyralisk Coffeehouse. The neighboring town of Barre has renovated its historic opera house, and the programs there are a successful, welcome addition to regional entertainment options.

Ethnic food choices are somewhat limited in Montpelier, excluding the usual college-oriented pizza and taco joints. The Pyralisk Coffeehouse is a favorite hangout for artists, actors, and other creative types, offering everything from a cup of morning joe to nighttime performances of rock, blues, and folk music. Rub shoulders with politicos and get a dose of local color at the Thrush Tavern. Vegetarian food is the emphasis at the Horn of the Moon Cafe.

Economic Impact of the Arts

Until recently there was little organization among Montpelier's art community, but in the past couple of years several strong, high-profile moves such as the establishment of a summer arts festival, the renovation of the Barre Opera House, and the formation of an active network of arts-oriented services have gone a long way toward bringing the town's artists and craftspeople a type of attention they've never had in the past.

Local Arts Agency

Onion River Arts Council, 43 State Street, Montpelier, VT 05602, (802) 229-9408.

"Most of our focus is on the performing arts," says executive director Janet Ressler, "but we do take care of visual arts—our performance programs include folk music, world music, dance, and some literature. Much of it takes place in the Barre Opera House or at the Montpelier City Hall. There are some important parts of the city that see us as an economic asset, especially now that the summer arts festival is helping so many restaurants and hotels get new business. Our staff includes an education coordinator who gets students in to see our performance programs, has entertainers do workshops at the schools, and organizes an artist-in-residence program with the school districts. Our programming tries hard to be mainstream. The feeling is that if people want something more sophisticated they can drive to Burlington for it."

Galleries and Arts Festivals

While there are several retail stores handling the work of Montpelier's many fine craftspeople, the community lacks a commercial gallery dedicated to the visual arts. There are, however, several nonprofit exhibition venues around town, including the Artisans Handcraft Coop, the Vermont Historical Society, and the Wood Art Gallery. The year's biggest arts festival is MidSummer, an event staged in a downtown park, featuring visual art exhibitions, craft booths, and eight stages for performance ranging from reggae to contemporary dance. Midsummer takes place on the second Saturday in July, attracting 5,000 out-of-town visitors into Montpelier.

What the Artist Says

"Central Vermont has a long tradition of supporting theater, and every small town seems to have its own group staging shows," says Kim Bent, artistic director of the Lost Nation Theater. "We're able to do a five-play summer season, and then travel the state during the winter months doing workshops at schools and in small towns. Here, artists have been innovative in approaching businesses for support—we're aware of the need to emphasize how that support will be good for their own business. We could use more collaboration between the arts community and local schools, as well as among the different art programs in town.

"There's so much artistic talent of all kinds in Vermont that we should try to position ourselves as an arts-exporting state, rather than looking to places like New York and Boston for importing artists. Younger artists find this a great place to start their careers. Many stay three years or so, make their contacts and establish their reputations, then move on to places where they can make more money from their work."

Floyd, Virginia

Location

The Blue Ridge Mountains of southwest Virginia form a rugged barrier between the gentle, pine-covered lowlands of the state's east and its steep-sloped, coal mining counterpart to the west. Floyd, a mountain community of 500 residents, is less than an hour's drive from Roanoke, and just a few miles west of the Blue Ridge Parkway.

Climate

Long, humid summers roll in around mid-May and don't let up until the first part of October, bringing 90-degree temperatures and an endless army of junebugs, fireflies, and mosquitoes. Autumn along the highlands flanking the Blue Ridge Parkway is spectacular, and Floyd isn't an exception to the rule. Leaf season starts in early October, and continues through the month, leading into a winter that can at times be extremely cold, windy, and snow-choked. Spring is riotous with color, if somewhat brief.

Living

Artists move here for Floyd's rural charm and its affordability. Recent years have seen increasing numbers of gallery owners from Washington, D.C., Atlanta, and Charleston making swings through Floyd to look at the work by area ceramicists, painters, furniture makers, and craftspeople. Today it's possible just to stay inside your studio, concentrate on becoming as strong an artist as possible, and wait for opportunity to come knocking.

The schools in Floyd are run by local folks who take their jobs seriously but have the tendency to create monarchies. The average 3-bedroom home in Floyd consists of a good chunk of land, a large garden, and a separate garage, all for $75,000. Artists end up building their own studios, because there's no surplus space in the town's few commercial structures.

Outdoors-wise, the hunting season is an important economic boost for Floyd's economy, not to mention the impact it has on local freezers and dinner tables. Summers are great for rafting and canoeing on the Little River, which meanders past Floyd on its way to Claytor Lake, a favorite sailing and water skiing site. Most local artists participate in the community recreation leagues organized by the city, and local softball fields are busy places when the weather's warm.

Out On the Town

Being close to Roanoke, Floyd residents satisfy their ethnic food fixes or mall-walking urges with a half-hour drive to the city—which also happens to be the site of the Mountain Mill Theater, a repertory company presenting a year-round slate of performances. There's also a concert hall and a surprisingly diverse cultural life in Roanoke.

Floyd's charms are much simpler, consisting of Friday night folk music at the Pine Tavern, which is also the area's best place to go to pass a few hours on a rainy day . . . and about the only place in town for dinner. Lunches at the Harvest Moon, a friendly place that shows and sells the work of local artists, is popular with visitors, and is the only place in Floyd to go for a vegetarian meal. The community hasn't yet been defiled by the presence of fast food restaurants, although someone who wants a fast buck has been pushing to see if the high-fat, low-nutrition palaces could be lured into town.

Economic Impact of the Arts

The arts community in Floyd is subtle (yet very much in tune with what goes on in town), and keeps a low profile. Artists moved here for a rural life, one where the town goes about its normal business and the artists go about theirs—not for a town built up with galleries and weekend-tripping yuppies from D.C. looking for art bargains. Here, the artists are recognized as having made a contribution to Floyd, and they're respected as being professional people who are serious about their work, as well as being good neighbors.

Local Arts Agency

There is no local arts agency in Floyd. "You can drive through town and see the improvements, see the ways that artists living here have made a positive impact on the town," says ceramicist Donna Polseno. "You couldn't possibly have a profitable gallery here, but there's evidence that people from different places are becoming attracted to what is here. Now, there are glass blowers, several very wonderful furniture makers, a few painters, lots of ceramicists, and plenty of serious artists who do what they can to stay here and make a living, even if that means holding down a part-time job or two. Occasionally artists give a class in the local schools, but those of us who work in art know that it's best to take the time to spark our own kids' creativity while they're at home, rather than depend on the schools to do it."

Galleries and Arts Festivals

Floyd's professional artists are, for the most part, working so that their creations can be sent outside the area to metropolitan galleries along the East Coast. There's a very small market for local work, mostly to visitors who wander into town from the Blue Ridge Parkway during "leafer" season. Blue Mountain Mercantile exhibits the work of some Floyd ceramicists and furniture makers, but the best way to check out what's being made in Floyd is to hunt out the artists' studios and call to schedule a visit. Each fall, there's a traditional crafts show at the Floyd High School, with a few dozen, mostly local, exhibitors.

What the Artist Says

Ceramicist Ellen Shankin has lived in Floyd for 16 years. "Once in a while the artists in Floyd will do their own open studio sales, but for the most part we're selling to galleries and doing some craft shows during the summer in other areas. Local people don't pry into what you're doing, and unless someone asks to come by your studio, it's sort of live and let live around here. For a potter, this is an inspirational place. There are some highly skilled artists here, and they'll take the time to help you solve problems in your work. You can always see the work of people who are much better than you are, and that helps set a standard. Floyd should be preserved the way it is. We have no need for new buildings."

Fredericksburg, Virginia

Location
Slightly more than an hour's drive south of Washington, D.C., the historic community of Fredericksburg (pop. 16,000) is filled with residential and commercial structures dating back to the mid-1800s and earlier. The Rappahannock River runs through Fredericksburg's business district.

Climate
The area has mostly mild winters that are characterized much more by rain than snow, although when it does snow, all hell breaks loose. Autumn is picturesque, but not as spectacular as in Virginia's more mountainous regions. Spring creeps in around late March and heralds the start of a long, humid summer.

Living
Close enough to the D.C. area to be a bedroom community for thousands of civil servants and corporate types who commute from Fredericksburg, the community is also attractive to artists, and has for a number of years pulled in creative professionals who wanted to live within an easy drive of galleries in D.C., Richmond, and Philadelphia. Fredericksburg is also an ideally located community for craft and art fair pros whose markets are on the Eastern Seaboard, because it's within a long day's drive of both New England and Florida.

The seashore at Virginia Beach is just a 2-hour drive away, and the mountain ski areas of West Virginia are even closer. The average 3-bedroom home in one of Fredericksburg's neighborhoods sells in the $135,000 range, while studio space in the historic arts district runs around $350 per month for a place with wood floors, high windows, and brick walls.

Out On the Town
Fredericksburg has some musical performance and theater, but with two metropolitan areas (D.C. and Richmond) nearby, local residents have easy access to some of the best the country offers. Still, Mary Washington College has an active performing arts orientation and produces a number of stage productions and classical music presentations throughout the year. During summer, there's a chamber music festival in Fredericksburg, and occasional recitals at St. George Church. The town's historic arts district has an offbeat theater troupe, the Rude Mechanics.

The dining scene is quite sophisticated, and one of the best restaurants, La Petite Auberge, has rotating shows of work by local artists. A favorite hangout for the arts crowd is Sammy T's, a bar/cafe that attracts a multicultural crowd. Family Pizzeria is a favorite for lunch, Irish Brigade is a popular nightspot, and vegetarian food is one of the specialties at Nader's Grocery.

Economic Impact of the Arts
Up until a few years ago, the arts scene was a quiet, enjoyable component of the community's lifestyle—some artists had studios in the town's older districts, there was a gallery or two that showed locally created work, and every so often an open studio tour would bring potential buyers

through the area. That has changed, and today Fredericksburg's arts community is growing so rapidly that even the town's government is trying to decide how to play catch-up with the potential of this newly created economic resource.

Local Arts Agency

Fredericksburg Center for the Creative Arts, 813 Sophia St., Fredericksburg, VA 22401, (703) 373-5646.

The center, located in an historic building along Fredericksburg's river front, operates a nonprofit gallery with rotating monthly exhibits. "The town's strength is in the fine arts," says Janet Payne, fine arts coordinator for the school district. "There's been a lot of progress made with artists forming their own working co-ops and their presence has changed the way local people think about the work created by Fredericksburg's artists—the feeling is that the more artists and galleries we have, the better off the entire community will be. The business community needs to understand that the expansion of our arts scene will directly benefit the community's economic development.

"Arts are starting to be viewed as a social equalizer, a way to bring the entire community together through creative interaction. The schools are starting to use artist-in-residency programs, not just visual arts, but also writing, drama, and fine craft. There's always a battle being fought between the back-to-basics crowd and the people willing to try new remedies for longstanding problems in our schools."

Galleries and Arts Festivals

One sure-fire indicator of the health of Fredericksburg's visual arts scene is the way galleries have begun popping up around town—there are now ten galleries with many exhibiting original painting, sculpture, weaving, and fine craft created by the town's growing community of artists. The year's biggest arts bash is Media, an early June celebration in Hurcamp Park that brings together more than a hundred performing and visual artists for exhibitions ranging from the mild to the scandalously experimental. There's also a fall and spring art fair held on the town's main square, with each show attracting 40 to 50 exhibiting artists.

What the Artist Says

Scott McKee, a stone sculptor, has lived in Fredericksburg for ten years. "We're a town that seems to like what's hot in the art world—that's what the galleries show and that's what people around here will buy. There's a broad acceptance of minimalistic and conceptual work. Fredericksburg has lots of studio spaces for artists, and a flood of new arrivals. I think the artists come here for friendship and advice, and because the town is developing a reputation as being a place where you can find strong, affordable art.

"Some galleries try and fail, but there always seems to be a new one going up somewhere. Here, artists like to organize: They enjoy going to meetings to discuss important issues, and putting together things like open studio tours and exhibitions of art work in local storefronts. Things could really be improved around here if Fredericksburg was to fund the development of a sculpture park—that would set us apart from most other places, giving people a whole new reason to come here."

Friday Harbor, Washington

Location

Victoria, one of Canada's largest coastal cities, actually lies south of this community in Washington's San Juan Island chain. Friday Harbor, with 1,500 residents, is the largest of the island's small towns, and is the government seat for San Juan county.

Climate

Folks in this part of the Pacific Northwest like to boast about living in something called a "rain shadow," which means the San Juan Islands receive more sunshine and less rain than nearby areas on the mainland. Now, for someone who lives in Seattle, that's great news, but don't get the impression that Friday Harbor is a desert paradise. It rains here . . . a lot. And it's chilly here most of the year. Summer is a different story, with lots of warm, sunny skies, but from October to May, you'd swear you were living inside a terrarium.

Living

Island life in the Pacific Northwest is ruled by the schedules of Washington's state-owned ferry system, but there are lots of ferries plying the emerald green waters between the islands and the mainland. You get to sit and chit-chat with friends while waiting to arrive at your destination, so the ferries serve floating town halls tying island people and small towns together. Artists move here for the opportunity to live in an environment where orca whales and bald eagles are practically everyday sights, and small-town living, friendliness, and personal safety are taken for granted.

Friday Harbor has a national historic park dedicated to the era when the island was jointly claimed by Britain and the U.S. San Juan is an island filled with bed and breakfast inns, small parks, and u-pick vegetable and fruit farms. Local residents take part in outdoor activities that include whale-watching cruises, sea kayak expeditions, fishing trips, and bicycling on the country roads criss-crossing the island. Downtown Friday Harbor has loads of available second-story studio space for around $350 per month. A 3-bedroom home on the island sells in the range of $150,000, with places on the waterfront costing considerably more.

Out On the Town

Friday Harbor is blessed with one of the nation's most active and visionary community theaters—it's a place that acts as the island's art center, producing everything from Cole Porter musicals to touring symphony orchestra performances and chamber music recitals. The San Juan Community Theater is smack in the middle of Friday Harbor, and its ambitious schedule of year-round presentations keeps local restaurants busy, and provides them with a vital cultural link to the world outside the islands.

The dining emphasis is on seafood, ranging from French bistro-style cooking (at the Duck Soup Inn) to Northwest contemporary (at Cafe Bissett) to elegant continental-style cuisine (at the Roche Harbor Inn). The San Juan Brewery and Ford's Bar & Grille are two local favorites for hanging out on a rainy afternoon. Ford's is also one of the best places to go for a hamburger. Vegetarians get their grazing willies worked out at the Maloula, and at the Way of Life Deli.

Economic Impact of the Arts

Considered to be an important aspect of what makes life in the islands both attractive and eminently livable, local residents are supportive of their arts scene—both by patronizing events at the San Juan Community Theater and by filling their homes with locally created art. Local businesses also provide an important financial foundation for the island's fine arts scene.

Local Arts Agency

San Juan Community Theater and Arts Center, P.O. Box 1063, Friday Harbor, WA 98250, (206) 378-3210. Publishes the newsletter *Theater Times*.

"We're a center of the island's diversity of arts tastes," says theater director Doug Scott. "Musically, there's everything from marimba to Scottish country dancing to ballet. Last year we had 102 performances of 57 different events. We have a year-round exhibition space that displays everything from school kids' art to touring shows from museums. Our summer technical and instructional programs are extensive, and it's all expanding to meet the community's needs. There's a lot of back and forth between the theater's functions and the programs offered through the Sunshine Gallery—what we have is a facility for the entire community to use."

Galleries and Arts Festivals

The 16 art galleries and artists' studios in Friday Harbor (and the rest of the island) are filled with local paintings, fine crafts, handmade furniture, and hand-woven textiles. There are two nonprofit exhibition spaces at the Sunshine Gallery and at the theater. The island's most popular arts event takes place around the annual San Juan Island Good Time Classic Dixieland Jazz Festival in late July.

What the Artist Says

"This is a perfect place for artists to come for inspiration and creative energy," says Emily Reed, writer and author whose guidebooks are filled with the whole scoop, and nothing but the scoop, on what's best to see and do in the San Juan's. "You can tell what's going on by seeing the impressive work in local galleries. Here, the artists are, for the most part, well past the arts and crafts thing. Most of them sell off the island in Seattle and other cities, but keep a local gallery presence since sales here can be quite good. Fiber arts are very strong because of the island's large community of wool growers.

"The concept of local art has really caught on with the people who live here, and we're seeing some serious buying going on. Sure, you can buy T-shirts in town, but I'd say we're a long way off from being overshadowed by that sort of thing. Yes, tourism is a mixed blessing: I think the best we can hope for is that the people who come here to visit, and those who decide to stay, have certain values they share with the people who have always lived here."

LaConner, Washington

Location
Across a tidal flat from the Swinomish Indian reservation, the 700 or so full-time residents of LaConner live on the edge of Skagit Bay, an hour's drive north of Seattle.

Climate
If you enjoy stormy weather, LaConner will seem like nirvana. Its summers are generally warm and crystal clear, with a day or two of rain thrown in just to keep the local population on its toes. Autumns are rather unremarkable, usually because they're experienced underneath the omnipresent cover of a dark, misty cloud. But spring in this end of the Skagit Valley is a spectacular affair, with nearby fields growing mile after mile of tulips and daffodils that bloom into technicolor vibrancy around mid-April.

Living
A convenient, affordable alternative to artists from the Northwest wanting to put a little distance between themselves and the ever-growing suburbs of Seattle, LaConner has a regional reputation as a haven for not only visual artists, but writers, poets, and retirees as well. Equidistant from both Seattle and Vancouver, British Columbia, it's a place that has attracted a fair share of interest from Canadian artists who, for tax reasons, set up their studios and weekend residences on the U.S. side of the border.

Ski areas in the Cascade Mountains are less than an hour's drive from here. Favorite outdoor activities center around the town's proximity to the Puget Sound, so sailing, setting out traps for Dungeness crabs, beachcombing, and sea kayaking are quite popular.

Studio space isn't too hard to find in LaConner, particularly if you're willing to hole up in an unused argicultural shed on the edge of town. In-town studios rent in the $500-per-month neighborhood. A 3-bedroom home in this part of the state (close enough to be within commuting distance from Seattle) lists in the $150,000 range.

Out On the Town
If you live in LaConner and you're looking for fun, the incomparable movie houses, micro-brewery pubs, and first-rate coffeehouses of Seattle are a short drive away, but this little town has plenty of great hangouts of its own. The LaConner Tavern is one fine place to pass a few hours on a rainy afternoon, and don't forget to try their cheeseburgers. Local residents bump into each other at the Cafe Pojante, a great place to slurp a cappuchino, and after dark it's time to give the Pub at Palmer's or the Conway Tavern a whirl. Classical music lovers need to make the drive to Seattle to satisfy their aural fixations, but there's decent theater nearby in Anacortes (at the Anacortes Community Theater), as well as at Skagit Valley College in Mt. Vernon.

Economic Impact of the Arts

LaConner may be scenic, but business owners need to realize that the candy shops and T-shirt dives aren't necessarily the attractions drawing in tourists (although these establishments seem to be on the verge of taking over prime downtown retail locations). In many disturbing ways, LaConner has wandered very close to the point of becoming a town that's sold its soul to the trinket shop lure of making a fast buck from one-time visitors.

Local Arts Agency

Valley Museum of Northwest Art, First Street, LaConner, WA 98257, (206) 293-4934.

Now housed in the historic Gaches Mansion, the museum is moving into new, 12,000-square-foot quarters in early 1995. "We're on a continual mission to educate the business community about the arts' economic impact," says Susan Parke, the museum's director. "Our emphasis is on visual arts and education. We produce a lecture series that runs along with a concert series, and our plans are to move more fully into art and education programs, as well as coordinating visiting artist programs through the local schools. Much of the art being created in town is reflective of the landscape work known as Northwest Tradition."

Galleries and Arts Festivals

"There's not really an art festival in LaConner, but there's a long-standing craft and art festival in Anacortes in August," says LaConner art insider Barbara James. "There's the Art's Alive festival in November, but once the new museum is in place, there will be a lot more going on. There are two serious galleries that sell original work, and for the rest there's Guy Anderson's gallery and the Janet Huston Gallery, which exhibit wonderful paintings by the valley's better artists, as well as some newer promising artists. We've also got a number of country galleries that aren't open full-time, but show very strong work by regional artists, and sell a surprising amount of work by people who are trying to work outside the mainstream galleries. Whenever they have shows it's a happy occasion."

What the Artist Says

William Slater, an oil painter who works in an expressionistic form of landscape imagery. "LaConner is the friendliest town I've ever been in. There are local farmers and fishermen who supported me by buying my work when I first got here. Now, I'm represented through a Seattle gallery and feel very fortunate to sell everything I paint. For a landscape painter, LaConner has good light, clear air, and lots of inspirational things to make you feel good about you and your environment. The town is into tourism, and that's causing problems with traffic, but there are still a lot of interesting artists, poets, and writers coming in."

Port Townsend, Washington

Location
The Olympic Peninsula juts out from the Pacific Northwest mainland like a green thumb, forming the land mass that harbors North America's only rain forest, as well as providing the Puget Sound with the sheltering barrier of the Olympic Mountains. Port Townsend, a community of 7,700, sits at the peninsula's northeast tip. It is a 2-hour drive (plus two ferry rides) from Seattle.

Climate
While not as rainy and socked-in as most of the Olympic Peninsula's communities, Port Townsend still gets its due when it comes to liquid sunshine. While weather fronts blow through this area rather quickly, the weather patterns tend to be large enough to last anywhere from a few days to a couple of weeks, which results in some stretches of rather gloomy weather. Summer is delightfully mild, as the town is surrounded on three sides by ocean waters. Spring and fall can be very, very squishy.

Living
Founded as a mercantile center and lumber-shipping community, Port Townsend is a remarkably well-preserved monument to the architectural genius of turn-of-the-century America. Its downtown district is comprised primarily of ornate brick commercial buildings with large window fronts and several upstairs floors, while the inner residential neighborhoods are filled with some of the loveliest Victorian structures north of San Francisco. There's still a lumber and logging industry in the area, although its presence and economic importance to the local economy has diminished over the years.

Port Townsend is now known as one of the West Coast's most attractive arts towns, a place filled with charming bed and breakfast inns, some worthwhile art and fine craft galleries, and a bunch of stores selling the local equivalent of rubber tomahawks. The average 3-bedroom home sells for $130,000, and there's an abundance of available studio space on the second and third floors of downtown commercial buildings renting for an average of $500 per month. Outdoors activities range from salmon fishing to mountain hikes into hot spring sites in the Olympic National Park.

Out On the Town
Because it's been a popular tourist stop for the past couple of decades, Port Townsend is also blessed with an abundance of great places to dine, from elegant Thai cuisine at the Khu Larb to first-rate vegetarian fare at both the Silverwater Cafe and the Salal Cafe. The town's best burgers (and a great place to sit for a while and watch the local residents come and go) is the Clubhouse Restaurant. Rainy days—and there are more than a few of them—are best spent hanging around one of the town's fantastic pubs: the Town Tavern, Back Alley, Uptown Pub, and the Hilltop are all fine places for micro-brewed ales, pool tables, and friendly conversation.

Port Townsend also has its own theater troupe at the Water Street Dinner Theater, and live music is performed at bars and clubs around town. Classical music performance is regularly staged at Ft. Worden State Park, a former military post that houses the offices of the Centrum Foundation, a nonprofit organization dedicated to promoting the arts.

Economic Impact of the Arts

Here, the connection between the community's economic health and the state of its artists is quite obvious: You don't have to go very far to find Olympic Peninsula communities that have had it rough as their fishing and lumber-based economies fell on hard times. Local businesses in Port Townsend are supportive of what the arts need not only to survive, but prosper, and government decisions are made with crucial input from the town's creative sector.

Local Arts Agency

Centrum Foundation, P.O. Box 1158, Port Townsend, WA 98368, (206) 385-3102.

"Fort Worden is our residential arts facility—a place for summer workshops, art training, and gifted student classes in the winter," says Joe Wheeler, Centrum Foundation executive director. "We also have (or had) a press, a recording studio, a lithography press, and a foundry. There are artists, musicians, writers, and dancers here on residency programs throughout the year. Lately, we've had music performance festivals grow out of our workshops, and our jazz, blues, and folk music weekends during the summer draw a lot of visitors into town. Another focus is to teach Washington schoolteachers about creative problem-solving techniques. More and more we're getting into teacher training. Kids from the schools in the Port Townsend area come in for our events, and we occasionally send visiting artists out to do workshops in the schools.

Galleries and Arts Festivals

While there are ten commercial galleries in Port Townsend, most show art work that caters to the tastes of tourists wanting a scene of a ferry, a waterfront, a pier, or a flock of sea gulls . . . and that's good news for artists who can fill that niche. There are dozens upon dozens of craft artists in the area, especially woodworkers, and in many of the town's galleries you'll fine exquisite craft objects. The town's nonprofit exhibition space, 1004 Gallery (considered to be one of the strongest galleries in the Northwest), shows primarily contemporary work. While Ft. Worden hosts regular music festivals throughout the summer, the year's biggest arts festival is the Quimper Arts Show and Sale in early June, attracting 50 or so exhibiting artists.

What the Artist Says

"Most of the artists living here have to hold down other jobs," says Ed Cain, painter and founder of the 1004 Gallery. "There's somewhat of a market for serious art, but the challenge is to be represented in a Seattle gallery—that's where you can make the sales. 1004 operates in the black, but that's in large part because of the generosity of its member artists. Here, artists here find their connection to the Northwest's spirituality. It's a small town and artists enjoy working together on projects."

Paul Harcharik, a landscape painter and three-year resident of Port Townsend says, "I've been surprised at the number of local people who have started buying my paintings. There's a sense of appreciation for fine art here . . . something that goes beyond the more accessible arts and crafts approaches. This is a place where an artist can find low-cost studio space and an environment that feeds your creative vision. It's also a magnet for tourists, and that makes a difference."

Twisp, Washington

Location
North-central Washington is a land of broad valleys and soaring mountains, a place where wheat fields and fruit farms shoulder most of the region's economic fortunes. Twisp, a community of 1,000 or so residents, is one of four towns dotting the 55-miles of the Methow Valley. If the weather conditions are favorable, Seattle is slightly more than a 4-hour drive away.

Climate
Hemmed in on three sides by 8,000-foot peaks, the alpine setting of Methow Valley has resulted in the area's winter tourism development as a center for cross-country skiing. Snows arrive early and stay late, even though spring's warming trend begins in late March. The summer growing season is rather brief, but gardeners who have a way with indoor seedlings can usually coax a few tomatoes out of their back-yard plots.

Living
Very rural and remote, many Seattle artists move into the Methow Valley as a low-cost alternative to the city's more hectic pace. Once here, they find a friendly and supportive group of a hundred or so fellow artists, most of whom work in the fine craft area, and are primarily represented through galleries in Seattle, Portland, and Sun Valley.

The low cost of living and the near absence of crime make the valley a great place for raising a family. Schools are well-regarded, and the region as a whole has a very straightforward attitude about dealing with governmental issues. A few years ago, the local residents banded together to shelve an out-of-state company's plans to build an alpine ski resort at one end of the valley, choosing instead to be satisfied with the vigorous cross-country ski economy that's developed parallel to the sport's increasing popularity.

Most artists have studios adjacent to their homes, but for those who want to put some creative distance between themselves and the family room, there are studio spaces in Winthrop and Twisp renting in the $200-per-month range. Three-bedroom homes on quiet residential streets generally list at around $75,000, although view lots and places with several acres of land can run considerably more than that.

While the valley is decidedly a prime area for winter recreation, the year's busiest season is summer. The eastern side of the Cascade Range experiences much less rain than does the Puget Sound area, and for decades part-time residents have built homes in the area to take advantage of the generally sunnier skies and warmer temperatures of eastern Washington.

Out On the Town
Because of its tourist business, the valley has a leg up on other parts of eastern Washington when it comes to dining and entertainment. It's a family-oriented atmosphere (except for the inevitable dive or two in each town), and the best places tend to be in Winthrop, which is the destination of most tourists driving through Twisp (just a 10-mile jaunt). The Winthrop Pub and Microbrewery is

one of the region's best places to pass a rainy afternoon. Duck Brand Restaurant offers regionally inspired cooking, and Queen of Tarts is a favorite spot for morning coffee and lunch. The Virginian serves grazing foods for the vegetarian crowd.

Community theater productions pop up every now and again at the Community Center and at Sun Mountain Lodge, and outside of summer-in-the-park sort of concerts and bands playing in bars, the music lovers in Twisp have to travel an hour or so to Wenatchee for the occasional concert or recital.

Economic Impact of the Arts

Small enough that each contribution made to the local economy is noted and appreciated, the valley's artists are seen as an integral component of what makes this area appealing to visitors. Visible primarily through the activity in local galleries, artists generally keep a low profile, but have definitely been able to make a difference when it comes to building the valley's economic base.

Local Arts Agency

Methow Arts Alliance, P.O. Box 723, Twisp, WA 98856, (509) 997-4004. Publishes the newsletter *Methow Arts*.

"I could tell we were getting to be a popular place when our gas stations started putting in espresso machines," says Debbie Nickell, chairman of the Alliance. "Most of our visual and performing arts programs are oriented toward exposing locals to things they normally wouldn't see in the valley, and getting tourists to spend money on the arts. We have the long-range goal of establishing an arts center that would give us performing, exhibition, and office space. Education is our main focus: We have artist-in-residence programs at the local schools, arts-in-education programming in the schools, and award a scholarship each year to a particularly talented art student."

Galleries and Arts Festivals

There are four commercial art galleries in the Methow Valley, the closest museums are in Seattle and Spokane, and the Methow Arts Festival in early July attracts 60 exhibiting artists and 15 performers for a weekend-long celebration of valley arts.

What the Artist Says

"The kind of artist who moves here has the idea in mind that they want to give some of their energy to the community," says Richard Wrangle, creator of sculpted, yet functional, furniture. "They're a skilled, creative, and eccentric group, and are occasionally hard to pull together, but their hearts are in the right place. The communities are trying to maintain their identities in the face of some development. There are younger artists moving in who take two or three part-time jobs in order to survive. We've been identified as a center for all sorts of arts, and that's attracting musicians, dancers, weavers, potters, and painters. The best things that have happened for the artists living here have come from people's own initiatives, like the gallery that was started in Twisp. It's a measure of the artists' integrity."

Berkeley Springs, West Virginia

Location
Overlooking the Potomac River from its perch on the West Virginia panhandle, Berkeley Springs (pop. 3,000) is a historic community less than a 2-hour drive from Washington, D.C.

Climate
Reflecting its distance from the lowlands to the east, Berkeley Springs' weather is more difficult in winter and more moderate in summer than that of nearby areas. Snowstorms that rip through western Pennsylvania are likely to hit this part of West Virginia just as hard, while spring arrives early and heralds the beginning of a lengthy, humid (though temperate) summer. Autumn is brief, but spectacular, with thousands of D.C. "leafers" winding their ways through the region, clogging country roads on the weekends in October.

Living
Commuters discovered Berkeley Springs in the 1980s. Fortunately, most who try to live here and hold down a job in D.C. eventually give up on the idea after realizing what they've ended up with is the worst of both worlds: They can't find time to enjoy the rural charm of Morgan County, nor muster adequate energy to focus on the fine points of the day-in and day-out requirements of their profession.

Local residents have this well-preserved community practically to themselves during the week, while on weekends they participate in the sport of stripping tourists of their spendable cash—and there are lots of places for these city-dwelling visitors to drop their dough.

Artists move into the area so they can take advantage of the ready-made market through local galleries and crafts stores, pulling down an income that's supplemented by participation in the lucrative arts and crafts fairs staged in this part of the country from early April through mid-November. Once an important mercantile center, the Berkeley Springs downtown area has single- and two-story buildings that are ideal sites for artists who don't want their studios at home. The average in-town studio rents for $250 per month, while a 3-bedroom residence on one of the town's quiet neighborhood streets lists in the $80,000 range.

Out On the Town
Being within easy distance of communities that have closer ties to the D.C. suburbs, residents of Berkeley Springs don't have to travel far to find ethnic restaurants, shopping malls, or community theaters. For the local potters, painters, metalsmiths, jewelers, furniture makers, and weavers who just want a quick bite to eat, the general prescription is to head over to Tari's Premier Cafe. Coolfront Resort, just a few miles south of town, is a popular place for more romantic dining, while those looking for nighttime fun, clog over to the Log Cabin for live music.

True to form for a traditional, small town, Berkeley Springs still has its downtown movie theater. The Star Theater, which normally runs mainstream fare starring macho studs like Steven Segal and Clint Eastwood, manages to occasionally sneak a late night presentation of films such as

Like Water for Chocolate and *Jamon, Jamon* into its schedule, and those are usually packed affairs for which the region's artists (and other cultural subversives) turn out en masse. Live theater lovers make the drive over to Shepherdstown for programs at Shepherd College, and there are occasional recitals at the Presbyterian church during winter. Summer brings folk concerts at the Berkeley Springs State Park.

Economic Impact of the Arts

It's well understood that Berkeley Springs' many bed and breakfast inns stay full most of the year, and out-of-towners are eating in local restaurants because of the town's reputation as an arts center. Sure, they come here looking for affordable bargains, and that in turn forces artists to keep their prices low, but without this sort of traffic, the Berkeley Springs economy would not be half as strong.

Local Arts Agency

Morgan Arts Council, Rt. 3, Box 191, Berkeley Springs, WV 25411, no phone. Publishes the *MAC Newsletter*.

"We're heavily into the performing arts for our programs," says Jeanne Morgan of the council. "We have an active concert series, and our newer members are very involved in the visual arts. We're a totally volunteer organization. We've been working with an adopt-a-school program, and we have school coordinators and teachers who are very cooperative in working visual arts, literature, and music into their curriculums. We'll continue to do lots of inexpensive, accessible programs for the community."

Galleries and Arts Festivals

The 50 or so full-time artists who live in Berkeley Springs have three art galleries and one specialized craft shop primarily selling the work of local creative professionals. The year's most popular arts event is the Apple Butter Festival in early October. It's an event that attracts more than 200 exhibiting artists and craftspeople, along with performers and street theater groups.

What the Artist Says

"Berkeley Springs is close to major highways and I see it as a good compromise location, not too isolated but still very rural," says Jean Pierre Hsu, a jeweler who sculpts pieces from anodized aluminum, woods, and acrylic. "There are many artists who spend their time on the road, using this place as a base for traveling to craft shows in the Northeast, the Southeast, and the Midwest. It's a community of artists and craftspeople, a place that seems to be changing for the better. Here, artists form a close-knit community that's interested in you and supportive of your work. Before you move here, try to develop your marketing strategy, and know how living here will effect you and your work."

Shepherdstown, West Virginia

Location
West Virginia's panhandle region is close enough to Washington, D.C. to be within commuting distance for thousands of federal government employees. Shepherdstown, a community of 1,300, is a 90-minute drive from Kennedy Center.

Climate
Set into a landscape of rolling, green hills, summers in this part of West Virginia aren't as stiflingly humid, nor as oppressively hot as those of the cities lying to the east. Autumn provides a colorful and noteworthy lead-in to winter, which has the capacity to turn bitterly cold and snowy, but is usually just cold and windy.

Living
Benefiting from the economic spill-over generated by the area's status as a bedroom community for some D.C. workers, and as a drive-to-the-country weekend destination for other city dwellers, Shepherdstown is just one of the many Jefferson County towns that has experienced an economic revival in recent years. Close enough to D.C. to allow folks easy access to the shopping malls, theaters, and restaurants spreading out through the surrounding areas, local residents enjoy a comparatively more affordable, and infinitely more secure, existence in this far eastern tip of West Virginia than do those living closer to the metropolis.

There's easy access to outdoor activities ranging from some of the nation's best white water rafting and kayaking sites on the nearby Potomac and Shenandoah rivers, to bicycling and horseback riding on the banks of the Potomac. Alpine skiing is within an hour's drive, and hikers can always head for the Appalachian Trail.

Artists whose work is represented in galleries from Philadelphia to Charleston find this part of the region to be not only convenient to their primary markets, but an affordable place to live as well. Studio spaces are mostly maintained adjacent to an artist's home. An average 3-bedroom residence sells in the $95,000 range, but that includes enough land for a garage, studio, large garden, and room for the kids to play.

Out On the Town
Fanciers of the exotic and the elegant can make their way back into D.C.'s suburbs if the urge for Thai cuisine hits, but Chinese restaurants are plentiful in this part of the state. China Kitchen in Shepherdstown is a local favorite. Rainy days and leisure hours are best spent down at the Mecklenburg Inn or the Yellow Brick Bank. Live music is presented at the Mecklenburg Inn and at the Shepherdstown Men's Club. The best burgers in the area are served at the Town Run Deli. Martinsburg, a 15-minute drive away, has the local vegetarian's number-one vote at Judy's Restaurant.

Music and theater presentations are surprisingly strong at Shepherd College, which produces a performing arts series covering classical, folk, and orchestral music. The college also stages the annual Contemporary American Theater Festival, using a variety of regional venues, including the restored opera house in nearby Charlestown.

Economic Impact of the Arts
Wrestling with the problems brought on by development, and trying to decide how to deal with both increased tax revenues and more demands for county and municipal services, have been the local priorities since the recession eased up in mid-1993. Here, the arts are not fully appreciated as an important component of the regional economy, yet there are festivals and performances held year-round that bring in vital tourist dollars, benefiting the entire community's financial health. Perhaps one of the reasons the arts are taken for granted is that local business people assume that there will always be more coming from the arts department at Shepherd College, and that the other artists living here are somehow associated with the college's programs . . . but that's hardly the case.

Local Arts Agency
Arts & Humanities Alliance of Jefferson County, P.O. Box 1036, Charlestown, WV 25414, (304) 263-3726. Publishes the newsletter *The Medley*.

"It's only been in the past few years that business groups have begrudgingly acknowledged the broad economic impact they receive from the arts," says Pam Parziale, a studio potter. "The Alliance is a coalition of existing organizations with board representatives from a number of groups that tries to implement long-range planning for the area's arts community. There's been three years of successful programming with adult and community education, and now we're moving toward a more aggressive plan to bring arts into the public schools. We have many artists in the area, but it's taking political controversy to pull us together."

Galleries and Arts Festivals
There are four commercial galleries in Shepherdstown and the surrounding area, all of which represent the work of local visual and fine craft artists. During performances staged at the Charlestown Opera House, the lobby is given over to nonprofit displays of locally created art work. There's also the nonprofit Boarman Arts Center Gallery in Martinsburg, and the Frank Art Center on the Shepherd College campus. The year's most popular arts events are the spring and fall stagings of the Mountain Heritage Arts and Crafts Festival in nearby Harper's Ferry, attracting over 200 exhibiting artists and craftspeople to each celebration.

What the Artist Says
"The local markets are good in this area," says Anne Bowers, a sculptural basketry artist. "If you hit the larger shows through most of the year, then get out in winter and do a few more in the south, you can survive on your art. The local galleries and craft stores are showcases of good, locally made work. The state runs crafts centers that promote what's made by artists living in the area, and the Chamber of Commerce is very good about organizing and promoting the Mountain Heritage Festival.

"Most of the local artists here work well together: We organize studio tours and print up driving maps. There are lots of antique stores in the area, and that's what originally started getting people from D.C. to drive through here on weekends. We're on the verge of entering the long-range planning process so that artists can have a voice in development-related issues. The artists here need to get organized and start speaking with a single, clear voice."

Mineral Point, Wisconsin

Location
A compact, historic town in the rolling farmlands of south-central Wisconsin, Mineral Point (pop. 2,200) is home to more than a hundred artists, many of whom moved here from large urban areas across the Midwest. The college town of Madison is less than an hour's drive away.

Climate
Local residents have the full force of all four seasons to contend with and that always means at least a few blizzards roaring through town during the winter months, as well as a moderate, occasionally humid stretch of midsummer heat. Autumn, which comes and goes in the blink of an eye, is an extraordinarily colorful couple of weeks and brings loads of tourists through town.

Living
Artists move here so that they can participate in one of the region's most robust arts-related economies. For years, Mineral Point has attracted creative types who gravitated toward the town's affordable, historic downtown district. Costs being what they were, many of these artists did what came naturally and opened up their own studios. That in turn pulled weekend visitors toward this part of the state, and soon there were bed and breakfast inns springing up to handle the carloads of curious folks.

Once the town realized the potential in the arts resource that had been deposited at its feet, it started promoting itself as an arts community, and today there's a year-round tourist flow through Mineral Point's many galleries and crafts stores. Many artists maintain their studios as street-level retail space, and in some instances the artist's family occupies the upper floor of a downtown building as their home. The average rent for a spot with good retail potential is $350 per month, while a 3-bedroom home on one of Mineral Point's tree-shaded streets sells in the $80,000 range.

Outdoor activities center around cross-country skiing in the winter, and the summer brings fly fishing and canoeing on the many streams winding their way through Wisconsin's unspoiled countryside.

Out On the Town
Long accustomed to handling tourists, Mineral Point has a number of good dining spots and those typical, country-charming sort of bed and breakfast inns. Here, artists like to pass their down time at the Studio on High, a coffee shop that does double duty as an artist's studio and an informal gallery space. The local delicacy is the pasty, and none serves a better version of this Welsh standby than the Red Rooster Cafe. The best burgers in town are served with a schooner of brew at Pilling's Pub, and vegetarian foods can be found 15 miles away at the Bountiful Bean in Ridgeway.

Nighttime fun goes on down at Folklore Village. Mineral Point's civic center is the home to local performances of a community theater troupe and occasional classical concerts. There's a summer repertory theater staged outdoors in nearby Spring Green, and the performance schedule in Madison, for everything from rock concerts to orchestral presentations, is first-rate.

Economic Impact of the Arts

Mineral Point's economic revival was largely based on the community's reputation as a place where artists lived and worked, and over the years, the downtown business community has come to include gallery owners and artists, whose voices offer an important viewpoint in the town's decision-making process.

Local Arts Agency

Mineral Point Artisan's Guild, 412 Pine St., Mineral Point, WI 53565, (608) 987-3656.

"We're working on pulling together the community's arts voices," says guild president Wendy Sundquist. "Right now, we have an arts festival that could be better publicized, a folk music festival that's done through a private promoter, and a newspaper that wants us to buy ads or else they don't cover our events. Local businesses display art in their windows, we've had a crafts mall open up recently, and there are art workshop programs using local artists coordinated through the schools."

Galleries and Arts Festivals

There are 20 commercial gallery spaces in Mineral Point, some of which are located in a crafts mall. The town lacks a nonprofit exhibition space and would probably do well to pursue the funding of a community arts center. The year's most popular arts event is the Mineral Point Arts Festival, a mid-August celebration in a downtown park, which attracts 60 exhibiting artists.

What the Artist Says

Bruce Howdle, a ceramic artist who works in large-scale vessels and mural relief installations. "Artists come here for the community's anonymous qualities—it's a friendly mix of the affordable, the creative, and the safe. The town could use an incubator studio facility—an arts center of some sort where we could place talented younger artists and have them work on establishing their careers.

"Mineral Point is starting to be discovered by people outside the Midwest, especially now that artists and craftspeople have come in here and prettied up the place. We're on the edge of change, but people who come here feel as through they've really found something. We've got a lot of craft and folk artists living here who travel on the show circuit. There's everything from western art to pottery, woodwork, weavings, and jewelry.

"I like the change of seasons here . . . it just hits you suddenly. Once you acclimate yourself to the types of outdoor activities the area offers, you really start to enjoy it. Yes, the pace is slower than what suits most people, and that takes some getting used to, but this is a good place to live if you want to own a hundred-year old home and be surrounded by other artists."

Cody, Wyoming

Location

In the shadows of northwest Wyoming's Absaroka Mountains, a magical part of the state where fingers of the Northern Plains nudge up against 10,000-foot peaks, Cody's 8,000 full-time residents live roughly a 2-hour drive from Billings, Montana.

Climate

Although it's certainly far enough north to merit warnings from anyone who has a problem with winter weather, Cody's climate isn't as severe as you would imagine. Other parts of Wyoming fare far worse when it comes to snowfall totals and below-zero freezes. Spring arrives quite early, heralding the start of a muddy season (that tries local tempers and maroons vehicles on farm roads miles from town) that ends in one of the most spectacular summers found anywhere. Autumn, which arrives in early September, goes by in a wink.

Living

Cody residents have been getting their fair share of attention in recent years, as the nation's love affair with Western interior design and clothing continues to be popular. Cody is home to dozens of furniture craftspeople who create contemporary versions of the elegant ranch furnishings pioneered by Thomas Molesworth. There are also those who use these more traditional designs as a jumping-off point for new schools of western-esque furniture, as well as metalwork doors, screens, and lighting fixtures. The types of artists who call Cody home are generally either Western realists or landscape painters, because that's the sort of work local galleries are able to sell.

This area has a reputation as both a ranching community and a frontier town, and it's filled with as much legend and lore as it is natural beauty. Inspiration comes in by the bucketfuls, whether from just driving through the countryside to look at mountain vistas, or from meeting the inimitable mountain men and cowpokes who call the Absaroka Range home. Outdoor activities are what living here is all about, from premier hunting opportunities in the fall to rushing trout streams in the spring and summer. The hiking terrain is second to none, bicycle excursions into the foothills are an easy bet for exhilarating adventure, almost everybody rides a horse at least a few times a year, and don't forget your fishing pole!

There are lots of commercial studio spaces available on the second floor of downtown buildings, with the average space renting for $450 per month. If that seems steep, realize that in recent years Cody has developed one of the West's most vibrant summer tourist trades. This is in large part due to the presence of the Buffalo Bill Historical Center, a sprawling museum that exhibits everything from Remington rifles to top-notch landscape work by deceased master artists. The average 3-bedroom home in Cody sells somewhere under $70,000, but prices are rising.

Out On the Town

This is Wyoming, and while there are a couple of good Chinese restaurants in town, ethnic food is still for the most part regarded with suspicion by locals. One of the best things about Cody is the bar scene—hanging out at the Irma Hotel's bar is a tradition dating back to the days when Wild Bill himself made this town his home. Don't bother asking anyone about vegetarian food—they'll wonder if you're asking for directions to the feed store. The Proud Cut, a tavern and restaurant, serves Cody's best hamburger and mountain oysters.

Nights out are best spent at Cassie's, a country and western nightclub. Theater-wise, there are summer performances of historical pageants at the museum, while occasional winter shows at the Thompson Auditorium pepper the calendar's leaner months. There's a popular jazz festival in July, a cowboy song festival in April, and occasional recitals at the auditorium.

Economic Impact of the Arts

Cody's economy is doing quite well from its tourism sector, and while the arts (outside of the historical museum's presence) are seen as a pleasant adjunct to what takes place here, the business community views its growth in terms not necessarily related to the economy. On the other hand, if you were to lump it all together—the furniture industry, Cody's painters and sculptors, and the impact of the historical museum—the bottom-line influence on Cody's economy would be substantial. Without the arts in all their forms, Cody would be just like a lot of other towns.

Local Arts Agency

Park County Arts Council, P.O. Box 1326, Cody, WY 82414, (307) 587-3129. Publishes the *PCAC Newsletter*.

"For many of the people living here, or those just visiting, there's a good awareness of Cody's art scene outside the context of the Buffalo Bill Historical Center," says Sarah Boehme, the center's chief curator. "The galleries are very well-known and are seen as an asset to the rest of the community's economy. There's art instruction in the local schools, but we're in the process of formulating a comprehensive plan that will provide a strong arts focus to Cody's educational programming. There's a concern about tourism's impact on the town and how it's expanding the lower end of our economic base, as it replaces the (shrinking) natural resources industries that paid their workers much higher wages."

Galleries and Arts Festivals

While there presently are six commercial galleries in Cody—selling work ranging from Western realist bronze sculpture to landscapes and campy, contemporary Western painting—several more are anticipated. The community's nonprofit exhibition space is operated by the Cody County Art League. The year's most popular arts bash is the Buffalo Bill Art Show and Sale, held in late September at the art league's exhibition space.

What the Artist Says

Reid Christie, landscape painter. "Having an historical center in town makes people want to take a close look at the local galleries. There's a surprising amount of work being sold right now, enough to keep most artists busy. For a reclusive artist, or one who's raising a family, this is a great place to live. There's a social scene you can choose to be a part of, but we're all still good friends. We could use more outlets for local art work. There's a high level of quality to the art made here, and that should be maintained. The art instruction in Cody's schools is good . . . there are lots of artists going into the classrooms to do workshops."

Jackson, Wyoming

Location
Spread throughout an alpine valley known as Jackson Hole, the 4,500 residents of Jackson live in an area framed by the Teton Mountains on one side and the Gros Ventre mountains on the other. The valley borders on Grand Teton National Park, and Yellowstone National Park is just an hour's drive away. The closest metropolis is Salt Lake City, a 3-hour drive south.

Climate
Brutally cold winters last forever in Jackson, a result of its being refrigerated by a ring of 11,000-foot peaks that hold in cold air and block the sunshine. Once spring begins to melt the mountains of snow piled up all over town, it's the start of mud season, an unpleasant period that lasts well in to May, which is about the time when night freezes go away for a few months. Summer is an explosion of alpine glory, with afternoon thundershowers a regular feature of each day's natural fireworks. Autumn is brief, but gorgeous, and then the snow starts flying all over again.

Living
The tourism and development boom that hit Jackson in the late 1980s has not abated, and that's been a mixed blessing for local artists and craftspeople. On the one hand, the surge of visitors and newcomer home-buyers has led to the opening of many art galleries, and has provided a lucrative market for dozens of gallery artists. On the other hand, it's also meant that for all but a few artists, the cost of living in this small valley has become unaffordable—not to mention the constant traffic and crowding that goes on in Jackson during the warmer months as well as ski season.

Some artists have turned to renting out their homes during the summer, a time when they can hit the regional art and craft circuit, returning to home base in the fall. Others have high-tailed it out of the valley completely, electing to relocate to more affordable towns in nearby Idaho. Still, many artists stay and some have even moved in (but most of the newer artists are trust fund babies who start their own galleries).

Outdoor activities are a strong lure for the artists living here. Most are dedicated skiers and river rafter types, some love the fly fishing and hunting in this part of the state, and others are painters and photographers who are simply inspired by nature's astounding beauty in this corner of the world.

Rents in the business district are so high that there isn't any studio space to speak of in town. Most artists work out of detached home studios, and most of those bought their homes years ago when Jackson was affordable. Today's price for an average 3-bedroom home is in the $225,000 range, enough to scare off most everyone except California artists desperate to escape their eroding state.

Out On the Town
It used to be that locals got to chit chat with friends and catch up on the town gossip whenever they went out for dinner or a cup of coffee. Now, tourism has changed that, and all over Jackson

there are lines of fast-lane tourists disrupting the scene. Still, the Cadillac Bar and the Stagecoach Bar are two places where locals like to gather. The best burgers are those dished up at Billy's, and Dynamic Health has a good selection of vegetarian food. Shades Cafe is a favorite place for lunch, the Pearl Street Bagel Shop pulls in an active morning crowd, and the Mangy Moose is a favorite nightspot for two-steppers. During the summer, Jackson is home to the Grand Teton Music Festival, while winter cultural needs are met by a variety of choral, orchestral, and classical music groups.

Economic Impact of the Arts

Continuing to grow each year, the Jackson arts community benefits from both the region's popularity as a tourist destination and from the interest out-of-state gallery owners have shown in coming here to take advantage of the influx of homeowners. Outside of the summer music festival, performing arts are not as strong in this area as you would expect them to be. Visual arts are growing in influence, but so is everything else in this valley.

Local Arts Agency

Community Visual Arts Association, P.O. Box 1248, Jackson, WY 83001, (307) 733-6379.

"We're promoting involvement for all age groups," says Susan Thulin, executive director of the association. "We have a pressing need for space, so we're using a number of venues for classroom instruction, exhibitions of art work, and our offices. We offer art scholarships to talented students, and are starting to coordinate artist-in-residence programs through the schools. Art in this area is appreciated for its salability—a commodity that builds up tourist figures. Growth is a problem, and we have to unify the valley's arts groups if we're going to get a cultural center built."

Galleries and Arts Festivals

There are 35 commercial galleries in this fast-growing town, along with one nonprofit exhibition space. The National Wildlife Art Museum calls Jackson home, and its new facility will have extensive exhibition areas. The year's most popular arts events are the Mountain Artists Rendezvous and the Art Fairs held in July and August, with over a hundred exhibiting artists and craftspeople.

What the Artist Says

"The work that does best in local galleries is plein-air landscape," says Deborah Wilson Lopez, a contemporary painter. "We see a lot of serious artists come here to paint, but their work gets sold outside the area. The newcomers have little desire to participate in our community, and that's why we're having trouble getting an arts center. We get a lot of type-A personalities who move here and don't know what to do with themselves, so they start nonprofit groups to serve their own interests, rarely participating in the other groups already established here."

Index

N

O

P

R

S

T

V

W